T0344962

"Doug Silsbee maps the territory of presence-based coaching and leadership with extraordinary rigor and nuance. Business educators will be intrigued by these insights into learning and practice, acquired in the crucible of the coach-client relationship."

—**Elizabeth A. Powell, associate professor,**
Darden School of Business, University of Virginia

"This book breaks important new ground for coaches, leaders, facilitators, and consultants. Doug goes far beyond basics to generously share the wisdom and techniques that built his reputation as a leading coach with over twenty years of success in helping his clients achieve and sustain results."

—**Anne S. Davidson, associate, Roger Schwarz and**
Associates, and coauthor, *Facilitative Coaching*

"Doug gets to the heart of the elusive yet foundational leadership quality of presence. This practical guidebook is clear and cogent. The liberal sprinkling of examples and exercises make it truly pragmatic."

—**Ann Fisher, managing director,**
Integral Coaching International, Shanghai, China

"I dare you to experience this book! I am amazed at what is happening— ease, stronger partnering, and joy with my team at work and my husband at home. This book delivers big on how to be present in important relationships!"

—**Connie Maltbie-Shulas, manager,**
V-22 Training Program, The Boeing Company

"*Presence-Based Coaching* is uplifting and practical. It is an essential read for coaches and for leaders wanting to be professionally effective while living a balanced life. This book radiates presence while offering pragmatic business examples."

—**Diana Whitney, president, Corporation for Positive Change,**
and coauthor, *The Power of Appreciative Inquiry*

"Finally, a truly great book that develops the *being* of a coach. Nothing else offers such clear and practical tools. A must-read for professional coaches and leaders using a coaching approach."

—**Henry Kimsey-House, cofounder,**
The Coaches Training Institute, and coauthor, *Co-Active Coaching*

"If intention and authenticity in relationships is of interest, this is for you. Doug offers a supportive and challenging invitation to explore growth and change in ourselves and others."

—**Nancy Light, senior associate director of philanthropy,**
The Nature Conservancy in Maine

"Presence is essential for the accomplishment of any critical task. Complete focus, totally connected—no less is required of coaches and leaders. Doug is a great teacher, using presence as a theme to probe deeply into human consciousness, the only place real transformation can occur."

—**Harrison Owen, author,** *Open Space Technology*

"Doug Silsbee nails it, giving us a doorway to experience the power of presence, and to bring it to bear on the development of authentic, purpose-driven leaders. This book is a sensible, grounded must-read!"

—**Richard J. Leider, founder,**
The Inventure Group, and author, *The Power of Purpose*

"Silsbee moves incisively into the core challenges of development. Rigorous methodology and practices show how to develop the authentic, resilient leaders we so need. Silsbee is the master he writes about, knowing the possibilities that await those willing to engage in the rigorous demands of accelerated development."

—**Rod Napier, coauthor,** *The Courage to Act*

"*Presence-Based Coaching* reminds us that our first step is the work we do on ourselves. This book invites us to expand beyond skill and technique to offer our presence—augmenting possibilities and choices for ourselves and clients."

—**Sharon King, editor,**
Center for Creative Leadership *Handbook of Coaching*

"Doug Silsbee helps coaches and leaders wake up and develop beyond their current level of effectiveness. He presents a compelling picture of the power of bringing presence to clients."

—**Mary Beth O'Neill, founder, MBO Consulting, and author,**
Executive Coaching with Backbone and Heart

"Doug delivers frameworks for developing real-world leadership skills, while expanding awareness of what's possible, even essential. Authentic and thought-provoking, I highly recommend this important new work."

—**Kelly Durkan Bean, assistant dean of executive education,**
UCLA Anderson School of Management

"Presence is the most important yet least understood coaching competency. Here is a path to effectiveness, life-long professional development, and joy for coach and leader."

—**Marcia Reynolds, author,** *Outsmart Your Brain,*
and former president, International Coach Federation

PRESENCE-BASED COACHING

Cultivating Self-Generative Leaders Through Mind, Body, and Heart

DOUG SILSBEE

Foreword by Richard Strozzi-Heckler

JOSSEY-BASS
A Wiley Imprint
www.josseybass.com

Published by Jossey-Bass
A Wiley Imprint
989 Market Street, San Francisco, CA 94103-1741—www.josseybass.com

This book is printed with vegetable based inks. The text paper was manufactured using a high yield thermomechanical pulp that utilizes as much as 80 percent of the harvested tree and is brightened using an elemental chlorine free bleaching process. Our use of lighter weight paper reduces the amount of paper (and trees) required to produce this book.

Readers should be aware that Internet Web sites offered as citations and/or sources for further information may have changed or disappeared between the time this was written and when it is read.

Jossey-Bass books and products are available through most bookstores. To contact Jossey-Bass directly call our Customer Care Department within the U.S. at 800-956-7739, outside the U.S. at 317-572-3986, or fax 317-572-4002. Jossey-Bass also publishes its books in a variety of electronic formats. Some content that appears in print may not be available in electronic books.

Library of Congress Cataloging-in-Publication Data
Silsbee, Douglas K.
    Presence-based coaching: cultivating self-generative leaders through mind, body, and heart / Douglas K. Silsbee; foreword by Richard Strozzi-Heckler. —1st ed.
      p.   cm.
    Includes bibliographical references and index.
    ISBN 978-0-470-32509-4 (cloth: alk. paper)   1. Executive coaching.
    2. Personal coaching.   3. Self-actualization (Psychology)   I. Title.
HD30.4.S562   2008
658.4'07124—dc22

                                                            2008032859

Printed in the United States of America
FIRST EDITION
HB Printing   SKY10077859_061924

Contents

Exercises, Practices, Exhibits, and Figures

EXERCISES

PRACTICES

EXHIBITS AND FIGURES

Foreword

AT FIRST GLANCE, DOUG SILSBEE'S NEW BOOK, *Presence-Based Coaching: Cultivating Self-Generative Leaders Through Mind, Body, and Heart* is a book for coaches. The book clearly describes how to develop the quality of presence and then how to offer that presence to the coach's work with leaders. Silsbee's book delivers for coaches who want to hold significantly deeper and more powerful coaching conversations with their leader clients. In addition, leaders in business, nonprofits, and education will benefit greatly from what is offered here.

However, this is more, much more, than a book for coaches or leaders. Essentially this is a book about waking up. At its core, everything presented here has application to all humans interested in their evolution and transformation. This is critically important in this historical time of accelerated change. As we face the environmental destruction of our planet, unmitigated violence worldwide, and the immoral plague of disenfranchisement, it is of utmost importance that we wake up and respond with skillful and compassionate action. This is a book for not only leaders and coaches, but for anyone else who hears the call to wake up and be a larger contribution to the world.

The profession of coaching is maturing. Government institutions, business, and the nonprofit sector regularly use coaches to assist their managers and executives and to improve team performance. There are a number of international organizations that certify coaches, hundreds of coach training programs, and countless coaching specialties.

As in any discourse, there are pretenders and opportunists and significant gaps in the training, but we can safely say that coaching is here to stay, and it shows promise in providing lifelong learning and transformation. Yet something is missing in the training of coaches.

As the profession moves into its next stage of maturation, there's a critical need to expand the coach's learning so that it goes beyond technique and skill acquisition and completing courses. The time has arrived in the coach's education to also emphasize the cultivation of the self. Clearly it's important what the coach can *do,* but it's more important how he or she is *being.* This requires the development of an embodied presence that is self-generating, self-healing, and self-educating. *Presence-Based Coaching* directly meets this need. This book will unquestionably advance how coaching is practiced and taught; it will also distinguish coaching as a far greater offer than it is now currently being presented. This is not a "how-to" book or a primer for beginning coaches. (For this, I recommend Doug's first book, *The Mindful Coach,* which sets a solid foundation for coaching.) In this new book, Doug goes directly to the heart of developing the purpose, presence, and awareness necessary for a masterful coach.

Presence-Based Coaching is the result of Doug Silsbee's many years of coaching leaders and teaching other coaches, combined with his ongoing commitment to his own personal evolution. What you will find in this book is the authentic voice of a person who has traveled the path that he teaches. Doug is not simply a highly refined intellect. He's learned from the varied terrain that he has traveled, and has integrated this learning into his life and work as a coach and teacher. He embodies and lives the distinctions that he offers; his writing voice is accessible without sacrificing depth. There's an intimacy in this book that makes the learning personal and very relevant. Doug has done, and is doing, the hard personal work of becoming a whole person that is necessary to be a master coach. He combines the scope of this journey with his powers of perception to create a pragmatic and poetically moving book. *Presence-Based Coaching* is a key contribution to the greening of the coaching profession.

This is an important book for two central reasons. One is that Doug brings forward the importance of the coach's self-organization as a unity of mind, body, and heart in order to be more effective in coaching. He doesn't do this by telling you what to do, but by inviting you into a state of reflection through questions and somatic practices. If you sincerely engage in these awareness and reflection practices, you will learn the moves and techniques of a coach; more important, you will generate the energy that fuels your own transformation. Very soon the reader begins to see that this book is full of gems that point to a way of being that includes the coaching discipline and then goes far beyond it. Most coaching books tell you what to do, how to do it, and when to do it. This is often useful for beginners as long as they realize that it's only a starting point. This is a prescriptive method, not an organic approach to the unfolding of a person's process. It has its place in the beginning stages of learning, but fundamentally omits how the living presence of the coach affects the outcome of the coaching engagement. In a very clear and grounded manner, Doug outlines how coaches can self-organize in a way that will improve not only their technical skills but open a new dimension of being and presence that will powerfully and positively affect the leaders being coached. Silsbee points out that when coaches fully embody who they are in an authentic and genuine manner, they will draw more deeply on their intuition, awareness, and energy field to be more effective in their coaching practice. This state of being he calls *presence*. This is a state of expanded awareness that brings one fully into a living relationship with a larger reality and is a deeply felt experience of timelessness. He grounds all this through the body so these are not simply good ideas or a rehashing of the perennial philosophies, but pragmatic and highly actionable distinctions. Doug does this skillfully and artfully by drawing on his rich personal experiences, offering practices the reader can engage in, metaphors that bring a living reality to his ideas, and models for how readers can increase their presence as a coach.

The other central point is the possibility that we all can be self-generating leaders. Through living deeply in our mind, body, and heart, we are led to a place of increased choice, a larger context in which to view our life, new possibilities for action, longer moments of awakening, and increased fulfillment that we can extend to others. The business, education, and nonprofit environments we work in provide each of us an opportunity to contribute positively to shifting the consciousness of individuals, teams, and communities. This book will open the way for a new generation of coaching and leadership.

More than that, it points the way to a state of being in which we can live our full potential.

Take this journey with Doug. Reflect on your purpose, commit to the practices, and embody a new way of being in order to benefit all.

Richard Strozzi-Heckler
Author of *The Leadership Dojo* and
In Search of the Warrior Spirit
Strozzi Institute

Acknowledgments

*No ray of sunshine is ever lost. But the green which it awakens
into existence needs time to sprout, and it is not always granted for the sower
to see the harvest. All work that is worth anything is done in faith.*

Albert Schweitzer

THIS BOOK REFLECTS THE LABORS AND CONTRIBUTIONS
of many people; truly, this has been a team effort.

I am deeply appreciative of the people who read part or all of
the manuscript and who gave me feedback that both challenged and
affirmed my thinking along the way. It was enormously restorative to
have such thoughtful encouragement and perspective. You were the air
under my wings. Thank you, Beth Davis, Elaine Floyd, Julie Harris,
Robyn McCullough, Rod Napier, Walker Silsbee, Carey Smith,
Richard Strozzi-Heckler, and Kathe Sweeney.

Thanks to Kathe Sweeney and the rest of the outstanding team
at Jossey-Bass, especially Rob Brandt, Brian Grimm, Nina Kreiden,
Maria Meneses, Bev Miller, Adrian Morgan, Rebecca Still, and Karen
Warner. It has been a delight to partner with such competence and
experience. Thanks to Don Carroll, Anne Davidson, Elaine Floyd,
John Flood, Les Landes, Mark Mooney, Lili Powell, Joel Rothaizer,
Roger Schwarz, Jenny Sheehan, Madeline Wade, Hannah Wilder, my
AL Team, and others who gave me significant support through the
unique gifts that are yours.

The legacies of countless teachers, living and ancient, are manifest in this work. I am acutely aware of the influence of some who have taught me directly: Rod Napier, Richard Moss, Darya Funches, Nancy Spence, James Flaherty, Sarita Chawla, Irmansyah Effendi, and Richard Strozzi-Heckler, among others. May you feel, in some small way, my deep appreciation for doing your own work with such commitment and rigor for the sake of becoming—and for sharing of yourself generously that those of us who follow might benefit. You, and your teachers before you, are each present in me. The legacy stretches back over millennia.

Thank you, too, readers of this book, the many clients I have worked with over the years, and participants in my retreats, from whom I have learned much, and all of whom I hope have benefited in some way from what I offer. Such is the nature of lineage.

My parents, of course, have been wonderful teachers for me. My mother, Ann, bequeathed me creativity and passion and self-examination. From you, Bob, I learned to marvel at the world, to be infinitely curious, to be gentle and kind, and to be a teacher in the absolute best sense of the word. I have deep gratitude to my three grown children: Alisia, Megan, and Nathan. You have each taught me, and continue to teach me, more than you ever can know about love and about letting go. And to Miles, my first grandchild, born the day after my initial manuscript deadline. You are simultaneously teaching me about unconditional love and providing an intimate view of the miraculous process of human development.

Thank you, Walker, for once again giving me the support to do what is mine to do. You are a committed, wonderful, and rigorous partner in the dance of life, and I'm so grateful to be hitched to the ever shining star that is you. Thanks for being my wife!

And, last but not least, thank you, True Source, for all the countless blessings of this life.

The Author

DOUG SILSBEE IS A LEADER IN THE FIELD OF presence-based leadership development. He is an executive coach, retreat leader, speaker, and author in Asheville, North Carolina. He specializes in coaching self-generative leaders in major corporations, small business, and education. His presence-based coaching encourages clients to enter into strong commitments and to take meaningful and skillful action to produce results they care about. Along the way, clients cultivate leadership presence, resilience, and aliveness.

A master teacher, Silsbee has worked with leaders in eleven countries on four continents, and he owns a mountain retreat center in North Carolina. He has studied with some of the pioneers in the coaching field, including James Flaherty and Richard Strozzi-Heckler, is certified as a Master Somatic Coach by Strozzi Institute, and is accredited by the International Coaching Federation (ICF). He serves as adjunct faculty at the Federal Executive Institute and is an affiliate of Pyramid Resource Group.

Silsbee is also the author of *The Mindful Coach* (2004). He has been a frequent and well-received presenter at ICF conferences, as well as conferences for the International Association of Facilitators, Association for Experiential Education, and OD Network.

More information on Silsbee's work can be found at http://dougsilsbee.com.

Introduction

We work on ourselves in order to help others, and also
we help others in order to work on ourselves.

Pema Chödrön

MANY YEARS AGO, I FACED A SIGNIFICANT PROFESSIONAL challenge. I was about to fly overseas to teach a ten-day seminar to a group of Latin American professors at a prestigious business school. It was early in my career, and I was terrified. I was positive that the participants in the seminar would be smarter than me, more knowledgeable about the subject matter, skeptical, resistant, and questioning of my competence.

I spoke with my mentor the day before I left. He saw capacities in me that I was not yet able to see in myself. He calmly reminded me of indisputable evidence about my competence, ability to design, and capacity to respond creatively to the unexpected. Remembering this evidence (which, in my panic, I'd conveniently forgotten) was reassuring. More important, an intangible quality in his voice—call it confidence, authority, or presence—invited me to relax, lean into my knowledge and instincts, and step openly and calmly into this unknown territory.

During this conversation, I experienced my mentor's presence through these particular qualities. At the end of the call, I was, in a subtle but real way, a different person. I had discovered a resourceful place within me that had lain undiscovered before the call. And I was then able to call on that resource later, when I needed it most.

In Costa Rica two days later, I learned, five minutes into the program, that two of the participants spoke no English. I would have to teach the entire ten-day seminar in Spanish. My first opportunity for creativity had arisen a bit too quickly! Drawing from my previous conversation, I accessed an immediate sense of myself as able to respond creatively and calmly. The potential disaster became an opportunity for flexibility and responsiveness. I switched languages on the spot and went on to have a wonderful and highly successful program with this open, sophisticated, and intelligent group of leaders. In that moment, I had experienced presence.

If I had been more observant at the time of this example, I might have wondered: What is the nature of the presence I experienced? How do I recognize it in him? In myself? How was this sense passed from my mentor to me? What is it about *his* presence that produced a different sense of *me,* and the capacity for new action? How can I cultivate my own presence? And how can I intentionally bring it to bear in my own work with others?

Since that time, I've become curious about presence. I have seen it in powerful leaders that commands the attention of an audience and evokes their commitment to something greater. I've seen it in sports figures at the peak of their game. I've experienced it in the gifted mentors, coaches, and teachers whom I've had the honor to work with in my own development. I've experimented extensively in the laboratory of myself and learned much about how to cultivate my own presence. And I've seen that presence has been central to my own efficacy in coaching executives and leaders through significant and sustainable change.

In fact, our ability to facilitate lasting, sustainable development in others absolutely rests on the presence that we offer to the relationship. Coaching requires that we first do our inner work; in fact, developing presence is the most important work we can do as a human being. Then, and only then, can we coach in a way that comes close to delivering what coaching often promises.

While coaching is the practice field and the focus for this book, what is offered is actually much deeper and broader. Presence is the key to more fulfilling family relationships, your own happiness and success, and a lifetime of purposeful action.

CORE ASSERTIONS

This book is based on several assertions of paramount concern to leaders in business, nonprofits, education, and government. These core assertions are the basis for everything that follows:

- There are three doorways into presence: mind, body, and heart. When we do practices associated with each of these areas, we become increasingly masterful over our inner state, and the experience of presence is more accessible.

- As leaders and as practitioners in any endeavor focused on human development, our quality of presence is central to our professional efficacy.

- Presence engenders creativity, agility, resilience, and authenticity, all key requirements of great leaders. When we are present, we are maximally resourceful and responsive to what our circumstances require of us.

- Living in a commitment to discover and cultivate this quality of presence greatly accelerates our capacity to learn and develop in any domain we choose. In fact, presence is central to our capacity to be self-generative—to choose, in each living moment, who we are and how we respond to life.

- Presence is a state available to all of us at any moment. While acquired habits and tendencies greatly constrain our experience of presence, our access to it can be intentionally and systematically cultivated.

Presence-Based Coaching explores these assertions in depth. I synthesize ideas from a number of important and influential streams into a clear and unprecedented statement of what presence is, why it is important, and how to develop and use presence to evoke change in others as well as in yourself. Importantly, this work is grounded in concrete business examples and in real-world application.

How to Use This Book

Presence-Based Coaching is not a basic how-to-coach book. (My first book, *The Mindful Coach*, offers a pragmatic, question-based coaching model, based on coach self-awareness. It is a good introduction to coaching, and to integrating mindfulness for more advanced practitioners.[1]) *Presence-Based Coaching* assumes some level of previous experience; it will not give you everything you need to start coaching from scratch. And it assumes a healthy appetite for your own learning and growth.

Given these two elements, whether you see coaching as part of your leadership role or you are a professional coach of individuals, the book invites you to take your work to the next level. While hard-driving business professionals may find it challenging at first to access presence, it is absolutely what is needed to get better results through efficacy and authenticity.

This material is broadly relevant to the fields of leadership, management, human resources, education, facilitation, consulting, and mediation. Having said this, the book is primarily written for people who coach and develop leaders in business settings. The microcosm of coaching illuminates distinctions that are easily extrapolated to other settings where human development is central.

In this book, the word *coach* applies to whoever is in that role, no matter their job description. The coach can be an outside professional, a boss, or an internal coach, among many others. (Some caveats apply to coaching one's own team members; this territory is tricky, and the boss's own agenda and concerns often make it difficult to provide the neutrality and trust that are essential to the coaching process.) Similarly, the word *client* is used generically to apply to the person being developed, no matter what the nature of the relationship is to the coach.

The book balances and integrates two threads. First, we explore presence as an essential element of human learning and development. I provide a comprehensive map of how presence supports, and in fact renders inevitable, this miraculous unfolding, and the concrete and practical tools to cultivate your own presence. This thread, which runs through the book, invites you into a lifelong process of self-development.

Second, we explore practical application in the domain of leadership development, and specifically coaching. In this second stream,

I offer clear distinctions for how presence evokes change in others and specific tools for accessing and using presence in relationships organized around the development of whole and effective leaders.

I have integrated a well-organized exposition of concepts with exercises and practical tools for developing and using coaching presence. My extensive experience as an executive coach, a teacher and mentor of coaches, and a lifelong learner ground the material and provide plenty of permission for the reader to be a work in progress.

The three chapters in Part One lay the groundwork for the rest of the book. Chapter One explores the nature of presence itself and the resourcefulness, connectedness, and joy that it produces. Chapter Two lays out the assumptions about human development and self-generation on which this coaching methodology rests. I also describe the process of self-generation and offer an illustrative business example. Chapter Three integrates all of this into a description of how presence-based coaching can provide the necessary structures and support for a greatly accelerated development process, grounded in a solid understanding of how we grow and change in the first place.

Part Two steps into the methodology of presence-based coaching and focuses on the inner moves that we can make as coaches to bring ourselves to the coaching conversation as the most useful possible resource. It will become clear in this part that inner mastery is a requirement for being fully present in the coaching relationship.

Part Three offers practical guidance about developing a coaching presence. The three chapters are organized around mind, body, and heart. Each offers an explanation of this particular doorway into presence and a set of practices. Doing the practices with some consistency over time will greatly increase your access to the state of presence and your ability to offer this to others.

Part Four integrates everything into a wide range of conversational moves that tremendously increase the pace, depth, and sustainability of our clients' development. On one level, this is presented as a tool kit. However, as a busy professional, if you decide to skip ahead to Part Four so that you can try out all these new techniques on your clients, guess what will happen? Yes, that's right. You will (correctly!) produce in your clients the impression that you are simply trying out new techniques.

I offer these moves with the caveat that unless you use them from a grounded presence within yourself (which can be developed only through practice), techniques just won't work very well. They'll fall flat or appear manipulative. In presence-based coaching, the work really begins with you. And it begins now.

A word about the exercises. In order for *Presence-Based Coaching* to provide not a grand tour of a conceptual realm, but rather an experience that moves you in new and perhaps unpredictable ways, I've offered lots of activities designed to provide fresh inner experiences and to stimulate inquiry. Some are cognitive in nature; others invite you to experience your own mind, body, and heart in new ways. Exercises are generally done once or twice in order to reveal something interesting. Practices, on the other hand, are to be entered into as a repeated, ongoing activity, much as we might commit to a workout program. Collectively, these experiences are central to fulfilling the promise of the book.

I strongly recommend doing at least some of the activities in every chapter. While it is not strictly necessary to do every one in sequence, you will fundamentally miss the point of the book if you don't dedicate some time to the inner work to which the activities provide a practical guide. Too, you will not be able to apply the coaching moves presented later in the book without having them grounded in your own way of being.

Simply put, we can't get the benefits of what is offered here without paying the ante of doing our own work. Our inner work gets us into the game.

MY PROMISE

Presence-Based Coaching offers a practical map to the territory of working with presence, both within yourself as a necessary and prerequisite step and in service to your coaching and developing of others. (Helpful templates, additional practices, and other resources can be found on the Presence-Based Coaching website at http://dougsilsbee.com/books/pbc.)

So here are my promises to you. If you read all of this book, use some of the Part Three practices with some diligence over time, and work with the moves described in Parts Two and Four, you will:

- Shift into the state of presence more easily and readily
- Increase your capacity to establish and hold a field of presence with others

- Increase your capacity to enroll and influence others through your authentic presence
- Understand how presence facilitates self-generation and accelerates development
- Apply a set of coaching moves that enable others to shift how they see themselves in relation to their challenges and to take new and creative actions
- Design unique practices for yourself and others that foster the capacity for presence
- Be experienced by yourself and others as more present, authentic, and alive

Presence is constitutional to being human. It is a birthright, a natural state of being. *Presence-Based Coaching* will help you rediscover your own capacity for presence, using inner (reflection and practices) and outer work (leading, coaching, holding skillful conversations) as the means.

READING AS EXPERIENCE

I want reading *Presence-Based Coaching* to be an experience. Throughout the book, I frequently invite you to experience presence in the act of reading. For example, at times, I introduce a *presence pause*. These are places where I anticipate that something I am saying may confront your belief system or open a new way of seeing.

It is easy, when reading, to gloss over these moments. However, these moments are the essence of the book. The moments when the experience of reading the book stretches you provide the greatest potential for real embodied learning. Moving quickly past these moments is an excellent way to protect what you already know.

In addition, pausing, sensing, and feeling what is being offered can open up something new. So I invite you to pause, sense, and feel anytime you are struggling with a claim I make. I invite you to notice your reactions. When you feel an internal tightening, resistance, or argument, be curious about it. You don't have to agree with anything; in fact, I ask you to take nothing on faith. Rather, I request that you allow the *possibility* of a claim's truth to permeate you, to work in you.

Let's try it. I'm going to make a claim. After you read it, take a break. Put the book down for a couple of minutes. Let the claim roll around in you. Open to it. Notice what your mind says about it, how your body reacts. See what might become possible if the statement were actually true. Then, let that sit. Be present with it.

So, here's the claim: If you read this book and try the suggested practices with an open mind, you will become a different person. This book will change you, loosen the grip of old habits, and support you in becoming more present, available, and resourceful in any situation that you face.

～ PRESENCE PAUSE ～

Now, what happened? Did anything open? Any arguments or skepticism take shape in your mind? Any new actions become possible as a result?

That's how I invite you to read. Notice your reactions. Be curious. When you see a presence pause, take it. And anytime you notice yourself with impatience, increasing energy, or judgment, then take your own presence pause to explore it. I want *Presence-Based Coaching* to evoke an experience for you, not just provide a pat set of ideas.

The book is designed to be eminently practical and invites you to validate every claim for yourself through experimentation. "Test this for yourself" is a recurrent theme. You have explicit permission to take this on, to experiment, validate, or refute every claim I make, and change anything you wish in order to make it work better for you.

Most of my readers have been deeply trained into a Western, Newtonian, reductionistic way of interpreting the world. As you read this book, you may be seeking mastery through a way of looking at coaching that supports the understanding you already have. If this is the case, you may well be disappointed.

Rather, I present some big claims and potentially disruptive practices intended to challenge what you believe you know. I invite you to let go of the understandable but limiting approach to reading in which you seek a new stasis, fixed and foundational, on which to base your coaching. I invite you to a new level of confusion and openness and, no matter your experience, to be willing to be a beginner. If you do so, your view will change. You may be less comfortable, but you will also be more generative, more creative, and more resourceful.

I have experienced some temptation to make this a rather academic book, a grand synthesis of all the literature on leadership development, coaching, presence, developmental psychology, and neuroscience. However, I'm a practitioner, not an academic. It was liberating to recognize that I'm not the person to write the treatise I originally had in mind.

I've had great teachers who contributed much to my learning and development over many years. My opportunity is to write from my heart, to share what I've learned in a way that's authentic, direct, and passionate, and to hold the possibility that it will touch open something new for you. That's a much smaller (and more achievable) premise.

I offer this as a working model. Although it is well grounded in research and in practice, it is also a work in progress. Rather than examining every aspect of the book to see how it fits with your current understanding, I invite you to try it on, validating or refuting elements in what I'm saying through your own experience.

Presence becomes possible through uncertainty and openness. Part of what makes presence so powerful in coaching is the openness of the team member or client to the possibility that things aren't what we thought, that greater things are possible. This book will have the greatest benefit for you if you approach it in the same way that you'd ask your clients to approach coaching: open, willing to try on new assumptions. What we have held as true becomes looser.

I'm aware that I don't live everything in this book. I can at times feel hypocritical in writing a book that so clearly advocates for the power of presence when much of the time, I'm not present myself! In my own efforts to be worthy of a book on presence, I've been reminded again and again that I'm a work in progress. The book offers a radical possibility. Through the writing, I'm living into that possibility more and more. I invite you to join me in being a work in progress yourself. Play. Experiment. Try on these ideas, and see what happens. Laugh at yourself along the way.

So who's the person reading this? Are you open and receptive?

PRESENCE PAUSE

I'm learning to simply take pleasure in the good fortune I have to be able to sit here and write about something I have passion about. I enjoy the feel of my little cabin at our retreat center in the North Carolina mountains. The sun is shining in the window and on the rhododendrons by the creek. My dog, Lyra, is lying on the floor next to me. While there are times of struggle and effort, at this moment, right now, I'm genuinely happy doing what I'm doing.

I hope you are enjoying reading as much as I'm enjoying writing.

Are you?

≫ PRESENCE PAUSE ≪

PART
ONE

Presence, Self-Generation, and the Role of Coaching

There is a vitality, a life force, an energy, a quickening, that is translated through you into action, and because there is only one of you in all time, this expression is unique. And if you block it, it will never exist through any other medium and will be lost.

Martha Graham

IT IS ESSENTIAL FOR ANYONE PRESUMING TO GUIDE others in a journey of change to be clear about the foundation on which they stand. We all have assumptions about what it means to be human, how we got the way we are, and how we change. Most of us have never questioned those assumptions, but they guide and restrict us whether we're aware of them or not.

The leadership training and coaching fields have often missed this questioning of core assumptions and have predominantly focused on training leaders to work with what's "out there." By this, I mean that leaders are accustomed to thinking about how they can make decisions that optimize the arrangement of materials or functions or humans, provide information that will advance their goals, or communicate in a way that will produce desired results. We train leaders to act on their worlds as if they were in a complex chess game, and their role is to make sure that the pieces do what they are supposed to do.

What's missing in this is the inner game. By separating ourselves from everything around us and treating people and other resources as chess pieces, we lose touch with the fundamental connectedness of all things. We forget that our inner state (meaning what we perceive, where our attention is placed, and how we experience ourselves in relation to the world around us) is central both to what information we can access and respond to, and to how we will be perceived by others.

Consider that the same leader, at two different times, responding to the same situation with exactly the same words, can produce radically different results. A primary determinant will be the inner state of the leader. For example, it is intuitively obvious to most of us that a rigid, controlling inner state is more likely to produce defensiveness or resistance in others. A relaxed, open, and optimistic inner state, and the same words, are much more likely to produce openness and acceptance.

Our inner state is not an accident. We can become familiar with it, eventually developing mastery in working with it. This mastery of our inner world is a requirement for our effectiveness and is key to accelerating our development as humans and as leaders. As coaches, this mastery is central to our ability to cultivate real and lasting change for our team members and our clients. (Given the challenges we face in the world, accelerated development of effective leaders should be of great interest to all of us.)

This inner state is fundamentally what *Presence-Based Coaching* is about. The most resourceful, ready, resilient inner state, available to all of us at every moment, we call *presence*.

CHAPTER 1

Presence

*It's not enough to simply understand intellectually that if we continue on
the path we're going on we're going to fall short of our goals ...
we have to feel it. When we have a deep enough emotional experience of the
impact of a behavior, our life changes permanently.*

Kevin Cashman

Doing the best at this moment puts you in the best place for the next moment.

Oprah Winfrey

I WAS COACHING A SENIOR VICE PRESIDENT AT A LARGE
financial institution with a business goal so radical and ambitious
it had never before been tried anywhere. My client had been extraordinarily successful, often by sheer energy, will, and force of character.
He was viewed as charismatic and inspirational, but was often criti-
cized for being a one-man band.

The goal had been agreed to by my client and his president with
little input from others. Wisely, my client recognized that being successful in this goal required a level of ownership and buy-in that his
senior team was sorely lacking. He knew it had something to do with
him, but no clue as to what to change in order to build this ownership. It seemed that the more he tried to inspire them to step up their
game, the more passive they got.

In one of our early conversations, I was feeling a bit stuck. He was expressing his frustration at the unwillingness of a couple of his key players to step up to the plate and didn't see how his leadership precluded their doing so. At one point in the conversation, I stopped in my tracks. Out of nowhere, I simply knew what to do. I experienced a sudden clarity, a sharper awareness. I suggested an experiment. I invited him to stand, to hold his body in an aggressive, forward-leaning stance, and feel what it was like to ask others for their ideas in that stance. Then I requested that he do the same while leaning back, in a receptive stance.

As he did so, the light of recognition came over his face. He sensed in that moment that his words were absolutely incongruous with the message that his body was sending. His words said, "I want your ideas." His body said, more loudly than his words, "This is MY show, and *I'm* going to make it happen. It's about me." He saw in a moment what his people had been watching for years. In that moment, my client realized that he had to shift how he interacted with people. He felt, in the core of his being, that he was inauthentic in his requests and that something deep in him needed to change. That awareness came from the power of presence.

This was one of many experiences of presence I've had as an executive coach. It has become clear to me that presence is in fact central to what it means to coach others from a centered place; be an authentic leader; and have a full, rich, and satisfying life. Presence is a fundamental capacity, inherent in being human. Our work as leaders and coaches provides us a unique opportunity to discover this within ourselves.

PRESENCE DEMYSTIFIED

There is no magic here; in fact, I intend to begin by thoroughly demystifying presence. So here are some additional examples. By seeing the range of the territory, you can first understand what presence is and then explore what it can show you about leadership, development, and coaching.

- Jerry had decided to let go of a manager, whom he had recently hired and was not working out. Jerry was frustrated, and the manager was both unproductive and defensive. He had gone way out on a limb for this guy, against the recommendations of almost everyone else in the hiring process, so letting him go was personally difficult. Jerry was conflict averse and had a strong tendency to keep people around, even when they weren't performing well. Confronting this situation also meant confronting his own habits. Jerry had a habitual tendency to tell himself stories to keep from having to hold difficult conversations. ("He just needs a little more time. I can work with him. He'll get this moving.")

In my work with Jerry, he spent considerable time in introspection, letting go of his frustration, recognizing his own contribution to the problem, and working with his emotional state. The story he was telling himself fell away, and it was instantly clear that it was time to take action. Then it became a question of how to hold the difficult conversation rather than what conversation needed to be held.

After this preparation, Jerry met with the manager. With calmness, caring, and candor, he explained that it wasn't going to work. He took responsibility for his own miscalculation and acknowledged that it also was a very difficult situation for the other man, who had relocated his family from the opposite coast. The conversation actually came as a relief to the other, who had felt a bit like a drowning man with few options. They were able to work out an equitable solution with mutual respect.

• There's a US Airways agent named Bob who frequently works behind the counter at the Asheville, North Carolina, airport, from which I frequently depart. As I enter the airport, preoccupied with my day, I scan for Bob, because I know that my day will be different if I find him. Bob is inevitably positive, even upbeat. He makes eye contact, addresses every passenger by name, and asks how people are doing (and he means it). I never fail to notice my own mood shift. After being around Bob, I always feel more alive, lighter somehow, and ready to enjoy my day. I've watched him for years and consistently notice how others lighten up around him. Bob is contagious.

• A few years ago, after filling my tank with gas at our local station, I pulled over to the side of the highway with a nagging suspicion that I hadn't replaced the filler cap. I looked and was shocked to see the entire nozzle and gas hose hanging from the side of my car! I'm not proud of this, but my first instinct was to take the hose and throw it in the weeds and drive off. Then I remembered a time when a colleague did the same thing, and the entire gas station flooded with gasoline from the broken pump. I visualized my local BP station engulfed in hundred-foot-high sheets of flame, and the stakes suddenly went way up. I also realized that if I threw the hose in the bushes, I would never be able to look my kids in the eye again and tell them not to lie.

This was an existential moment, with a very clear choice between following my baser but nonetheless seductive instincts, or the values I'd always espoused. I experienced that familiar "deer in the headlights" paralysis, knowing that my values were on the line and that either choice had real consequences. I stood, not knowing what I was going to do. Then it became absolutely clear that there was no real choice. I loaded the twelve-foot, heavy, smelly hose in the passenger seat and headed back to face the music.

• Most of us remember starkly and clearly, wherever we lived in the world, the morning of September 11, 2001. (I was lingering over breakfast with my parents, who were about to leave to drive home three days after my daughter got married at our retreat center.) We each heard, or saw, the news at a particular moment. At some point soon after that moment, we had a realization that something fundamental had changed. How we each interpreted that change depended on many factors: where we live, our cultural assumptions and beliefs, our personality and orientation in life. But before our interpretation kicked in to provide our own meaning from those difficult events, the world seemed to stop. Our internal world shifted; we became aware of a larger truth, and we could never go back to being the same. This too was a moment of presence.

These examples provide wide-ranging examples of experiences involving presence. The commonalities may not yet be readily apparent. While you may not have named your own experiences of presence as such, we've all had them, and we've witnessed them in others. Some of yours may have been large and dramatic, like the events surrounding 9/11, while others may have been matter-of-fact and practical, like my client's conversation with his manager.

Given this range, let's explore what presence is, and how it's relevant to your work as a team leader, coach, or executive.

EXERCISE 1.1.
Experiences of Presence

- Consider times when you have had an experience of presence. Remember a time in nature when you felt moved by a waterfall, a sunset, or a grand view. What was that feeling like? What specifically did you experience within yourself?
- Remember a time when you felt a spontaneous wave of affection or love for a spouse, a child, or another person. What happened in that experience?
- Remember a time when you were confronted with a choice, the choice said something about you, and there was no place to pass the buck. What was your experience in that precise moment when you knew the implications of your decision but not what you were going to do?
- Recall a time when you were being with someone who was upset, perhaps a crying child, perhaps an upset employee, or as the first person at the scene of an accident. Intuitively, perhaps, you understood that being calm was central to how you could help. Somehow your calm presence helped another. How did you access that calm?
- Remember where you were on the morning of 9/11. Consider anything that seemed to come sharply into focus that morning. Was there anything that touched you, that you suddenly perceived differently, or that emerged as more important than previously?

These are examples of presence. And, I suspect that with a minimum of diligence, you were able to identify something for each question.

So, What Is Presence?

Presence turns out to be a devilishly slippery and challenging word to define. Other writers have approached it in a variety of ways. As you look at the following descriptions from gifted observers, notice what reactions you have. Is this something you want more of? What strikes you about the definitions?

"Presence means bringing yourself when you coach: your values, passion, creativity, emotion, and discerning judgment—to any given moment with a client."[1]

"Presence ... a deep listening; of being open beyond one's preconceptions and historical ways of making sense."[2]

"The ability to connect authentically with the thoughts and feelings of others, in order to motivate and inspire them toward a desired outcome."[3]

These descriptions generally describe what we are doing. They assert that *presence* is largely a verb. Presence, in these views, lends itself to the development of skills and techniques and is useful for bringing resourcefulness and a certain quality of being to relationships with others. I can imagine that being with someone who is doing what these writers describe might lead to an experience of openness, of being listened to in a profoundly different way. The descriptions imply what we can do in order to produce simultaneous authenticity and a different way of being with others. That's practical.

I propose a different, broader, and more inclusive definition of *presence*. I suggest that presence includes every one of these pragmatic definitions. However, if we limit our concept of presence to its applicability, we are depriving ourselves of something profoundly significant.

Here's a broader definition that I offer: *Presence is a state of awareness, in the moment, characterized by the felt experience of timelessness, connectedness, and a larger truth.*

- Presence is a *state*, not a verb. It's subjective, personal, internal.

- It's *in the moment*, meaning right now. This moment. And this one.

- Our felt experience of *time* changes radically. Future concerns and past memories drop away, and there is only this moment.

- We experience ourselves as *connected* to others, to ourselves, to our environment and circumstances.

- Presence brings us into direct experience of a *larger truth*. This might mean seeing clearly and directly who we are, who another person is, how we fit into a bigger picture, what the situation really is, what is possible for us, or what choices are available to us.

> ### PRESENCE
>
> Presence is a state of awareness, in the moment, characterized by the felt experience of timelessness, connectedness, and a larger truth.

This definition is, I believe, more inclusive of a wide range of experiences than the useful descriptions of other writers. It is true that presence serves our efficacy as a leader and a developer of people; *Presence-Based Coaching* offers practical, tested wisdom about bringing this experience of presence into the domain of work.

It's also true that presence opens the door to a radically accelerated pathway for our own development. The state of presence turns out to be a central and essential element in the capacity for learning itself. Working with presence opens the floodgates to an ever deepening experience of yourself that will touch every area of your life.

EXERCISE 1.2.
Presence Now

Let's experience presence. Here are two quick experiments that you can do. Read the directions through for each exercise until familiar, and then do the exercise without reading.

First, sit in a comfortable chair, without distractions. Close your eyes. Relax. Now, notice the short space between your thoughts. Notice that there is a moment of stillness between the end of one thought and the beginning of the next. Bring your attention to that stillness. Watch, expectantly, for the beginning of the next thought, like a cat waiting, with total alertness, for a mouse to emerge. That moment, between thoughts, is presence.

Then, sit in front of something that moves you: a picture of a loved one, a view of nature, a special work of art. Close your eyes, and visualize it. Consider what it means to you. Hold it in your mind's eye, concentrating on the image. Now slowly open your eyes, and look at the object *as if you were seeing it for the first time*. Simply let yourself feel, with freshness and curiosity, this thing that you're seeing anew.

So, what did you notice? What did you feel? That's presence.

IMPLICATIONS OF PRESENCE

Presence itself is an inner state, a fleeting kind of awareness that often lasts for only a moment. For now, let's explore some of the implications of this state, given the previous anecdotes, and see how they might bring this definition to life and establish useful meaning and grounding for our work together. A little later in this chapter, I tie this back into coaching.

Presence reveals a larger context. Sometimes our perspective shifts suddenly, and we clearly see a larger truth that somehow had eluded us. We can resist this (as in the wonderful Gary Larson cartoon with two cowboys in a defensive circle of covered wagons, flaming arrows coming in from all sides. One cowboy turns to the other and says, "Hey! They're lighting their arrows! Can they DO that?") Or we can allow this expanded perspective to call us to something new. Leaders who make decisions with a more inclusive view are less likely to fall into the trap of myopic, symptom-driven decision making.

Presence unveils new possibilities for action. Through the direct view of a more inclusive context, we see things clearly and expansively. This felt experience can illuminate new actions. On the morning of 9/11, in each individual's moment of realization, his or her world changed. Some people, like Pat Tillman, the National Football League star, were moved to enlist. Others responded by donating blood. My wife and I called neighbors and friends to join us around a bonfire, realizing the precious and fleeting nature of our community. Each of these decisions was taken as a meaningful, chosen response to a felt experience.

Presence lays bare our freedom of choice. The gas hose dilemma provides a wonderful example of the immediacy of choice in the moment. I was acutely aware of the decision and the implications of each alternative. I could face an embarrassing confession (and, in my mind, the potential liability for the largest conflagration the small town of Weaverville had ever seen) or do penance with a lifetime of reflection on my hypocrisy. There was no one else to pass the buck to, and time stopped as I realized it was all up to me. Ultimately when the chips are down, each of us performs in the moment, or we don't. Being aware of that moment of choice results from presence.

Presence provides an intelligent moment. Presence produces a feeling of waking up. Things come into sharp focus, and we immediately experience more energy, alertness, and resourcefulness. We can see this in every example set out in this chapter. In that moment, there's nothing else. The fuzziness in which we spend most of our hours drops away, and things are suddenly clear and elemental.

Presence is an invitation. Bob, the US Airways guy, is so clearly and visibly in a different mood from most other people in airports that it calls us up short. His mood is so stable and contagious that he opens a new possibility for everyone around him. He is an invitation into a shared state of happiness. His presence confronts people with a clear choice: in that moment, they can become happier, or get onto the plane feeling like a grump. The invitation is there, and my experience with Bob is that it's easier to accept than decline.

Presence is the opening to fulfillment. The present is the only moment in which we can actually have joy and fulfillment. We think about happiness like this: it will come when we get the perfect house, the next promotion, a new job, the latest iPod, or a bigger paycheck. Those beliefs, well conditioned by our marketing culture, defer our happiness to a perpetually future circumstance. Presence opens us to joy now.

SOME IMPLICATIONS OF PRESENCE

- Presence reveals a larger context.
- Presence unveils new possibilities for action.
- Presence lays bare our freedom of choice.
- Presence provides an intelligent moment.
- Presence is an invitation.
- Presence is the opening to fulfillment.

Let's explore how the characteristics of presence might be relevant to the development of a number of essential leadership traits:

- *Agility:* A commitment to considering the implications and context for decisions, and discovering new possibilities for action, is critical. On an organizational level, this engenders agile, responsive, innovative cultures. On an individual level, this is a recipe for fast-track development and learning.

- *Accountability:* Any meaningful definition of business and personal efficacy must include both measurable results and the

LEADERSHIP TRAITS SUPPORTED BY PRESENCE

- Agility
- Accountability
- Resourcefulness
- Resilience
- Authenticity
- Vitality

effects of those results on colleagues, employees, customers, communities, and ultimately the whole of life on earth. Presence makes us accountable to considering an ever-larger context for every decision we make.

- *Resourcefulness:* Presence invites us out of habitual ways of doing things and into the real possibilities available every moment of every day. It's about choice—about living life as a creative, generative process. If we are interested in building a culture of innovation and creativity, we must begin with ourselves.

- *Resilience:* Presence is foundational to leader resilience. The experience of presence is antidotal to the grinding effects of stress and unpredictability, and feeling overwhelmed, that tire even our best leaders over time. In the present moment, we find a respite to which we can turn, over and over, in order to become more resourceful and less caught up in things that pull us away from ourselves.

- *Authenticity:* Presence is a central attribute in authenticity. The presence of an authentic leader is an invitation to join in something that is ennobling, that is greater and more worthwhile. If we are looking to address retention, motivation, and organizational effectiveness, what better way to do so than to be the kind of leader people want to follow?

- *Vitality:* Rather than experiencing "slow death" at work as so many people do, presence invites us to wake up.[4] When present, we can see that every moment is an opportunity to learn something, to experience our energy and aliveness. Presence opens us to a full experience of our lives and our connectedness to the people and environment around us.

The cultivation of presence as a business or nonprofit leader, an educator, or coach is inextricably linked to efficacy. Presence allows us to make choices grounded in an understanding of the implications of our decisions and to become bolder in choosing new courses of action that we might habitually avoid. Presence therefore is fundamental to enduring human change and development. It is central to our creativity and resourcefulness as professionals and is a major factor in how we are perceived and received by others.

What I am offering here is about all of life. Widely used, the tools and practices presented in this book will lead to better leaders in corporations, associations, and nonprofits. I am also deeply committed to seeing stronger educators in our schools and coaches in all walks of life who are able to support their clients in becoming more compassionate, grounded, and powerful contributors.

Presence and the Products of Coaching

I presume that, given the title of the book, you're reading this because you have a commitment to the learning and development of others, whether or not you actually call yourself a coach. Right?

I define *coaching* broadly as *that part of a relationship in which one person is primarily dedicated to serving the long-term development of competence, self-generation, and aliveness in the other.*[5] Coaching is a central and critically important activity for any leader in any organization who sees himself or herself as working with and through others. It is unlikely that anyone reading this book doesn't fundamentally understand coaching as a component of what you do.

This definition excludes group coaching. Although presence is just as relevant to group coaching as to individual coaching, it's my desire to keep this conversation focused on the essential elements.

COACHING

Coaching is that part of a relationship in which one person is primarily dedicated to serving the long-term development of competence, self-generation, and aliveness in the other.

These will be much simpler to see and apply to one-on-one conversations than to group conversations. I will leave it to practitioners to make the easy extrapolation into other contexts.

My definition of coaching also excludes one-on-one interactions that are not dedicated to the learning and development of one partner. Thus, I exclude supervisory interventions and other conversations that are driven by organizational goals and priorities rather than the learning and development of an individual. Although presence is clearly relevant to those conversations as well, there are additional complexities that are beyond the limited scope of this book.

With these caveats, I hold that coaching is something that all business leaders and educators do, whether or not coaching is included in their job title. Coaching in a business context is intended to support others in developing competence in behaviors that are effective and authentic and produce results. At the same time, coaching seeks to develop the ability of people to contribute, to be competent learners who drive their own development, and to find fulfillment.

I distinguish three essential products of coaching:[6]

- *Observable competency in fulfilling the client's commitments.* The client's specific commitments will generally determine much of the focus of coaching. Resulting competencies will be observable by both the client and others.

- *The capacity for self-generation.* We explore this in more depth in the next chapter. For now, I assert that the capacity for, and ownership of, one's own ongoing learning and development is a central product of coaching. This often provides benefits far beyond the original outcomes sought from coaching.

- *The experience of greater aliveness, fulfillment, and joy.* Presence-based coaching puts us in much more direct contact with our moment-by-moment experience. Increased sensitivity and awareness of our own experience are the keys to the intangible rewards that we seek in our lives. This too predictably results from skillful coaching.

Presence is central to each of these three products. As coaches concerned with both the efficacy and fulfillment of ourselves and of our clients, it follows that we should be acutely interested in the development of presence.

THE PRODUCTS OF COACHING

- Observable competency in fulfilling commitments
- The capacity for self-generation
- The experience of greater aliveness

Presence is not something we can produce in others by a reliable magic wand or a carefully practiced set of techniques. We're not in control of others, and we can't manipulate others into presence.

I suspect that if you picked up this book, you are already onto the notion that your own development is inseparable from your efficacy as a developer of others. It's not just a matter of modeling, although that too has a role. I'm saying that your way of being is fundamental to your ability to produce genuine new shifts, insights, and behaviors with those you coach. The coach is an instrument for the client's development.

Presence is an invitation. When we are present, we stand as an invitation. Coaching begins with our own inside work; it is through this development of the capacity for presence in ourselves that we evoke the experience of presence in others. *Presence-Based Coaching* will help you to greatly increase your capacity for the presence that is fundamental to developing yourself and others.

Then, and only secondarily, you can explore coaching moves that make it more likely that your clients will also experience presence in a way that is liberating and leads to the possibility of new actions.

✌ PRESENCE PAUSE ✌

In the example of Jerry above, presence was essential to the successful resolution of a difficult situation. Jerry had to do his own inner work in order to own his responsibility for the problem, be compassionate with his manager, and bring a graceful end to a situation that was working for neither. In speaking candidly and compassionately, Jerry made it clear that he was going to terminate the current arrangement and invited his manager to join in an exploration of the best possible resolution. The quality of Jerry's presence was sufficiently inviting that the other man responded undefensively and they were able to create a mutually satisfactory solution. This also redounded to the credit of Jerry, and the company.

CHALLENGES TO PRESENCE

Many factors in the coaching environment and limitations in the coach make maintaining presence quite challenging. If we are to maintain our own presence, toward the end of evoking presence and capability for more effective action in our clients, we must be aware of the challenges as well.

Here are some of the things that make our own maintenance of presence difficult:

Internal Impediments to Presence

- Our own habits of thought, which tend to run in narrow grooves worn by years of practice
- Our desires to look good, avoid conflict, be perceived as smart, and so forth
- Our investment in maintaining equilibrium in our relationship with the other person
- Our needs to be seen, or to see ourselves, as a particular kind of person or coach

External Impediments to Presence

- The pressures we feel from organizational agendas or other stakeholders
- External pressures from other stakeholders, such as a boss's agenda for our coaching client
- Organizational goals, cultural attributes, and performance measures that may be dissonant with our clients' interests
- Business drivers of coaching outcomes
- Time factors and pressures
- Dual roles (for example, we're the person's coach and supervisor), which set up internal dissonance
- Contractual limitations on how long we can work with a person or on what can be discussed
- Cultural impediments (for example, our cultural bias toward separating mind and body and valuing thinking over being)

Here's an example of a brief coaching conversation, illustrating how some of these factors might impede the conversation. Like most of the examples and dialogues in this book, this conversation is based on actual coaching conversations. However, the names and particulars have been changed to ensure anonymity, and some of the conversations are composites of several clients. In all cases, they have been edited for clarity and conciseness.

In this conversation, June is an internal coach to Rick, the head of a product division. June is reopening a conversation that she had with Rick a week ago. In the previous conversation, Rick had committed to having a difficult conversation with a direct report with some performance issues. She knows this is a tough situation for Rick.

This is going to be dicey; I bet it didn't go well. I'm going to start very neutral, she thinks, before opening the topic with Rick. "So, how did your conversation go with Jim? The one we planned last week, in which you were going to discuss the schedule delays on the development project he's managing for you?"

Rick responds, somewhat tersely, "We held the conversation. That's the best thing I can say. It didn't go well. He was really defensive. I tried to listen to what he was saying, and to empathize, but he didn't react well to my feedback."

That's predictable, the coach thinks to herself. *Seems like Jim is always defensive when Rick talks to him about this, but I don't see Rick recognizing that he might be contributing to that.* She asks, "How do you know he didn't react well?"

Rick explains, "He avoided my questions. When I kept probing, he became angry. He gave an excuse for everything that didn't go well with the project. Everything was outside of his control."

Dang. Here we go again! He's frustrated with Jim, but doesn't see his part. June feels a little caught by Rick's story and has often experienced Rick as defensive. However, she hasn't shared that perspective with Rick. She asks, "So, do you see any part that you played in his being defensive?"

Rick responds, with some energy, "I figured you'd ask that! Actually, I've tried to see my part, but I don't see how I could have done anything differently. I asked him what he thought,

I asked him where the delays came from, I asked him what he thought he could do differently. I listened to him, I really did. He said there wasn't anything he could do differently. No ownership. Nothing."

Well, Rick asked a lot of questions. But he never shared his concerns or assessments. He was trying to get Jim to volunteer the problem, but Jim just can't see it. This isn't going well. She had hoped that Rick would see what he could change, but he wasn't getting it. She feels impatient and frustrated. Distracted, she thought, *Rick's boss is going to ask me how this is going when we get together this afternoon. I really want to coach more in Rick's division, but he has to show people it works. So, I've got to make something happen.*

June asks, "So, what do you see that you could do differently?"

"I make of it that some people just aren't going to be willing to listen to feedback. It feels like beating my head against the wall. I'm really not sure that he's the right person for the job."

He's just not getting it! June begins to feel some self-judgment, and the tension in her gut increases. *I feel stuck. I'm not very good at this. This is wasting Rick's time, and he knows it. And if Rick doesn't begin modeling some new behaviors, this initiative is going to be dead in the water.*

Maybe Jim really isn't the right person for the job. That could be a way into some new actions for Rick. "Rick, we have a choice in front of us. Is it more important to you that we look at how your conversation with Jim could have gone differently, or that we explore how you can make the decision about whether Jim is the right person in this director role?"

The conversation continues. But you probably noticed that the ground of the conversation has shifted. June began by working with Rick on his behaviors in difficult conversations, which tend toward the indirect, manipulative technique of asking Jim to identify a behavior. Rick has already identified what he thinks is the problem, but doesn't want to risk speaking out loud. Now they're in a very different conversation. Why the course change?

Two main dynamics are preventing June from being fully present and resourceful with Rick. These dynamics are limiting June, and because of her limitation, neither is getting what they need. First, there is an internal impediment. June is actually doing the same thing that frustrates her when she sees it in Rick. Her discomfort with directness is keeping her from sharing her assessment, which Rick is apparently not able to discover for himself. Second, there is a significant organizational dynamic that provides an external impediment: the shared hope of June and Rick's boss to bring coaching more into the division. This creates implicit pressure in this conversation to get some kind of results visible to others in the system, a reasonable goal. However, in this moment, that felt pressure expresses itself in June's apparent willingness to accompany Rick on a rather dramatic tangent that may or may not be fruitful, prevents Rick from learning from the present situation, and could potentially cost Jim his job.

June's discomfort with being direct with Rick, and her organizational objectives, are impeding this conversation. If June were able to be present:

- She would recognize her own aversion to directness and make the most useful choice possible for Rick's learning.
- She would recognize the organizational dynamics influencing her view of the conversation and set them aside for now.
- She would be both compassionate and direct with Rick and able to share her assessment candidly with less likelihood of provoking his defensiveness.
- She would bring more presence to her conversation with Rick, which might open up new possibilities for him.

Here's a replay. Let's see how this might go differently if June is more present:

June is preparing to enter the conversation. *I'd better get some results here. I know that Rick's boss wants others to see him doing things differently. Whoa, wait a minute! That pressure's not helpful to me right now. Let's just set that aside. This is now . . . This may be dicey; I bet the conversation didn't go well. Center myself, just be present with Rick. Frame a clear question.* "Rick, let's talk about the conversation with Jim. I know this was going to be a tricky one, and you had the intention to be direct and candid with him. How did you practice directness with Jim?"

Rick responds, "We held the conversation. It didn't go well. I wasn't very direct, because he was really defensive. I tried to listen and to empathize, but he really wasn't open to my feedback."

I wonder what Rick was doing that produced this defensiveness? Seems like Jim is always defensive when Rick talks to him. What's Rick up to here? She asks, "How do you know he didn't react well?"

Rick explains, sounding irritated, "He avoided my questions. When I kept probing, he became angry. He gave an excuse for everything that didn't go well with the project. Everything was outside of his control."

Dang. Here we go again! Rick sees Jim as the whole issue. June notices her own impatience, and some judgment of Rick for not owning his part. She brings herself back. *This is familiar; I'm starting to feel hooked; there's that tension in my gut, that trapped feeling. Breathe. Stay present. Ahh. That's better.* "So, Rick, I wonder if you can identify how you contributed to Jim's defensiveness?"

Rick responds, with some energy, "I don't see it, June. I asked him what he thought, I asked him where the delays came from, I asked him what he thought he could do differently. I listened to him, I really did. He didn't own a thing. Nothing. I don't see what I could have done differently."

Here it is. There's that gut thing again. I'm picking up defensiveness. It's right here in our conversation. Here's an opening. Breathe. Be present. Soften. How can I be an example of what we're talking about? June notices her energy increasing dramatically, although she feels intensely focused and calm at the same time. "So, Rick, I want to offer my experience. Right now, I notice some tightness in my gut. I'm watching my own reluctance to be direct with you. And I notice your increased energy when you stated so clearly that you did everything that you could." She pauses and touches her heart, feeling her compassion for Rick. Then, more softly, she asks, "Rick, I'm curious. I'm wondering what you see happening right now in our conversation?"

Rick looks startled and his face tightens. "Well . . . I don't know." He pauses. "I see what you're getting at. I'm being defensive right now. Is that right?"

June can see Rick struggling to understand what she is saying. She feels compassionate, remembering her own struggle to be more direct with him. She feels her heart soften as she speaks. "You'd have to make that call, Rick. I just noticed that when your energy went up and you were emphatic that there wasn't anything you could have done differently, I found myself reluctant to share my views with you. It seemed to me that it would have taken a lot of energy to get through to you."

"I can see that. But, I really don't see what I could have done differently yesterday."

"Maybe we'll get to that. For now, Rick, can you identify where your energy came from?"

"Well, you were asking me questions about what I could have done differently and I didn't see it. I felt clueless, and somewhat accused. So I guess I got defensive."

"Thanks, Rick. I can see that. Of course, I don't see you as clueless. We're simply exploring for a new way of seeing things. I wonder if this present moment sheds any light on what happened with Jim?"

Rick has that startled look again. "Yeah, it does." He pauses; June can see his face shifting. His body seems to relax, his shoulders drop, his eyes soften. He looks up and almost smiles. "Yeah. I think I get this now. I was just asking questions of Jim, trying to get him to confess. I was trying to manipulate him into saying it because I didn't have the courage to tell him what I really thought. He got defensive just like I did. But I was really protecting myself, June." He pauses. "I could have done that really differently."

And so forth. We could continue the conversation, but the point is made.

Notice in this second pass through the conversation that things play out very differently. June is working with her own presence. First, she recognizes the potential for the organizational pressures to come into the conversation and consciously chooses to set them aside. Later she recognizes her own discomfort and impatience. And a couple of times, she has to work with herself to bring herself back into presence.

Midstream in the conversation, she speaks about what was going on for her right then. June becomes an invitation into an immediate, present moment of experience. Rick, when he comes into presence, discovers a new way of seeing his situation. And new actions become possible when he sees the truth more clearly.

We might also notice that once present and in the moment, the organizational dynamic with Rick's boss and bringing coaching into the division doesn't enter into June's thinking process. The quality of presence electrifies the conversation, and the level of energy and engagement in the conversation simply doesn't leave room for it to reenter.

What June does in this conversation is to create a space of presence into which she can invite Rick. Rick discovers a different perspective of what went wrong in his conversation with Jim because he becomes aware of a similar dynamic in the present moment. This illuminates a clearer understanding of what was driving him in the conversation with Jim and what his options might have been.

Developing our presence as a coach, in the face of the challenges of both internal habits and the organizational dynamics at play, requires continual attention and inner work. This is both a requirement for professional efficacy and an invitation into the ongoing process of doing our own professional, and ultimately spiritual, development work.

CHAPTER SUMMARY

- Presence is a state of awareness—a felt experience of timelessness, connectedness, and a larger truth.
- We have all had experiences of presence, whether or not we identified them as such, and we can practice and cultivate our access to this state.
- Presence has significant implications for leadership. As leaders, through being present, we will be perceived by others differently, become more resilient and resourceful, and be better able to make decisions from a larger context.
- As coaches and developers of leaders, our capacity for presence affects both our resourcefulness and our ability to authentically and effectively extend presence to our clients.
- Coaching produces observable competency, the capacity for self-generation, and the experience of greater aliveness. Presence is central to all three of these products.

- A number of factors, both in the external environment and in the inner world of the coach, make it difficult to stay present. Building familiarity and attention to our particular challenges to presence is essential to self-mastery.
- Doing our own inner work is both a requirement for professional efficacy and a prerequisite to using presence-based coaching moves in a grounded way with our clients. We must be rigorous about our inner work in order to evoke the best from our clients.

How Humans Change: Conditioning, Identity, and Self-Generation

We first make our habits, and then our habits make us.

John Dryden

The beliefs that for a time feel so comfortable that we may not be fully aware of them somehow reach the limits of their effectiveness for us and begin to get in our way. . . . Development is . . . always a matter of transcending some earlier way of knowing and including it in a newer, more complex way of knowing.

Bill Drath and Ellen Van Velsor

THE WORLD NEEDS LEADERS WHO ARE RESILIENT, optimistic, resourceful, authentic, and committed. As leaders and coaches, it is our business to understand what it takes to develop these capacities, first in ourselves and then in others whom we propose to develop through our coaching.

While humans can't help but change and evolve, this development tends to proceed slowly. The deep biological needs for self-preservation, adaptation, and conformity tend to habituate us rather than accelerate the development of ways of being that are responsive to the emerging political, economic, social, and natural environment.

We are biological creatures, and as such we tend to embody the traits that have been required for survival over millions of years, but may not necessarily be relevant to our unique circumstances now.

Accelerating the development of leaders requires understanding how we become shaped into the people we are. We must be clear about the assumptions we make about how humans grow, change, and develop because useful coaching methodology rests on these assumptions.

In this chapter, we appear to diverge for a few pages in order to explore the nature of human conditioning. How did we become the leaders that we are? What holds our personalities and behaviors in place? And how do we work with the nature of that conditioning in order to become self-generative and embody the qualities listed above?

These are big questions. Philosophers, neuroscientists, geneticists, and psychologists have explored these topics in great depth; I won't pretend to offer a new explanation of how this occurs. However, as practitioners concerned with both our own development and that of others, it is critical to have a working model of how humans develop, form personality, change, and resist change. This is foundational for our work.

CONDITIONING

It is essential to have a narrative that can guide our work. Our capacities and achievements as executives, teachers, authors, coaches, and entrepreneurs are enabled, shaped, and limited by a myriad of elements embodied in who we are. To know ourselves is to understand our nature as biological organisms who received certain stories we came to hold as true, as people who have unique genetic endowments and histories, and as the inevitable cumulative products of both our own deep histories and every choice that we have ever made.

Similarly, who we will be in the future is in some way shaped by the choices we make now.

✎ PRESENCE PAUSE ✎

By becoming conscious of how we became who we are, we can wake up to the unfolding story of our own lives and see ourselves in a developmental framework. We can, in fact, become conscious of our own developmental process and can choose and greatly accelerate how we enter into it. By becoming more present, we begin to author our own story rather than living unconsciously in the story that we are only slowly waking up to.

The Developmental Impulse and Shaping

Each of us is the inevitable product of the miraculous process of unfolding we call development.

Like all of us, my grandson, Miles, came into this world helpless and dependent. Yet he arrived pre-wired with a deep instinctive urge to root for the breast. He didn't have to be taught how to do this; he simply knew. For Miles, the behavior of rooting around was quickly rewarded with warm milk, and nursing quickly became familiar and habitual.

As I write this, Miles is eight weeks old. He is incessantly in motion. His face changes moment-by-moment, and his little arms and legs flail around, seemingly at random, with no conscious control. He is adorable, and we can't help but respond with instant and total love for this little perfect creature.

As the miracle continues to unfold, his neural system develops through these random movements. As he discovers what works and what doesn't, the random movements will develop into crawling, walking, and, who knows? Maybe eventually pole-vaulting! As I watch my grandson, I am in awe that I am witness to the early stages of a primal and powerful development process, driven by the deep impulse that propels us all forward.

We are shaped throughout life by the interaction between the primordial impulse for creativity and experimentation, and continuous feedback from the world about what works and what doesn't. Our early years are particularly formative. Some behaviors get rewarded: parents are thrilled over our first stumbling word, crying brings a caregiver running to our comfort. We learn to do the things that get us what we want: approval, love, food, a good feeling. Other behaviors don't get rewarded: poking the cat's eye results in a painful scratch, or crying elicits a strong reaction from an already overtaxed parent.

Implied by this is a self-adaptive learning capacity: when something works and is fun, we do it more. We learn to suppress the impulses that first bring pleasure but lead to consequences we don't want. Our bodies come equipped with a natural orienting mechanism that has the function of guiding us toward or away from certain kinds of experiences as we learn and develop.

While the impulse for experimentation and creativity is always available within us, patterns of behavior begin to form that constrict our creativity. Although this is necessary, it also damps our fullest expression as a human being. We can begin to see that we are products of all the experiences that we have had. We can say that we are conditioned by the world around us. As the poet David Whyte says, "We shape our selves/to fit this world/and by the world/are shaped again."[1]

Habit Formation

Over time, emerging patterns of behavior become embedded as habits; we can think of our particular accumulation of habits as the basis of a unique personality. Habits are part of who we are in the world, and the nature of a habit is that we no longer have to think about them.

Think of driving, and how awkward and tentative we were at first. As driving became more familiar and practiced, our brain internalized the complex coordination of movement and balance required. Now, some of us drive so automatically that we (erroneously) believe we can safely dial a phone or check e-mail as we drive in traffic. This is true for more than mechanical habits like driving. Think of the rote way we ask "How are you?" when we don't expect or even desire a real answer, or how we eat our food, often without tasting it, while carrying on a conversation.

These habits are just part of who we are. They are defaults, learned over years, that shape how we interact with others and respond to what life offers. Habits are like worn grooves in the parts of our brain that drive behavior. Without a conscious decision to do something else, we nearly always act consistently with these habits. Collectively, our habits determine who we are as a person, how we show up in the world, and how others perceive and respond to us.

After years of practice interacting with the world in ways that make us feel comfortable, we have internalized our habits to the degree we no longer have to think about them. Others may well notice them and remark on them as our unique personality. Yet we remain largely unconscious of these habits because they're in the background. It is our nature to learn habits well; it is the nature of habits to be invisible and automatic.

EXERCISE 2.1.

Identify a Habit

Identify a habit of your personality. This might be something that another person observes in you and considers as your quirk, or something that you do fairly consistently that someone else finds mildly annoying. Briefly describe this habit.

- Where and when did you start doing this? How did you learn it?

Habit Nature

Habits, which consist of a constellation of related phenomena, are the predominant means by which we experience and respond to our world. Generally a habit consists of practiced behaviors intertwined with emotions, sensations, and a story, or interpretation of reality, that justifies and produces the behaviors.

Our habits are stored in the very shape and hard-wiring of our bodies. They are triggered by events and people around us, which, in our internal story, provide a full justification for our resulting behavior.

For each of us, our world consists of these sensory experiences and the interpretations we make of these experiences. Our world is unique to us, and no one else can fully understand it.

ⅆ PRESENCE PAUSE ⅆ

For example, teenagers go through a natural developmental stage in which their brains are developing new pathways and capacities. This is an extraordinarily creative, and often dangerous, time. Teenagers feel immortal, are discovering what they can be in the world, are socializing with their peers, and are differentiating themselves from their parents. Unfortunately, this natural and healthy process often results in tension between independence-seeking teens and parents concerned over their safety.

In the teenager's story, very real to him, the parents don't understand him, are old and irrelevant, don't trust him, and are unnecessarily controlling. This interpretation is accompanied by strong emotions and justifies not listening, pushing limits, and sometimes outright deceit.

In the parents' (equally correct) story, the teen is overconfident, hanging out with friends who are bad influences, not yet mature enough to make sound decisions, and in need of firm boundaries for his own good. This interpretation leads to strong emotions and behaviors of clamping down, limits, and behaviors. The teen interprets these as overly controlling.

Both the teenager and the parent live in their own story. They feel completely justified in the habitual actions they take to, respectively, defy and assert authority. Their conditioned emotional reactions and behaviors, natural and developmentally appropriate, make perfect sense in their world. The difficulty results from the fact that teen and parent literally live in different worlds that are rendered incompatible by the power of interpretation. (Fortunately, the development process ensures that parent and teen usually transcend the identities that clash so readily during those years and find harmonious ways of enjoying each other's company.)

EXERCISE 2.2.
Identify Your Story

Consider the habit that you identified in Exercise 2.1. Now identify the story with which you justify this habit.

- When someone else points out this habit to you, what are you likely to say in reply? How do you justify or explain the habit?
- How might a reasonable person see it differently?
- What other story might be true?
- How does your story serve you?

Our world is limited because it is determined by our interpretation, which inevitably excludes everything that we're not able to see or understand. Show a member of certain tribes in Africa a photo of an animal with which she is very familiar and she won't recognize it.

It's not because the animal is not recognizable to her; she's seen thousands of them. It's that there is no way for her to interpret what a photo represents. Photos are not part of her interpretive structure and therefore not a part of her world.

In summary, our habits comprise our personality and way of being in the world. They include the specific behaviors that we have learned to engage in to get what we want (and avoid what we don't want) and the sensations, emotions, stories, and interpretations that construct meaning in our world and justify our habits. We can say that our stories produce, and are produced by, our habits. By their very nature as defaults, they represent a restriction in our range of ways of seeing, interpreting, and acting.

IDENTITY

We are driven through this process of development, differentiation, and individuation to form a unique identity in the world. Our identity is our self-conception: what we hold to be true about ourselves. We might have an image of our self as a strong leader, capable of motivating and inspiring others. This identity is linked to a behavior of talking in front of groups. Positive feedback from our audiences affirms and reinforces that identity, making it stronger.

In addition we often, consciously or unconsciously, set up situations where that identity will be reinforced. We construct in our lives the circumstances that support the identity that we are seeking to create. This allows the development of a healthy ego and a sense of self as competent, accepted, and worthy in the world. By relying on what we do well, we get better and better at those things.

Our identity also tends to constrict us. In a very real sense, our identities become their own champions—self-perpetuating, unconsciously working around the clock to ensure their own survival, and constantly alert for threats. Other behaviors tend to atrophy as they become less practiced. Left unchecked, this tendency leads to an increasingly narrow range of behaviors. At the extreme, our personalities become a caricature of our greatest strengths as we lose the capacity to respond flexibly to what the world throws at us.

Our identity, and specifically the behavioral and interpretive habits that make up that identity, inevitably run up against circumstances in which they no longer match what is required of us. While we came by our habits honestly, through years of hard work, adaptation, and self-preservation, our identity has reached the limits of effectiveness. Our very strengths have become our liabilities and are getting in our way. We are called to being something new, and yet every fiber of our being wants to rest in the familiar home of our tried and true identity.

This is a crux moment in both personal and professional domains. External circumstances and job requirements change. However, unless a leader is able to reinvent the identity she has built over years, which has been endlessly reinforced by others and has arguably been essential to her success so far, her career may derail. This is a tragic loss for both the leader and the organization.

Development inevitably requires that we transcend ourselves. This requires a significant and sometimes difficult letting go of old habits. Coaching, and presence, can help us enormously.

A Case Example: Janet's Identity

A former client of mine (I'll call her Janet) had been rapidly promoted to the highest levels of a large national financial services firm. Growing up as the oldest of three children, she had significant responsibilities for looking out for her siblings. She was an achiever and had been the first in her family to go through college.

I experienced Janet as a wonderful, generous person, and sharp as a tack. She had built a strong identity as a quick problem solver with superb analytical skills. And she was always willing to go the extra mile to help out her colleagues. Both traits had been noticed and rewarded with quick progress up to the national office.

Coming from the field, Janet had extensive knowledge of the technical issues that people faced. She was also hard-wired to help. She felt significant pressure to prove to her new boss that his confidence in promoting her was justified.

Janet frequently got calls from people in the field, and her habitual structure of interpretation led her to see each of these calls as an opportunity to help and a chance to solve a problem. Knowing that she would quickly be able to identify the root cause and organize the various players to solve the problem by going to their site, Janet would fly to the regional office to work with the people there to solve the problem.

By doing this, Janet's dual identities as a helper and a problem solver were reinforced. Her habits, formed early in life, were still being reinforced as a senior professional in her fifties. The people in the field welcomed the high-level support, and their problems were solved fast when she came. They were effusive in their appreciation and rated her very high on company 360-degree reviews, reinforcing her identity. Janet's boss heard frequent compliments from others at the vice president level about her effectiveness. It seemed an ideal marriage of Janet's identity and the needs of her people in the field.

You can see where this is going, can't you? Janet's habits were becoming stronger and stronger as she reaped the rewards that her particular identity in life craved. Although she was grateful for the opportunity for higher responsibility, Janet's life had no balance: her marriage was suffering, she was often stressed and sick, and her job was becoming bigger and bigger.

Like all of us, Janet was a creature of habit. Driven by her attachment to helping others and solving problems, her tremendous strengths were becoming her very limitations. Not only were her people not learning to solve their own problems, but Janet was often in the field when she was needed elsewhere. Clearly the emerging picture was not healthy for Janet or for the company, although she was receiving plenty of positive feedback and appreciation that reinforced the behaviors. Janet came to coaching because she didn't like where this was going.

Coaching provided an opportunity for the automatic nature of Janet's habits to loosen their grip and for her identity to begin to shift as she discovered a new view of her contribution. This led to the development of new, more appropriate habits that served her and the company better.

We'll come back to Janet in a bit, after we explore more about what holds habits in place and how we can loosen their grip to become self-generative.

Attachments and Aversions

Underneath each visible habit, and inextricably bundled with our behaviors and narratives, are specific sensations and internal experiences that we can learn to observe. This is because it is intrinsic to our conditioning that habits are stored in the body.

EXERCISE 2.3.
Identity: Who Do You Hold Yourself to Be?

Spend a little time reflecting and journaling about the following questions.

- Who are you? List about four or five positive adjectives that you believe describe who you are. Think of this as a short description of your identity.
- Now describe something that you've done recently that, consciously or not, was designed to get recognition from others for these same qualities. What habits of yours can you identify that serve to protect and build that identity?
- Finally, choose one of your positive qualities, and consider how it limits you. How does your drive to reinforce this trait eliminate other ways of responding? What possibilities might open if you didn't have to keep building that particular aspect of your identity?

Our identities, and the habits that comprise them, are deeply embedded in the physical shape of our bodies—in the default neural pathways in our brains and throughout our bodies, the unique chemistry of our brain, and the predisposition of our muscles and sinews to respond in certain ways. Habits, learned behaviorally, have become biological. Thus, change on a biological level is required in order to reshape these defaults and respond creatively.

With practice, we can begin to bring awareness to the sensations and experiences associated with the triggering of our habitual behaviors. This connects us directly to the biological roots of our behavioral dispositions, providing a powerful window into the fundamental drivers of our habits and therefore the identity formation process itself.

For example, we can think of the underlying urge, or pull, to move toward pleasurable things as an *attachment*. If we are attached to a belief that more money, a promotion, a new commitment, a particular holiday, or an experience will provide us what we want, we organize ourselves and our actions toward this end. We are attached to things that produce pleasure or validate the identity that we have built in the world.[2]

Similarly, there's an underlying urge to move away from things that bring us pain or difficulty. We call this an *aversion*. For example, receiving feedback that conflicts with our comfortable view of our own identity often produces a defensive reaction. At a fundamental level, this automatic defensiveness is driven by underlying biological survival energies, now directed toward the preservation of our built identity rather than our physical self. Aversions organize us by driving specific behaviors. The strength of our own aversions and subsequent reactive habits can sometimes be surprisingly strong.

Consider a difficult feedback conversation with a team member. The employee, anticipating the conversation, braces himself and tells himself simply to listen. Yet once he is in the boss's office, those good intentions crumble. The feedback triggers some ancient place in his nervous system that erupts in a strong defensive reaction, and he angrily blurts out a justification for the action he took.[3] No matter who's right, the conversation is polarized, no one is learning, and performance doesn't improve.

EXERCISE 2.4.

Experience Attachments and Aversions

Attachments and aversions can be sensed directly. Here's an easy way to experience this. While this is somewhat different from experiencing the urges that propel our behaviors, it is nonetheless a realistic way to experience an urge.

First, get a small quantity of a substance that you sometimes crave: coffee, dark chocolate, potato chips. You get the idea.

Now, without putting the substance into your mouth, sense it fully. Look at it. Smell it. Feel the possibility of ingesting it. Notice what urges arise in your body—sensations of craving, changes in your mouth. Notice any stories that you are telling yourself to justify ingesting it immediately. Stay with the experience for a minute or two before actually ingesting it. That is the experience of attachment.

Depending on your tolerance for aversions, you may do the following either as a thought experiment or as a real one. Take a clean spoon, and spit a small quantity of saliva into it. Look at the saliva in the spoon. Notice the sensations, thoughts, and feelings that arise. Then place it back in your mouth. Again, notice what arises.

Most people find even the idea of this revolting. Yet it's obvious that it's clean saliva, taken from your mouth by a clean spoon, and put back where it came from. No big deal, right? Wrong. The power of a conditioned aversion can be quite strong.

It is significant to work with this and to discover that, with practice and attention, the aversion loses its strength.[4]

This defensive reaction is driven by an urge, by an aversion to the unpleasant experience of what our employee interprets as unfair criticism. It is automatic, and even the strongest intention can sometimes fail to override our practiced instinctual responses.

Attachments and aversions are deeply rooted directional urges in our bodies that serve to guide us through life. They provide the orienting mechanism that holds our identities in place. They drive nearly every aspect of our behaviors, yet generally operate below our level of awareness. We can learn to feel both our attachments and our aversions directly. Becoming aware of how they operate within us is becoming aware of the underlying drivers of our behaviors.

Significantly, we don't generally have to deconstruct why we came to be a particular way. That is the realm of traditional psychology and therapy. In coaching, the story of how team members and clients became who they are is interesting but mostly extraneous.

As coaches, our concern is that our clients learn to author their own stories. This begins with the competency of observing, at a moment-by-moment level, how they are shaped by their attachments and aversions. Becoming familiar with their habits, and the underlying attachments and aversions, is the ticket to freeing themselves from the grip of habits that are not serving them. By noticing their urges as they arise, our clients can choose to follow them or not. This is change at the root. Change at the level of the automatic habits that form our very identities requires being deeply present with ourselves.

When we open to and directly experience the essential nature of our functioning as a human, we're no longer bound by what we've been. We see, and can respond to, a universe of new possibilities. This is a critical step into transcending ourselves to become something new and bolder.

The central challenge in development is to move beyond an identity that no longer serves us. Development is essentially about engaging intentionally in the business of transcending an existing definition of our identity, in order to literally conceive of ourselves in a different, new sense. We learn to loosen the grip of our conditioned way of being—our habits, stories, ways of interpreting the world, and customary responses—in order to act consistently with new and more generative commitments.

This is a big request given the deep biological roots of our conditioned nature. To do this, we work at the level of the attachments,

EXERCISE 2.5.

Challenging Your Identity

Choose an automatic interpersonal habit that's strong in you and part of the identity you have built in the world. It could be interrupting people in meetings, or saying "How are you?" to your colleagues without making eye contact or listening for the answer. You choose.

Now, change it. Give up the habit for a week, and notice what it takes to change it. Notice if it's hard to pay attention to it. Notice how quickly your commitment to change this habit recedes into the background; you may even completely forget about your commitment or decide that the experiment is over. Notice any stories you have right now about doing this.

As you conduct the experiment, note any urges, or pulls, to do what you usually do. Observe the strength of your habits and how they work to keep you from changing.

aversions, and structures of interpretation that drive our behaviors in the first place. We come to recognize and suspend worn habits and aspects of our identity that no longer serve us. We focus on deep change, on shifting the assumptions and narratives from which we make decisions, assess our potential contribution, and orient our self in life and work.

This doesn't mean tearing apart what we have been in order to become something entirely new and unrelated. Rather, we author an ongoing, unfolding story of our own development. We come to see ourselves as engaged in an ongoing process of transcending what we have been, while including the history, skills, and values that are core to who we are. We learn to discover and reorganize around a new identity, and we acquire and master new behaviors that are relevant and effective for current commitments.

BECOMING SELF-GENERATIVE

Let's now explore what's required to make the shift from automatic, conditioned behaviors focused on survival, fitting in, getting validation, and achieving success to new and creative actions linked to purpose, contribution, efficacy, and fulfillment.

We can choose to live with a less desperate focus on achieving competence for current circumstances and a greater explicit commitment to our growth, change, and evolution. Within this commitment, we become conscious of learning not just because there's an immediate need, but because we have a long-term view of our own development. We understand life's challenges as our personal curriculum; learning to navigate these challenges provides meaning and context for our lives. Learning becomes a central capacity for how we want to live in the world.

When we are *self-generative*, we have *the capacity to be present and a learner in all of life in order to make choices from the inner state of greatest possible awareness and resourcefulness.* Self-generation is one of the three products of coaching mentioned in Chapter One.[5] It requires approaching every moment as a beginner and being open to responding as a learner. Self-generation produces resilience, creativity, self-awareness, authenticity, and a passion for learning.

SELF-GENERATION

Self-generation is the capacity to be present and a learner in all of life in order to make choices from the inner state of greatest possible awareness and resourcefulness.

We can consider self-generation in two related senses. First, we mean that it is the *self* that is generating new choices and actions. Here, being self-generative is in the sense of having autonomy and agency.

Second, we are being generative *of* a self. In other words, when we take new and creative actions in life, we are in fact producing a new and greater self. Taking creative, effective actions inevitably furthers our own development.

Self-generation is a fundamental capacity. When we combine the two meanings, we are constantly generating new actions and possibilities, which in turn lead to a new and expanded self. We are taking responsibility for our own learning, development, and aliveness in the greatest possible way.

Self-generation can be specifically encouraged and developed. In fact, supporting team members or clients in becoming self-generative is a central promise of coaching. As coaches, we design our work so that clients understand and ultimately self-guide their own development.

Self-generation is ongoing. We can distinguish four components, each of which can be supported by specific development activities, practices, and exercises. Sometimes the components appear sequentially, but to call them stages implies a linearity that is not always present. These four components are self-observation, realization, reorganization, and stabilization.

Self-Observation

In self-observation, we learn to observe ourselves in action. It is useful to think of this as the creation of an artificial split between two parts of ourselves. One part acts in the world: eating, facilitating a meeting, building a spreadsheet, running through the park. The other part, which we can call the observer, stands back and watches, as if we were seeing ourselves on a movie screen.

This observing part can describe what it notices: "I'm eating now. I'm facilitating a meeting. I'm building a spreadsheet." The cultivation of this observer self is the basis of self-awareness. Although self-awareness, by itself, does not lead to behavior change, it is foundational.

The more skilled we become as observers, the more subtle and complex the phenomena that we can see. From "I'm talking to Joe," we progress to "I'm feeling a little tense," to "There's a subtle tension in my lower stomach. I notice my breathing is shallow and my shoulders are hunched." The more complete our noticing, the more information is available to us from which to base decisions and the more familiar we become with our reactions to life's events. This is how we observe the subtleties of our attachments and aversions.

Self-observation is powerful because it requires disidentification. Think about the fact that we can watch a dog playing. Logically this means that the dog is separate and distinct from us as observer. Similarly, the fact of being able to observe our own behavior means that the behavior itself is a distinct phenomenon, independent of us.

$\approx$ PRESENCE PAUSE $\approx$

This disidentification is central in behavior change because it implies a choice. We are not our behaviors. As observers, we can both see the behavior we are using, and alternative behaviors; we can then choose which to put our energy into.

Self-observation is particularly useful when focused on a particular behavior that we want to change (a habit that is not producing the results we want) or a behavior that we want to cultivate (a habit that we want to become more available to us). By paying attention to these habits over time, we become more familiar with them and better able to be more self-aware when we are engaging in them.

Self-observation separates us from our reactions to things and opens the possibility of seeing that we are making one choice and that many others are available to us.

EXERCISE 2.6.
Self-Observation

Observe yourself right now, as if you were in a movie. Notice yourself sitting where you're sitting, reading this book. Notice how you're sitting, what your mood is, what is being provoked in you by what you're reading. Notice how your energy level is. Notice what stories you are telling yourself about the reading. Notice any self-assessments or judgments about the book present in you right now.

This noticing is the function of the observer; the act of noticing invokes the observer.

Realization

With practice, self-observation builds familiarity with our habits. Self-observation, however, is often a retrospective activity. For example, I might ask a client who is struggling to let go of certain responsibilities to write down, on a daily basis, examples of her reluctance to delegate. By tracking this over time, she builds the muscle of awareness. She begins to notice more and more examples of situations when she makes the choice to keep a task to herself rather than pass it off. With this increasing familiarity, she becomes more and more finely tuned to this particular phenomenon and is more and more likely to notice, in the moment, that she is in the act of holding on to a task that she could delegate. This realization is the moment of presence.

Realization provides a present moment simultaneous awareness of what we are doing, that we are at choice, and that there are multiple directions to go from here. Realization provides the intelligent moment. There's a palpable expansion, a sense of being in possibility. This is the moment of choice, the moment from which everything else in our lives proceeds.

In a big sense, realization is the powerful spiritual experience toward which Buddhist masters and other spiritual leaders have been talking about for millennia. In the context of our daily lives, it's these little "waking ups" that happen more frequently when we are paying attention. It is the immediate awareness that you could ask your administrative assistant to make your travel arrangements. It is the recognition, in a heated moment with a colleague or spouse, that you usually avoid conflict with this person and could instead stay engaged and talk the issue through.

Where self-observation requires a distance between the observer and the action that's happening, realization happens when that distance collapses and we're just present with ourselves, in the naked moment. Realization is the moment of choice and can result only from being present.

Realization, and the state of presence, disappears as soon as we observe and name it. When we notice that we are present, we are able to say, "Oh, there it is! That's realization. *That's* being present. That's what Doug is talking about." However, in the act of naming the phenomenon, we've once again split out the observer, immediately taking us out of the state of presence. Self-congratulation paradoxically immediately cancels out the "achievement" of being present in the first place.

So throughout this book, while we work at becoming more present, we also can't make it happen. It can even be counterproductive to call it a goal, because then we begin to measure ourselves against it, and the measurement is, by definition, self-observation again, and not realization. Realization tends to be fleeting.

Another way to describe this is that realization represents a moment of freedom from our automatic habits, driven by attachments and identity. In this moment, there is the possibility of entering something new.

EXERCISE 2.7.
Realization

At the end of this paragraph, I'm going to ask you to stop reading and wait for a long pause, perhaps twenty or thirty seconds, before resuming reading. In fact, I'm inviting you to just wait and to watch what happens. In that pause, you are completely at choice about when to begin reading again. Feel yourself in the pause. Don't think about when to resume; simply experience yourself at choice, at any point being able to stay in the pause or to resume reading, and not knowing which will happen.

Now, stop reading. Pause . . .

Wait . . .

Wait . . .

What did you experience?

Reorganization

The moment of choice is existential, and every moment is a moment of choice. Realization is simply waking up to that fact.

The future is always unwritten. Any choice will launch a succession of phenomena that we can never really fully anticipate. What we can know is that a choice has consequences. When, in the moment of realization, we choose something that is habitual, it's easy. There's often a sense of relief, of collapsing into something familiar. The succession of resulting phenomena is fairly predictable. This is true because there's little or no reorganization of ourselves that's required. It could be said that we are already organized internally to follow our habits. Our habits are a form of organization, and defaulting to them is, in a sense, like falling asleep. When we choose a new behavior or a different path, the consequences are less familiar. A new behavior feels awkward, unfamiliar, sometimes even scary. It requires a reorganization of ourselves behaviorally, cognitively, and somatically.

The more something is new and different, the more we need to prepare for it. We might find ourselves taking a deep breath, feeling energized, rehearsing in our minds what we're going to say, changing the shape of our body, drawing ourselves taller in readiness. This is reorganization: organizing ourselves toward the new action or behavior. We have to discover how to be a body that can take the new action.

Similarly, when we default to known behaviors, there are few repercussions in our relationships with others. When we behave habitually, the people who see us every day are not surprised; they'd expect nothing else. In fact, their identities, and their orientation in their relationship with us, may require us to behave habitually. To do otherwise would rock the boat.

As we change our habits and become a different person, we may need to renegotiate with others. This is a different kind of reorganization; reorganizing ourselves internally is followed by an external kind of reorganization that involves others.

EXERCISE 2.8.

Reorganization

Experience reorganization right now. Place the book down, stand up, stretch, walk to the window. Take a couple of minutes to stretch and feel your body. Take some deep breaths. Get your circulation going. Reenergize yourself. As you do so, be conscious of reorganizing your attention to reengage the reading in a more alert, more conscious state than before you stood up and moved.

Then sit back down and bring your fullest attention to the reading. You can think of this as a presence pause writ large. You're actually taking a brief time-out to invite your attention to reorganize.

Stabilization

The final component in the self-generative cycle is stabilization. Here, we've made a new choice, reorganized ourselves around this new choice, and are proceeding toward integrating it into our lives and our way of being. Stabilization is fundamentally about practice.

Our old habits became habits precisely because we practiced them over and over until we didn't have to think about them any more. They became embedded in us. So why should we think we can let go of an old habit and replace it with a new one simply by resolving to do so? Those of you who have made noble New Year's resolutions, only to have them fall by the wayside by the middle of January, know what I'm talking about.

Practice, essential for stabilizing ourselves in a new behavior or in a new way of being, is about building capacity through repetition. We are building a body that can reliably call on the new behavior, even in circumstances that formerly, and reliably, evoked the old behavior. Practice, with full attention, of new choices over time leads to enduring shifts in our stories about what is possible and in the physiological underpinnings of our actions.[6]

It's not that, with practice, we will reside permanently and stably in this new state or habit. Our old habits will occasionally get triggered by events, and we will be thrown off. Stabilization requires

---

EXERCISE 2.9.
Stabilization

To practice stabilizing a shift in attention, commit three hours or so, without demands from others, in which to conduct an experiment. Find a digital watch with a countdown timer or a kitchen timer that you can set for ten minutes. A timer that automatically repeats is best but not necessary.

Set the timer to go off every ten minutes (or plan to reset it every ten minutes if it's manual). Each time it goes off, reorganize your attention, as you did in Exercise 2.8, taking thirty seconds to a minute to stand up, stretch, breathe, and bring your full attention back into whatever you're doing at the time.

Many people notice two opposing trends. The first is to become more competent at the shift in attention through practice and repetition. The second is to become bored with the exercise, to stop doing it, or to justify a halfhearted attempt with "Okay, I got the point already!" and then to end their commitment.

This tension is fundamental to stabilization and sustainable change. Experience that tension within yourself in this practice. No judgment. Just notice how you respond to the exercise.

---

a certain faith that wobbling is part of the process. This wobbling requires self-regulation: managing ourselves and our internal state through constant attention and vigilance.[7]

The most rewarding moments in coaching for me are when a client reports, after weeks or months of work together, that he has responded in a new way to a difficult situation that formerly triggered a habitual and unhelpful response. The indicator that stabilization has taken place is not that the client has responded in a new way, but rather that the response seemed so normal. Rather than being challenged by the situation, the client simply responded, easily and effectively, with the new habit. Often he is surprised by how easy it seemed. We can say that, through practice, he has become stabilized in the new behavior.

How Coaching Supports Self-Generation and Sustainable Change

Developing self-generation in ourselves (and in our team members and clients) establishes the foundation from which specific skills and competencies can be chosen and executed. As coaches, we are continually working at becoming more self-generative in our own lives. Similarly, to focus our coaching efforts simply on measurable outcomes while ignoring the calling to the inner work of self-generation misses the extraordinary leverage for learning that self-generation provides.

A central question, then, is how we as coaches can support each of the four components of self-generation: self-observation, realization, reorganization, and stabilization. Let's explore how coaching with Janet helped her gain traction toward a different way of leading.

When we left Janet, she was in the throes of a self-induced difficult situation. Recently promoted, she was taking personal responsibility for solving field problems, at which she was greatly skilled. Her job requirements had changed, but she was the same person. Her strong identity as a helpful problem solver was supported by the appreciation she received from others. In spite of her best intentions, Janet was paying an enormous price, and it was beginning to become evident, at least to herself, that she was overextended.

Coaching Self-Observation

In self-observation, the client gains practice in observing her behaviors in action. Mostly this takes place after the fact. With practice, however, comes familiarity. And with familiarity comes recognition, in the moment, that a particular behavior or response is happening.

The coach is critical in inviting the team member or client into this process. People are generally unable to see their own habits. However, as coaches, we are often able to see the limited and habitual nature of how our client senses, interprets, and acts in her world. (Lest we become arrogant about our own perceptiveness and wisdom, it is important to remember that we are also creatures of habit, by definition unable to see our own limitations.)

The coach invites the client to observe her own habits and offers the structure of a self-observation practice so that, over time, she becomes increasingly familiar with their nature. The coach connects what happens in the moment with relevant context.

In our conversations, it quickly became evident that Janet's urge to help was pretty automatic. When someone needed something of her, her body responded with an increase in energy, and she quickly organized herself around helping (read: rescuing) the other person. While the urge began in her body, there was also a story (probably learned many years ago) that she could solve the problem faster and more easily than others.

Through coaching, Janet began a regular body practice to help her become more skillful at noticing the subtle experiences within her body, particularly the increase in energy that was the first indication of her habitual urge to help. In addition, she began a rigorous self-observation practice to become more familiar with how this habit arose.

Within a few weeks, something that had previously been automatic became more conscious. She was able to see, in fine detail, exactly what happened within her when someone came to her with a problem. This included being able to describe the direct, sensory experience of her attachments to being kind, helping, and solving others' problems. She could sense the pull of her need for validation from others in her still new role.

Through becoming skilled at observing the minute details of her habits, she became intimately familiar with her own habits. She was now a conscious witness of something that previously had been automatic.

Coaching Realization

With familiarity comes recognition. This is the waking up to the moment of presence. The shift is from self-observation (in which we are observing a phenomenon, usually with hindsight) to realization (the recognition, in the moment, that this *is* the phenomenon). With realization come increased energy, expanded awareness, and simultaneous recognition that our habit is simply a phenomenon and we can choose whether to indulge it or do something else.

Realization tends to emerge naturally from a rigorous practice of self-observation. As we've noted elsewhere, the practice makes realization much more likely.

Soon Janet had moments of realization, the Aha! moments. A call would come, Janet would be on the phone with someone in the field, and she would recognize the familiar urge to rescue. In this moment of recognition, Janet realized that she had a choice. The automatic nature of the reaction had been interrupted, the future was unwritten, and a new landscape of possibility was revealed.

The coach can also support the waking of realization by reflecting to the client when the habit is arising during the coaching conversation itself. (Recall from Chapter One that June, in her conversation with Rick, provided a real-time assessment to Rick that invited him into a moment of realization that his defensiveness was arising right then.) This real-time experience, in the presence of the coach, can provide significant new insight.

Coaching Reorganization

The moment of conscious realization makes reorganization possible. In this present intelligent moment, we have many choices available to us. The practiced, automatic response means following the default tendency. Self-observation and realization provide the possibility of interrupting a habit and replacing it with a new response. Reorganization is the actual shift from this default habit to something new. We mobilize our bodies, our energies, and our nervous systems toward a new action.

Coaches serve this component through several means. The first is by supporting the client in recognizing and describing what an alternative response to the triggering situation might be. In essence, this makes available to the client a new distinction that constitutes a more life-affirming and effective response. The second is by helping the client experience reorganization in real time, thus providing a direct experience of a reorganization move that can serve as a reference. And the third is to design practices with the client that she can work with, between coaching conversations, to build competency in the new behavior.

> *We explored a range of alternative responses, as well as the potential benefits of placing more responsibility in the hands of Janet's field people. Along with alternative behavioral responses, she discovered that she could learn to interpret the field problem as a development opportunity for her people rather than as a rescuing opportunity for herself. This new interpretive choice led to an emerging identity as a developer of problem solvers rather than as the queen problem solver herself.*
>
> *With this new view of her emerging identity, Janet learned to take advantage of her moments of realization. She learned to reorganize herself, in the moment, to explore with her people how a problem could best be solved without her. This was a new competency, and it took practice and discipline at first.*
>
> *In these conversations, it usually became quickly apparent that there were other good alternatives. While a few of her direct reports initially leaned on her to travel, she discovered that most didn't actually expect her to jump on a plane. This came as a bit of a surprise and also as a relief.*
>
> *Janet's new identity made intellectual sense to her, but it still took conscious attention, even effort, to override her historical urges to care-take and problem-solve. She actively practiced letting go of her need to be of help in the ways she had previously defined it. This was essential in order for her to build, and sustain, a new identity and role in the organization.*

Coaching Stabilization

The final phase of self-generation is stabilization. This phase requires that we practice the reorganization and the new behavior to the point that it becomes our new default.

Repetition is key. As leaders, we tend to move to the level of our training, of our practice. It's not cerebral knowledge of what we should do that drives our actions in a crunch situation; it's what we've embodied through practice and repetition.[8] When we practice a habit, that's what we come, more and more, to embody. When we practice a new behavior, first it becomes increasingly available to us, and eventually it becomes our new default. The body's capacity to learn and incorporate new responses is much deeper than previously thought.

As coaches, we support this process by designing repetitive practices with clients that they can work with over time as they learn to embody the new behavior. The client takes these practices out into the world. Some practices may be done in the morning or evening outside work hours as a solitary activity; other practices require the participation of others or are best done in the context of a work environment with all the opportunities and challenges that go along with that environment.

It is through practices that clients become different people, capable of responding to inevitable difficulties in new and creative ways. If we want to change, we must practice something new.

Janet became able, with practice, to stabilize her new behavior. She articulated her new role to her people and found, with few exceptions, that they welcomed her redefinition of her identity in relation to them. She practiced exploring alternative ways of responding to field issues. While she still traveled to the field, it was now a conscious choice made in consideration of a number of factors rather than an automatic default.

It was essential for Janet to be heartful and compassionate with herself when she lapsed. There were a number of breakdowns, and Janet had several periods of real anxiety that she was abandoning those who counted on her. When these occurred, it became important to practice forgiveness and compassion and to remind herself about the new leader that she was becoming.

She came to take great pleasure in her new identity as a developer of others and found herself looking at field problems through the bigger lens of overall organizational resources and priorities. She also found that it was much easier to keep a reasonable balance between professional and other priorities. She came to really enjoy the new role and went on to great success.

Janet, Resolved: Self-Generation and Identity

We can see in Janet's story the development of a strong identity, rooted in childhood. She had become a competent, well-liked professional with a reputation for doing whatever it took to get the job done. Clearly, the behavioral expressions of this identity had led to success and rapid promotions. But although her professional behaviors were simultaneously great strengths, they also had become limiting. A different understanding of her role was critical if she was to be successful in this new role. Janet had to become someone new.

With coaching support, Janet embarked on a process of *transcending* and *including* who she had been to become a different kind of leader.[9] We can see the four components of self-generation in her development of this new identity and the associated competencies.

Increased self-awareness of her strong default tendencies resulted from self-observation over time. Familiarity with her habits and how they arose in response to triggers in her outside environment provided moments of realization. She became aware that she had a choice between acting consistently with her old story of who she was, or doing something that produced a new identity.

This new identity required both an internal reorganization (new behaviors, actions, narrative about her contribution, sources of affirmation) and external reorganization (managing expectations of others, creating new processes for solving problems). Reorganization happened both in the precise moment of realization and choice, and in the longer time frame of months, as she renegotiated expectations and practiced new behaviors. Janet learned to recognize and let go of her attachments associated with the former identity, and the pressures from the system around her to stay the same.

Over time, this new identity became stabilized in Janet. Practice led to a place where it no longer took discipline to explore alternatives to traveling to the field. She thought of herself primarily as a developer of people rather than as a solver of problems. She asked questions from that identity and felt validated and successful when she saw her people learning and solving problems themselves. Janet had shifted to a different way of being that was stable. It was a new "normal" for her.

In our later conversations, Janet frequently reported to me that she responded to a previously challenging circumstance in a new way that had become effortless and normal. In fact, she sometimes didn't even notice the situation until afterward; the old habit simply didn't arise. A moment that previously would have triggered her desire to rescue passed so easily that it was unremarkable. The ground of Janet's being has changed, and she has literally become a different person.

LIVING IN SELF-GENERATION

We live in a field of presence; presence is always available to us. Yet when we live habitually, we are not aware of this, and naturally organize ourselves around our attachments and aversions. We live to maintain and protect our identity.

Figure 2.1 shows how we can respond to the events in our lives in one of two fundamental ways.

Our lives consist of a range of evolving situations. Within each situation, an event often happens that presents us with a challenge; something in our habitual nature is triggered by the event. Most often, we move automatically into the responses, practiced over decades, that have made us who we are.

This habitual response, as we've discussed above, is characterized by related phenomena that arise nearly simultaneously: a story or interpretation, emotions, and bodily sensations. When we are triggered, we are most likely to act unconsciously; our habits and practiced inclinations largely determine our actions. Unaware, we default into the *habit loop*.

Like it or not, we all spend much more time in this habit loop than we realize. Because we live in it, the habit loop feels comfortable and normal. We don't even see that we're in it. (In fact, to see that we're in it, from a place of relaxed awareness, is already *not* being in it!)

FIGURE 2.1. *Habit and Self-Generative Loops.*

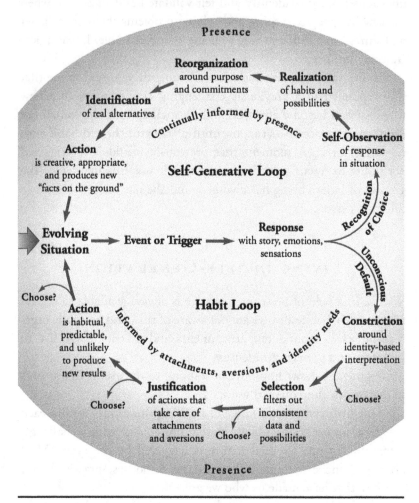

The habit loop works like this. As we respond to an unfolding event, we unconsciously default into our predictable ways of interpreting and responding. Specifically, our view becomes constricted around our interpretation of that event. Because our interpretation is identity-based, it is inseparable from the attachments and aversions that also produce that identity. Without knowing we're doing so, we see selectively, filtering out all data and possibilities that are inconsistent with our identity-based interpretations. We simply don't see other truths. Our awareness becomes self-sealing.

Our interpretation serves our identities by justifying habitual and predictable actions that take care of our attachments and aversions. In a sense, these actions are serving us well. However, identity-driven actions are much more effective at preserving and strengthening our identity than producing new results. We continue in our patterns, others do the same, and we get frustrated when things don't change. We see our difficulties as someone else's fault, or simply "just the way things are."

Informing this habit loop, and expressing themselves at every stage, are our attachments, aversions, and identity needs. Although this is not inherently a bad thing, this fact limits the range of what we can perceive and respond to in any given situation. For better or for worse, we humans organize ourselves in life primarily around preserving and perpetuating our identities.

Contrast this with the *self-generative loop*. Through practice, presence becomes increasingly available to us. We learn to see challenging moments as opportunities to wake up. Recognition of this possibility of choice brings us immediately into presence. The simple thought "A-hah! This is an opportunity!" invites us into self-generation, continually informed by presence. (At any time, even when deep into our habit loop, there is the possibility of recognizing that we're in the loop, and choosing to wake up into presence.)

In the self-generative loop, self-observation allows us to discern the first arising of our habit. Realization of our habit wakes us immediately into a vaster landscape of possibilities: we become self-aware and resourceful. Depending on how spacious and aware we are, more or fewer possibilities may be revealed.

With realization, we can reorganize ourselves around our purpose and commitments. Relaxed and present, we are not constrained by habit and are much more likely to see new possibilities that may have been available to us all along. From this expanded sense of what is possible, we can identify real alternatives, and choose new actions that are creative and appropriate. Taking these actions from a centered presence then creates new "facts on the ground." Our relationship to the situation has changed, and we're now able to produce something new and different within it.

Over time and with practice, we stabilize these new behaviors or actions so that we are comfortable and competent using them. (This is not shown in the diagram, as it results from repeated passing through the cycle.) Repetition stabilizes not only our new and more constructive behaviors in the specific situation (which we can think of as more useful, more evolved habits that will eventually become limiting themselves), but also our competence at living in the self-generative cycle itself (which, I suppose, we could conceive of as a meta-habit).

Presence informs every step of the self-generative loop. It is always available and serves as the oxygen, if you will, that allows self-generation. Presence endows us with the possibility of responding in creative and positive ways to anything that comes at us.

We can see that Janet began to reside more consistently in the self-generative loop. And we can see the possibility for ourselves that this learning cycle, in which we are constantly opening ourselves to new information and new ways of seeing and responding, can become a way of being in the world. The basic requirements for this are the components of self-generation. These can be learned and practiced, such that being self-generative is increasingly embodied in who we are and in how we lead.

This understanding of development, and specifically how self-generation supports our development of a new identity, is foundational to our work. It naturally begs the questions, What is our role as coaches in supporting this kind of development? How do we develop our own presence? And, how do we make the coaching moves to support leaders in their unfolding of a more powerful identity?

The answers to these questions are essential for responding effectively to the crying needs of our organizations, our communities, and indeed, our very planet.

CHAPTER SUMMARY

- The human journey of development is largely a conditioning process by which we habituate ourselves in order to adapt, fit in, and be successful according to the prevailing models of success. We are creatures of habit, and these habits are largely invisible to us.
- Habits are hard-wired into our nervous systems and held in the shape of our bodies. We *are* our habits: our behaviors, interpretations, sensations, and emotions. Changing requires change on a biological level.

- Habits are held in place by our attachments and aversions. These are subtle urges that can be directly experienced and that steer us toward experiences we hold as positive and away from those we hold as negative.
- The sum total of our habits we can think of as our personality or our identity; it's how we hold ourselves in the world. We seek to get our identities reinforced. At the same time, our identities eventually become limiting, and we are required to let go of old habits that don't serve and replace them with new ones that do.
- We can think of development as an ongoing process of *transcending* our identities, and *including* them in a new and more expansive way of being in the world.
- Self-generation is *the capacity to be present and a learner in all of life in order to make choices from the inner state of greatest possible awareness and resourcefulness.*
- Self-generation can be described as a cycle of four components: self-observation, realization, reorganization, and stabilization. Each of these components can be supported through specific practices, coaching moves, and learning activities.
- Self-generation is a capacity that can be developed and is the central capacity for building a new identity. Living in a self-generative way, we move toward continual self-awareness and the capacity to consciously choose new actions and behaviors most appropriate for fulfilling our commitments.

CHAPTER 3

Coach as Development Partner

The rung of a ladder was never meant to rest upon, but only to hold a man's foot long enough to enable him to put the other somewhat higher.

Thomas Henry Huxley

In everyone's life, at some time, our inner fire goes out. It is then burst into flame by an encounter with another human being. We should all be thankful for those people who rekindle the inner spirit.

Albert Schweitzer

BUSINESS, RUN WELL, PUTS A PREMIUM ON REPLICATION, efficiency, and scaling up well-designed processes. This extends to learning as well; businesses have poured billions of dollars into performance coaching to increase the productivity and skills of their human talent at all levels. The overarching promise of performance coaching is an increase in employee contribution toward organizational goals. At the same time, the complex processes used to systematize human development and take it to scale are a reflection of the mind-set that, ultimately, even the development of leaders can be managed and controlled.

Complex development maps are necessarily generalizations. They may be a good entry point to coaching, but they won't get us where we need to go. The cultivation of authentic, resilient, effective leaders always requires deeper approaches to development than can be easily replicated at the scale of most corporate coaching initiatives. Coaching can and must, in furthering the sustainable and robust development of leaders, contain elements seldom included in performance-driven coaching.

Developmental approaches take coaching to the next level. In one sense, we are still committed to the development of specific and observable competencies; they are the first of the three products of coaching I described in Chapter One. However, developmental coaching views these competencies, whether technical or "soft," as primarily a means to an end.

Presence-based coaching is my approach to developmental coaching. Through this approach, coaches can express a deep commitment to cultivating leaders who are fully awake, resourceful, and connected to themselves, their people, and their environments. These leaders demonstrate excellence in their professional domains, but we propose to develop them in other, perhaps more important, ways. Self-generation, and the aliveness that comes with it, are predictable products of coaching, and we are committed to these qualities as specific outcomes of our work with our clients.

This chapter explores what makes this developmental approach to coaching distinct, identifies the three essential structures that allow developmental coaching to be successful, and lays out the specific work of the presence-based coach in allowing this to happen.

PERFORMANCE VERSUS DEVELOPMENTAL COACHING

Let's begin by differentiating between performance coaching and developmental coaching. The former generally refers to coaching driven by organizational standards and metrics. Competency models, 360-degree assessments, and other tools are used to diagnose development needs and prescribe learning approaches that will develop the requisite skills to either close performance gaps or prepare for greater responsibility. In the process, the client presumably is learning new skills and becoming more motivated. Win-win.

To illustrate, I'll use the example of Roger, a former client and a chief financial officer at a university medical facility. He was a likable, brilliant, energetic man. He was the first person in his family to go to college, had earned an M.B.A., and, through hard work and ambition, had quickly risen to his current position.

Roger worked very hard, being rather driven and competitive. He seemed to believe that if he didn't keep his hand in every project, it would go off the rails. He tended to micromanage and was sensitive to others' judgments and opinions. Roger sometimes didn't seem to trust his good fortune in being in this position. Others frequently commented that he seemed to think that if he relaxed his vigilance for even a moment, the entire house of cards was going to fall. He didn't trust others to do their jobs and was frequently pulled off track by the needs and priorities of others.

The CEO had suggested coaching after a difficult 360 review to which Roger had reacted quite defensively. Roger was in real danger of career derailment because of being so reactive and not managing his time and projects well.

A traditional performance coaching approach would support Roger in organizing his projects, learning time management and delegation methods, implementing these with accountability to the coach, and measuring what happened. This would, if effective, result in Roger's being more efficient, managing his time better, and getting deliverables to the CEO on time. The problem would be fixed, and Roger would get to keep his job. All would be well!

That's fine and well, and there is a place for performance coaching. It is particularly appropriate for learning needs with a clearly defined scope. Roger may have benefited greatly from this approach. However, performance coaching has limitations. First, because it is driven by organizational imperatives, there is sometimes a tension between the organization's goals and the client's goals. I have coached many leaders who have significant questions about how their goals fit with what the organization is looking for and whether they can find success and fulfillment in that setting. Performance coaching may be unlikely to address a client's deeper concerns.

Second, when coaching is driven by performance metrics, a standard for performance is at least implied, if not stated directly. This comparison to specific metrics can make learning more difficult, because deeply rooted ineffective habits can actually be strengthened when a learner is experiencing the stress and tension produced by the performance gap.[1]

A development agenda works by supporting a client in being curious, opening to new possibilities, and acting on those possibilities in order to see what happens. To produce a new identity, a client must become open to significant new ways of seeing, interpreting, and behaving. It feels fundamentally different from the often gap-driven process of performance coaching. A developmental approach uniquely infuses a spirit of discovery into the entire process.

Third, performance coaching can build new skills. However, if those skills are not grounded in a higher level of self-awareness and self-generation, they often make things better for a while, but are not sustainable or embodied. They are quick fixes, symptomatic solutions.

Let's come back to Roger, and see how a developmental approach simultaneously supported Roger in building necessary competencies and becoming more self-generative in the process.

Clearly, to be successful, Roger needed to build competencies around managing his time and priorities, staying on track, and leading his organization with a greater sense of consistency. With this in mind, our developmental coaching together began by exploring the attachments and aversions that drove Roger's behaviors in the first place. Rather than organizing our work around resolving the symptoms of reactivity, disorganization, and inefficiency, I invited Roger to be curious about how he got off track in the first place.

Self-observation showed Roger that the times when he got pulled off his plan were often when others came to him with requests for help and when he was highly attached to being seen as competent. Roger had a strong aversion to the judgment of others; when he felt judged, he tended to become disorganized, insecure, and anxious and to jump into noncritical tasks in order to earn respect.

With practice, Roger became able to realize this habitual reaction in his body. He learned to relax and accept the reaction as something that just happened, without interpreting it as evidence of failure. He learned to reorganize himself internally to take a stand for the priorities he knew he should focus on. This self-generative capacity for Roger began to show up in every domain of his life: his marriage, his golf game, his church, as well as at work. He began to experience himself as calmer, clearer, and more direct. Others frequently remarked on the change, seeing Roger as more relaxed, easier to be around, and less stressed.

Later in our work, this capacity for self-awareness and reorganization provided a solid ground in which practical new skills in time management and delegation could take root. However, it's important to note that the ability to observe, accept, and self-regulate his inner state preceded the development of the specific skills most directly tied to his performance issues.

Roger went on to be very successful, as well as being much more fulfilled and less stressed. In a very real way, his changed relationship to his work, and his new-found capacity to accept and self-regulate his anxiety, had contributed as much or more to the difference as any specific time and task management skills.

We can see in this example that developmental coaching transcends and includes performance coaching. There may be elements of gap analysis and performance standards that come into a developmental coaching process. However, developmental coaching includes many elements beyond the organizational imperatives and competencies on the table.

PRINCIPLES OF DEVELOPMENTAL COACHING

Here is a brief set of principles to illuminate the developmental coaching territory. These are the basis for describing the coach role:

- *Development is deepest and most sustainable when focused on learning, not performance.* Real learning takes place best when we are open, relaxed, and curious. Coaching produces new competencies that the client will carry for a lifetime; it is the competency we're after, not simply a short-term result. While new skills can reasonably be expected to produce better results, driving learning through performance measures can actually make it harder for the learner to learn.

- *Coaching is freely chosen.* At the root of behavior change is choice. Pressure reduces the bandwidth for learning. Granted, sometimes a client's choice to enter coaching is illuminated by the stark fact that he will no longer have a job unless he addresses some performance issue. Still, unless there is an opening in the form of a genuine desire to learn, coaching is unlikely to succeed.[2]

- *Coaching is possible because coach and client exist in different worlds.* Our world is composed of what we sense and our interpretation of what we sense. Since that interpretation is a result of our unique conditioning, my world is distinctly different from yours. A coach asks questions, offers distinctions, and invites new ways of seeing and interpreting based on her own world. At the same time, she establishes relevance for these distinctions in the client's world.

- *New distinctions invite the client to expand her world.* From his own world, a coach offers new distinctions by naming phenomena that, once described, the client can observe for herself. Distinctions emerge as the coach, gently and insistently, invites the client to allow the limits of her own world to become more porous, make new observations, and discover possible new actions that, though hitherto unseen, have always been available to her.

- *Self-generation is the central capacity for sustainable change.* A well-coached client learns how to coach himself. Thus, clients need to acquire not only the competencies required for the particular domain of application, but also the underlying "technology" of self-regulation and of development itself: self-observation, realization, reorganization, and stabilization. When the coaching process is transparent, this work leads inexorably to a lifetime of discovery and increasing depth.

- *Self-generation provides a foundation for specific leadership and management skills.* It is shortsighted to coach a client in specific management skills without also cultivating the ability to observe herself and make conscious choices to actually use these new skills. A self-generating client will discover what she needs to know. But a leader with brilliant technical skills who doesn't have a grounding in self-awareness, self-regulation, and the ability to intentionally choose new behaviors will always be limited.

- *Developmental coaching is biological.* In Chapter Two, we explored the nature of conditioning and saw that the habits that make up our identities are deeply embedded in our bodies. Exercising any new behavior requires awareness, activating new neural pathways, and reorganizing the shape and functioning of our bodies. Stabilizing it requires a biological process of establishing new default patterns in our neurological and muscular systems. In my experience, although people are sometimes capable of making transformative leaps, stabilizing significant new behaviors and identities usually requires engaging the body over months.

- *Coaching is iterative.* As distinct from training and other event-driven learning experiences, coaching directs attention to development over time. Coach and client come together for a conversation, usually on a periodic basis. The client emerges from each conversation with actions to take, new practices for building competencies, and self-observations. This iterative process provides opportunities for practice in real-life situations and for continually honing the development approach.

PRINCIPLES OF DEVELOPMENTAL COACHING

- Development is deepest and most sustainable when focused on learning, not performance.
- Coaching is freely chosen.
- Coaching is possible because coach and client exist in different worlds.
- New distinctions invite the client to expand her world.
- Self-generation is the central capacity for sustainable change.
- Self-generation provides a foundation for specific leadership and management skills.
- Developmental coaching is biological.
- Coaching is iterative.

THREE INTEGRATED STRUCTURES FOR DEVELOPMENT

Presence-based coaching accelerates the development of authentic leaders by providing three critical structures for an integrated development methodology.[3] The structures themselves have been around for millennia in traditions that value the cultivation of character and leadership. We can think of coaching as simply a modern form, relevant to our times, for providing those structures.

EXERCISE 3.1.

Differentiating Between Performance and Developmental Learning

Consider a time when you were learning a specific new skill or competency for a particular purpose, or to meet someone else's requirements of you.

- What was the situation?
- Who helped you learn this?
- How did you go about learning what you needed to learn?
- How did learning this skill build a certain identity?
- What identity was being built?

Now identify a time of significant change when you had to rise to a fundamentally changed circumstance and become a different person.

- What was the situation?
- How did you go about learning what you needed to learn?
- What aspects of yourself did you have to let go of to become someone different?
- What did you come to understand about yourself in the process?
- What identity was being built?

Now, grounded in your own experience, how do you see the difference between performance and developmental learning?

The first structure is *engagement with a competent partner* (coach, mentor, teacher, elder) who can expand what we are able to observe and act on. The partner lives in a world distinct from ours and is deeply committed to our development. This partner offers a different perspective and constructs a relational process that places our challenges and opportunities in a developmental context. The partner offers assessments and invites us to engage with him in new ways that require new awareness and more generative responses.

Generative practices are consistent, ongoing practices that increase our self-awareness and the ability to self-regulate. They provide a powerful foundation for presence and self-generation, and are the means through which we come to master our inner state and a "commitment to a way of being in the world."[4] Generative practices serve us wherever we are. Centering ourselves, for example, will help us be more present in our marriage, when having a difficult conversation at work, and when preparing to go on stage for a major speech.

Outcome-specific fieldwork complements generative practices with targeted and specific learning activities. Fieldwork, like generative practices, is done between coaching conversations. It includes exercises, practices, and experiments that develop and stabilize the actions and behaviors we require for competence. Fieldwork is the means for training ourselves in specific skills in the domains of our commitments. Performance coaching generally focuses on fieldwork, omitting the underlying generative practices.

These three integrated structures focus and accelerate the often sluggish developmental impulse, which is easily sidetracked by our own attachments and the hypnotic effect of the systems around us. Presence-based coaching delivers these three products of coaching in an integrated and coherent approach.

INTEGRATED DEVELOPMENT STRUCTURES

The three critical structures for development . . .

* engagement with a competent partner
* generative practices
* outcome-specific fieldwork

produce . . .

* observable competency in fulfilling commitments
* the capacity for self-generation
* the experience of greater aliveness

PRESENCE-BASED COACHING: FOUNDATIONS INTO METHODOLOGY

Up to this point, we have been addressing the nature, core structures, and products of developmental coaching. We now have a solid foundation on which to build a methodology.

Fundamentally, presence-based coaching is the means through which we deliver the three development structures. We provide these elements for the client. Simultaneously and inextricably, we pay consistent attention to our own development, remembering always that we too are works in progress.

- In coaching, we are a competent development partner for our clients. We create intimate conversation with our clients, in which our presence and our coaching moves reveal a new world and energize new actions and self-generation. *To do this, we must be constantly engaged in our own learning. We work with teachers and coaches who can help us by revealing our own learning edges. We experientially develop mastery in the territory of development.*

- We challenge our clients to engage in generative practices. With them, we design practices that are both relevant and sustainable in their lives. *We are consistent in our own generative practices as well, recognizing that they are integral to embodying who we want to be in the world.*

- Our presence and coaching moves engage our clients with fieldwork to develop specific competencies tied to their outcomes. Their fieldwork changes their context; in turn, they are required to listen and respond differently. *Coaching is our fieldwork, in which we practice the skills and presence required to be a useful resource. We are always learning through our coaching, and this in turn shapes who we are.*

Now we shift into a thorough exploration of the inner moves, supporting practices, and relational moves that comprise presence-based coaching. All of these are rooted in presence and evoke presence.

To disillusion you of the notion that you are in control of what happens in coaching, I primarily use the term *move* rather than *tool.* The distinction is important. A tool is something we use to carry out an operation on something or someone "out there." The recipient of this operation is distinct, separate from us, an object. A move is simply a shift, a change, something that we do. It's an action, taken with certain intentions. However, we are never in control of our clients. We are in relationship with them. We make moves that change the dynamic and invite, or evoke, a particular response. A move is an invitation.

A move produces something useful when we are present and attuned to the client. Our coaching moves do not change our clients;

rather, they change the field within which the client perceives, interprets, and chooses. A skillful coaching move makes presence and new insight more likely.

We differentiate between an inner move (primarily intended to shift the awareness of the coach) and a relational move (primarily intended to invite a shift in awareness in the client). The line is gray, of course, and because we're connected with our clients, our inner moves often produce a shift in the client as well. In some sense, everything is relational.

As a necessary prerequisite and to earn the privilege of guiding others on the path, we are deeply committed to integrating the three structures into our own development. We find competent partners, coaches, and teachers who can challenge our own assumptions and hold us as learners. We engage in generative practices in mind, body, and heart that enable us to bring a crystalline presence to our work and to be self-generative in our own lives. We do our own fieldwork, using coaching as our own laboratory for self-cultivation. Our self-cultivation is the foundation that allows everything else to work. The centrality of this cannot be overstated.

The rest of this chapter begins to define some of the inner and relational moves of presence-based coaching, using Roger as an example to bring them to life. Following this overview, the rest of this book explores these distinctions in depth.

Inner Moves

Inner moves in coaching are the means by which we work with our own inner state to be the best possible resource we can be for our clients. These moves require a level of mastery only produced by practice. Let's take a look at two areas of inner moves, which will illuminate the nature of the practices required to support them.

ORIENTING The first set of moves involves orienting ourselves before and during the coaching conversation. Orientation is a powerful way to stay present. Through orienting, we are intentional about what we invite into our awareness. We can:

• *Orient ourselves to a coaching model.* A good coaching model provides the distinctions for self-observation, grounds us in a theory of how humans change, and guides us in structuring the conversation.

- *Orient toward the client as a whole and resourceful person,* as someone with a story and a past and a future, as someone with tremendous potential. We can be intentional about how we view our client.

- *Orient toward our own purpose as a coach.* Why are we in this coaching relationship? What is our purpose as a coach? What is being served by these conversations? Knowing the answers to these questions grounds us in the conversation.

- *Orient toward the client's purpose.* Our knowledge of the client's purpose provides a foundation in the conversation. Orienting ourselves strongly to this makes us a powerful resource for the client.

- *Orient toward specific, competency-based outcomes.* Agreeing on outcomes at the beginning of coaching makes both coach and client more accountable and provides a beacon toward which we can frequently orient during our conversations.

- *Place the client, and the conversation, into a larger context.* This bigger picture (time frame, organizational view, or strategic perspective) lowers the stakes on the situation itself and allows greater spaciousness and resourcefulness than when we constrict ourselves around a specific situation.

Orienting requires a certain internal agility. Rather than organizing ourselves blindly around what is being thrown at us, orienting requires making a deliberate and conscious choice about what we invite into our awareness and what we exclude. Before and during the coaching conversation, we are managing the content of our own awareness in order to be the most helpful possible resource for our client. From a state of presence, oriented in what is important and real, we extend toward our client. Chapter Four explores this.

> *I begin preparing for my telephone meeting with Roger ten minutes before our call. I mentally set aside other things I have been working on and center myself in my body for the conversation. I touch my heart lightly with my fingers and I smile, feeling my caring for this person who has willingly entered this privileged relationship with me.*

I orient myself in my office, looking out the window at the knoll, shrouded in mist. I sense the distance between my office and his, hundreds of miles away in an office park outside Chicago. I visualize the busyness of his office, remembering the people he interacts with. I recall his sharing about his upbringing as a highly competitive athlete with a demanding father and consider how our formative experiences shape all of us.

A mental picture of Roger with his wife and teenaged son comes up and passes, and I feel within myself the love he has for them. I think about his boss, whom I know well; she truly believes in Roger and is simultaneously frustrated with recent events. And I recall Roger's poignant words when he and I first talked: "Doug, I really want this to work. And I don't know how to do my job differently." I sense the intensity of his commitment to being successful.

Holding all of this as context, I review the notes from our previous conversation and jot down a couple of reminders about things I feel important to bring up. I recall my own commitment to be deeply present with my clients.

Oriented, I let it all go, settling into the chair. I wait, present, alert, and expectant, for the phone to ring.

EXERCISE 3.2.

Orient to a Client

Take a moment to consider someone you work with as a coach or in some other developmental capacity. Think of this person's concerns and aspirations.

Now, consider how reading this book might allow you to be different with this person. How might what you've been reading inform your work together?

Orient to this person, and then return to your reading. Allow this person and his or her concerns and aspirations to reside, undemanding but present, in the background. By inviting this person into your awareness as you read, you are more likely to make connections between the reading and your work together.

HOLDING A RELATIONAL FIELD In any interaction between two or more people, there is a relational field that we can sense and tends to elicit a particular response from us, whether or not we are conscious of it. "A relational field can be described . . . as an energized space that exists between two living presences. . . . Relational fields exist between any two (or more) people in relationship. . . . Both parties . . . contribute to, and connect through, the relational field. Therefore, the relational field is a field of consciousness, which is at least to some degree, shared."[5]

Consider the differences in your internal experience of the moment, in each of the following interactions: meeting a business appointment and sizing each other up through a handshake, seeing your child or spouse after some time apart, a tension-laden conversation with that same child or spouse, a conversation with someone in your workplace in which you are requesting that he take some action. Each of these interactions feels different. We can think of them as distinct experiences of the relational field.

We respond in conditioned ways to the fields in which we find ourselves. Think of a person with whom you immediately feel at ease, relaxing and trusting. Now think of a person whom you instinctively mistrust, tightening and guarding yourself in his presence. Each of these fields produces a different reaction in you.

To be sure, the way you respond also affects the field. Think of a situation in which one person came to a meeting hot under the collar, and the calmness and acceptance of another person settled a potentially difficult conversation and allowed a useful exchange of ideas. The more solid and intentional our presence, the more our presence can shape the field.

Coaching requires us to be intentional about how we contribute to, shape, and hold the relational field. Practices train us to generate and hold a field within which the most relevant experiences can arise for our client. In coaching, we:

- *Maintain awareness of the relational field* and are intentional about how our presence shapes and holds that field. We sense and extend, through our attention, particular qualities that are conducive to resourceful learning.

- *Remain unshakably certain about the possibilities* that exist in the situation and convinced of the client's potential for generative learning, no matter what happens.

- *Allow silence.* It is within silence that new possibilities often arise; the unrelenting and fragmenting demands of our everyday work lives are anathema to presence and to learning. Times of silence during coaching conversations can be restorative as well as productive.

Chapter Five explores holding moves in detail.

Roger is describing a situation that arose at work with a direct report who had created a crisis situation that Roger had to step into and fix. It was entirely preventable, and Roger is frustrated because it kept him from doing the work he really needed to focus on. He doesn't know how he could have dealt differently with it and is feeling self-critical for letting the situation develop in the first place.

As I listen, I am focusing on what he is saying. At the same time, I am extending my attention toward Roger. I am experiencing his desire for me to tell him how to handle it. And I'm noticing, but not indulging, my urge to offer a solution.

I am holding Roger as whole and resourceful, sensing his anxiety and tension, his commitment to learning, and his genuine desire to support his managers in their jobs. I am experiencing Roger in this moment as a brilliant, good person in the middle of conflicting commitments. I'm seeing the possibility that Roger could have engaged very differently with his manager, both before and during the actual situation. I don't know exactly how; at the same time, I know there is something significant for Roger to learn in this.

I feel energized. I'm smiling on my end of the phone and ready to be curious with Roger in discovering what there is to learn.

EXERCISE 3.3.
Play with a Relational Field

Consider a conversation you're about to have with someone: a colleague, friend, or loved one.

Just before the conversation, think about what you really like and appreciate about this person: the unique qualities and personality traits that make this person special to you. Allow yourself to feel your appreciation for the person before you begin the conversation.

As you interact, stay in touch with your appreciation. Simply let it be there as you talk. Smile as you talk, extending that appreciation through your smile to the other.

Doing this shifts your own inner state. Afterward, consider whether the conversation felt different to you, and if so, how.

Generative Practices for Presence

It should be apparent from the examples that ongoing self-awareness and self-regulation are part and parcel of the inner work required to coach. The quality of the relationship proves the primary factor in whether a coaching intervention is likely to produce the desired outcomes. Coaching is a relational activity, and our presence is fundamental to the quality of our relationships.

While presence is an awareness that is always available, our conditioned ways of being limit our access to it. Our constant efforts to prop up our identity in the world have produced the collateral damage of living, much of the time in a reactive, constricted way. This deprives us of much of the rich sensory and creative experience that comes with the state of presence.

There is more.

PRESENCE PAUSE

It is essential to rediscover our capacity for presence. It is both necessary for our efficacy as coaches and for experiencing the aliveness that is our birthright. We can cultivate our presence through three primary doorways. Each offers a set of generative practices that, when done regularly, greatly increase our access to the state of presence.

Because presence is there, waiting, we simply have to practice opening to it. These doorways, then, are doorways into what is already there.

PRESENCE PAUSE

Here are several doorways, available to you, through which you can develop your experience of presence:

- *Mind.* Mind is the organ of awareness. By becoming familiar with its workings, we become much better able to direct and focus our attention. It is through mind that we self-observe. And it is through self-observation that we become aware of the attachments and aversions that are so often the drivers of our behavior. Mind is the source of choice, of free will. This doorway is the subject of Chapter Six.

- *Body.* It is through our bodies that we experience our own aliveness. While we live constantly in sensation, the busyness of our mental activity usually overwhelms the realm of sensation, and we lose touch with it. For some of us, it's only through the pursuit of sensory pleasure that we remember that we even have a body. By connecting to the sensations in every part of our body, we can become more fully alive, more present, in any moment of any day in any place. The body is a powerful doorway into present moment awareness and a rich source of information about what is going on within ourselves and in our relationships. Chapter Seven shows you how to do this.

- *Heart.* We are accustomed to thinking of our heart as a physical organ that accomplishes certain functions. However, there is also a distinct intelligence available through our heart. While connected to the rest of our nervous system, the heart has its own way of understanding and teaching. This doorway into presence includes both the spark of romantic love and, more relevant to the coaching world, gratitude, compassion, and spiritual connection. The practices in Chapter Eight will support you in building your capacity for experiencing this intelligence. Through the heart, you will come to embody a compassion that invites your clients to become more self-accepting, less defended, and more open to possibilities.

THREE DOORWAYS TO PRESENCE

- Mind
- Body
- Heart

Practicing in all three areas is central to the premise of presence-based coaching. The generative practices offered are the bass note on which we build the fundamental capacity for presence in our lives. Practicing to be present is about living life fully and recovering our own aliveness. Clearly this is relevant, indeed essential, for coaching at a deep level. It is also ontological, in the sense that the capacity for presence will show up in every aspect of our lives.

In our professional domain, we are committed to the development of others. A prerequisite is our commitment to our own development; prerequisite to that is being as awake and alive and human as possible. That's the game we're in. We:

- *Engage in regular practices of mind,* outside the coaching conversation, that enable us to self-observe, notice and release attachments, and be more present.

- *Engage in regular body practices* that build our capacity to be centered and ready no matter what is going on around us. Body practices are a quick path to presence.

- *Engage in heart practices* that build our access to the heart's intelligence and cultivate gratitude, compassion, and spiritual connection.

- *Invite our clients into mind, body, and heart practices.* Grounded in our own experience, we extend our presence toward our clients. We stand as an invitation to practices for self-observation, self-regulation, reorganization, and centering under any circumstances. These are generative capabilities, relevant to every context that the client will ever be in.

I am committed to my regular practices. This wasn't always so. I've historically been someone who struggles with routine.

A former teacher invited me to "begin a tai chi practice, and enter it as if you are going to do it for the rest of your life." Typically, I resisted. I joined a class, but it was off again/on again for months. After six months or so, something shifted, and it became integrated into who I am to the point that it is simply how I start my day.

Now I begin each day by walking to the river with our dogs. At the river, I do a series of movement practices from tai chi and aikido, two martial arts that cultivate an embodied presence. Then I sit on the bench facing the river for sitting meditation. I follow my breath, bringing my attention back every time I notice my mind drifting. I close with a compassion practice of sensing and connecting through my heart and a prayer of gratitude.

I walk back over Hound Dog Hill, stopping to deeply experience the magnificent sunrise view east over the mountains, and throwing tennis balls for Lyra on the road back down past the cabins.

Each of these practices, in its own way, is a way to be present with myself and to build the muscle of awareness and the aliveness within me.

While I coached Roger, I did these practices in the background. While I don't do them because I am coaching people, they are fundamental to who I am becoming. Generative practices provide a foundation for my work and directly affect the resourcefulness and connection that I bring to my relationships.

They also allow me to speak, with grounding and authenticity, about how similar practices will be helpful to Roger. I invited Roger into several regular practices that proved to be instrumental as he learned to respond differently. Sitting practice allowed Roger to observe himself quietly and notice what was going on inside him. Centering provided the means to stay present and at choice when others made requests of him. A heart-centered compassion practice helped him relax and be more accepting when he lapsed into old behaviors. (I provide specifics on each of these practices in later chapters.)

EXERCISE 3.4.

Settle Yourself

Take a minute to try this. First, scrunch up every muscle in your face, closing your eyes tightly, and holding this for a few seconds. Then let it go completely.

Hunch up your shoulders to your ears, tightening them; hold this for a few seconds, then let your shoulders drop, exhaling at the same time. Let them hang.

Straighten your back so your chest opens a little, not straining, just straightening. Take three deep and slow breaths, inhaling, then letting the air go completely. With each exhalation, let your shoulders drop even more.

Now notice your inner state. How do you feel? How are you different from how you were two minutes ago?

This is a simple example of practice.

Relational Moves

Within the field created by these inner moves and the structure of the coaching conversation, we also make relational moves that are visible to the client. These specific coaching moves both depend on and evoke presence. They tend to produce new ways of seeing, expand the client's world to include new distinctions, and provide in-the-moment experiences relevant to the client's commitments.

Relational coaching moves are generally correlated with the components of self-generation. No matter the specific content and focus of our coaching, we remember that self-generation is one of the fundamental products of coaching. We are fostering self-generative leaders who, regardless of their job description, are maximally capable of responding to the demands of any circumstance with self-awareness, resilience, resourcefulness, and vision.

Keeping the components of self-generation in mind, we have a great range of moves available to us.

Self-Observation and Realization

- *Share our present-moment observations and experiences during the conversation.* We are a resource; standing outside the world of the client gives us a unique and useful perspective. When we share our experience, we make it possible for our clients to observe distinctions they previously couldn't.

- *Direct the client's attention into her present moment experience.* Something is always being revealed. We invite our clients to inquire, to be curious, to look inward. We invite them to pay attention to what their bodies are revealing.

- *Focus the field.* We introduce relevant information. We create immediacy by bringing the context into the conversation and establishing relevance for the client's experience. We spotlight habits as they arise.

- *Challenge limiting assumptions in the client's identity.* We expose the client's assumptions and structure of interpretation, thus broadening what she is able to see and respond to.

Reorganization

- *Invite, in the present, new perspectives and future possibilities.* We are curious about what will be revealed with a different perspective.

- *Practice centering and reorganizing around a specific commitment.* The coaching conversation provides many opportunities for the real-time experience of reorganization. Doing this during the conversation provides practice and a successful experience to reference later.

- *Build competency in reorganizing.* We can do this by stabilizing our own presence and identifying specific experiences and resources that are helpful for the client in reorganization.

- *Mobilize commitment in the present moment for new actions.* The energy for a future action is put into place now, and the coaching conversation provides opportunities for practicing this move into commitment.

Stabilization

- *Design, with the client, fieldwork to operationalize new distinctions and skills* that come out of the coaching conversation. Fieldwork is action. Joint design increases the client's ownership, readiness to coach himself, and ability for self-generation. Fieldwork includes practices, exercises, self-observations, and other learning activities that build competency and self-generation.

- *Engage the client with changing "facts on the ground" produced by his fieldwork and actions taken.* The client's development, and the new actions and behaviors taken, will affect others. Action produces a changed context, and new data, for the next conversation.

This may initially appear like a menu. However, these distinctions are intended to support your own intuition, not replace it with a carefully proscribed process. The descriptions reveal a territory that you'll come to navigate creatively with your own clients.

The risk is that we come to think of these moves collectively as our "presence tool kit." We can indulge in the belief that by making a certain move, we will give our client a specific experience, a new perspective, or energy to meet his goals. However, coaching techniques delivered without a grounded presence will appear as, well, techniques. They will appear disingenuous and will either fall flat or be counterproductive.

It is our own presence that imbues moves with meaning, grace, and elegance. Offered with presence, coaching moves can be received as invitations. The conversation unfolds naturally and easily.

We are in relationship, as a committed partner, with another human whose development is the purpose for the conversation. Given a period of practice and increasing mastery, coaching moves eventually arise intuitively as creative responses to the relational field that envelops us and our clients. They can be integrated into almost any existing coaching model and can serve to make any conversation more real and relevant.

This is what I want for you, and is worth far more than what this or any other book could provide in out-of-the-box tools.

Here's an abbreviated excerpt of coaching with Roger, based on a telephone meeting. This does not illustrate every move described above but provides a sense of a presence-based coaching conversation.

> *Roger pauses in his story of frustration. He sounds resigned and I ask, "What are you experiencing in your body right now?"*
>
> *He responds, "I feel discouraged, somewhat heavy and dense. My shoulders are tight; my chest feels compressed. My head is slumped forward. It's similar to what I experienced Tuesday when I realized that we were going down the same road again, after several conversations with this manager."*
>
> *I sense my own body's reaction to what he was describing. I reply, "Listening to you describe this, I'm noticing myself as feeling pessimistic and not very resourceful. What are you experiencing?"*
>
> *Roger responds, "No, it's hard to feel optimistic. This kind of stuff happens every day; this was just a recurring one, and a big one."*
>
> *"Yes, that's challenging. When you're feeling like this, how are you at resolving these kinds of issues?"*
>
> *"I'm snappy with others and not very creative. I manage the crisis, but we don't get to a root cause, so we just go down the same path again later."*
>
> *"Okay. Now let's practice reorganizing yourself. Center yourself, and describe to me what you're doing."*
>
> *Roger reorganizes himself at his desk, as he has been practicing for the several weeks of our work together. He describes, over the phone, exactly how he's doing so. Pauses show me that he's experiencing this as he talks. "I'm dropping my attention . . . centering my attention in my belly . . . straightening my back . . . looking up and out . . . shoulders drop . . . jaw letting go . . . taking a couple of deep breaths. I'm touching my heart . . . smiling."*
>
> *I follow his narrative, allowing myself to experience the same things within my own body.*
>
> *"Nice, Roger. So now, in this different body, tell me what's most important for a real resolution of this issue. Tell me how this situation*

can be really different, say, three months from now. Describe it to me as if it were already true. Don't worry about how to get there."

Roger begins, slowly at first, then with more energy, "Well, the manager has a really clear understanding of the new process. She's trained her people on it. And she has a backout schedule for the week of closing. All her people understand what their role is and where they plug into the schedule, so no one downstream gets surprised by not having what they need."

"Who is it that is describing this, Roger?"

There's a long pause, as Roger has a moment of realization. "It's me! Well, it's a different me from five minutes ago!" He pauses again, sensing into the question. "It's the resourceful, creative part of me. This part is lost when I'm in the discouraged, triggered body. However, it's immediately accessible in this centered, more powerful body. I definitely know how to solve this problem."

"Okay, great. Now anchor that feeling. Be the centered, resourceful body." I pause for twenty seconds or so as Roger stabilizes in this different body. "Now let's talk about some practical next steps to get there."

The actual conversation was considerably longer. However, in this conversation, we can see the coach:

- Inviting Roger to self-observe and describe his inner experience.
- Connecting Roger's in-the-moment experience to the context of the situation, thus establishing relevance.
- Staying present with his own experience and sharing that experience with Roger.
- Inviting Roger to reorganize himself and describe what he's doing to make it visible and explicit.
- Inviting Roger into a moment of realization: this different body enables a different level of resourcefulness in the situation.
- Encouraging Roger to stabilize himself in the new awareness.
- Inviting Roger to generate some fieldwork: specific, practical steps to address the problem.

Performance coaching would have skipped over much of this and focused on generating the practical steps to develop Roger's manager and solve the problem. However, this would have skipped over the crucial self-generative aspect of working directly with the recurring triggering that undermines Roger's confidence and keeps him reactive.

The developmental coaching conversation addresses both the root of the problem "out there" and the root of the problem within Roger. We can imagine from this brief conversation that some iterations of this process could lead both to improved management skills and a greater ability to work with his inner state in ways that cultivate resourcefulness, authenticity, and resilience. That's the premise of presence-based coaching.

Part Four provides descriptions and business examples of relational coaching moves for each component of self-generation.

CHAPTER SUMMARY

- Performance coaching is driven primarily by organizational standards and metrics; developmental coaching addresses the development of the whole person.
- The principles of developmental coaching underpin a deeper approach to development focused on self-generation and sustainable, lifelong competencies.
- Accelerated development rests on three core structures: a competent partner or coach, generative practices that lead to self-generation, and outcome-specific fieldwork that targets specific competencies in the domain of the client's commitments.
- Presence-based coaching is a particular approach to developmental coaching, built on inner moves in which the coach is self-regulating her inner state to be present and useful, and relational moves in which the coach invites the client into greater presence and resourcefulness. The relational moves are organized around the four components of self-generation.
- Coaching moves should not be viewed as a linear process of steps to be mastered or as a set of techniques guaranteed to produce certain results. Rather, they are an artist's palette. When offered with presence, the moves are received as an invitation, and something new can emerge in the conversation.
- The cultivation of presence requires engaging in ongoing generative practices that build self-awareness. The doorways of mind, body, and heart offer distinct practices that cultivate unique qualities of presence essential to leadership, coaching, and aliveness.
- Through practice and mastery, coaching moves come to arise intuitively.

PART
TWO

Inner Moves for
Presence-Based Coaching

We must be the change we wish to see in the world.

Gandhi

PART TWO EXPLORES THE INNER MOVES OF ORIENTING AND HOLDING a field. Here, we are managing our inner state in order to be the best possible resource for the client.

It could be argued that the generative practices that are the major thrust of Part Three should precede this material, as some facility in inner awareness and focusing of attention is required for the moves described here. However, you may well be impatient to get into application. The exercises in these two chapters will give you a taste of things to come, and the text will provide a case for the foundational practices of presence that follow.

As always, the self-awareness and self-generation provided by your practices are essential for being able to work in a grounded way with this material. If you're in a practice, you'll know the moves to make. You will be an invitation. If not, you will be executing techniques rather than embodying an invitation.

Chapter Four presents a number of ways in which we can orient, or selectively organize our field of awareness, to include particular elements that help us serve clients. In Chapter Five, we explore the nature of the relational field and the inner move of holding that field with the intention that something new, and perhaps surprising, will emerge.

Orienting

It is time we steered by the stars, not by the lights of each passing ship.

Omar Bradley

The rose is a rose from the time it is a seed to the time it dies. Within it, at all times, it contains its whole potential. It seems to be constantly in the process of change; yet at each state, at each moment, it is perfectly all right as it is.

Timothy Gallway

O RIENTING OURSELVES MEANS KNOWING WHERE WE are in relation to something that we have selected from a broader set of possibilities. We orient ourselves in a room by scanning to assess who and what is there; only then can we determine how to proceed. We orient in time by looking at our watch to see that we have fifteen minutes to our next appointment. Depending on the circumstances, that may be reassuring, or may add urgency. Either way, we know more of what is required of us. We are oriented.

This chapter presents *orienting* as a means to become a different kind of resource for coaching clients. By orienting, we make a conscious choice about what we invite into our field of awareness. Two core assumptions underpin orienting. First, what we include in our field of awareness will affect our resourcefulness as a coach, the possibilities we can see and articulate, and the distinctions and context we can offer to our clients. Second, the resource we are, which depends on the perspective and interpretations we represent, directly affects the client. Our presence, and what we extend into the relational field we hold with our client, affects what our clients are able to perceive in immediate, undeniable, and tangible ways.

Some perspectives narrow our view; some broaden it. You can choose. As an initial experiment, take your eyes off this page, and focus your gaze intently on the details of your fingerprint, held a comfortable foot or so away. Fix your gaze on it as if there were nothing else. Let the rest of the room disappear. Now soften your gaze. Shift your focus to the background, but allow your peripheral vision to gain strength as you bring in a sense of the room around you. Feel and sense yourself as being in the room, taking it all in without focusing on anything in particular. Let your body soften with your gaze. Now toggle back and forth several times between these two views, exploring the distinction.

How were you different in these two experiences? What shifted in you? Were you aware, in the latter state, of information that wasn't available to you in the former?

✎ PRESENCE PAUSE ✎

Orienting is intentionally bringing resources into our field of awareness that encourage greater creativity and new ideas to emerge. By orienting, we evoke greater resourcefulness in ourselves and in our clients.

Beginning with this chapter, the activities are described as practices, rather than exercises. You can do a practice as a one-time experience, and something interesting will likely be revealed. However, the

---

ORIENTING MOVES

- Orienting to a coaching model
- Generative orienting to your client
- Orienting to your purpose
- Orienting to your client's purpose
- Orienting to coaching outcomes
- Expanding the context

real power of practices comes from repetition. The more you commit to doing practices over time, the more available will become the resulting shift in attention and inner state. This is the road to mastery.

A COACHING MODEL

Orienting ourselves within the context of a coaching model provides a road map of where we're going and how we're getting there.

There are many schools of thought and coaching approaches; some are profound and useful, and others lack foundation and depth. A coaching model should provide a certain rigor in this work. To be useful, it should serve at least these four core functions:

- Ground our work in a robust theory of how humans learn and change.
- Organize our coaching work according to a road map that includes beginnings, coaching for specific outcomes, and endings.
- Offer distinctions that provide the basis for self-observation and presence.
- Integrate rigorous self-development for the coach into the coaching itself.

When we orient to a coaching model, we bring the model's structures, tools, and ways of seeing into our awareness. They become resources, and we are in turn a greater resource for our clients. With practice and as we develop ourselves further, we use these resources flexibly rather than as a script to follow.

Using the approaches in *Presence-Based Coaching* will help you bring more presence and depth to your coaching in any model you use.

The Septet Model for Mindful Coaching

The Septet Model is the subject of my first book, *The Mindful Coach*. Unlike most other coaching models, it is specifically designed for the four functions listed above. I describe it briefly here to illustrate how a strong coaching model supports our development as practitioners.

The model provides seven clearly delineated voices integrated into a road map for coaching conversations. Each voice has relevance and utility at particular points in the conversation; we strive to be mindful in choosing which voice to use in any given moment.

The Septet Model is designed to support the kind of rigorous self-observation I advocate in this book. Distinct coaching behaviors provide a foundation for self-observation. Through mindful attention and an understanding of how our attachments and aversions drive behavior, we start to see when our urges might override our discernment about what the client needs from us. Furthermore, self-observation leads us into greater presence in our coaching relationships and to self-generation as coaches. (Unique, free self-assessments that provide additional perspective about coaching habits can be found at http://dougsilsbee.com/books/tmc/assess.)

The investigator voice is central in the model and encompasses three distinct lines of questioning that interact to produce creative tension. These questions lead to additional voices that sharpen the conversation and open up new ways of seeing and action possibilities: the reflector (providing feedback, and encouraging self-assessment and reflection), the teacher (offering new information and distinctions, and challenging the client's thinking process), and the guide (encouraging the client to take action, and sometimes suggesting or

---

THE SEVEN COACHING VOICES

- Master
- Partner
- Investigator
- Reflector
- Teacher
- Guide
- Contractor

These voices invite:

- New and expanded perspectives on the client's situation
- Clearly articulated outcomes
- Grounded action steps to move toward that outcome

recommending specific actions). The contractor supports the client in translating new insights and commitments into specific action steps, and builds structures of accountability that support the iterative learning that makes coaching so powerful.

Foundational to the five voices described so far are two other critically important voices. The master voice describes the way of being of the coach and requires us to do our own ongoing work, bring presence and deep listening to the conversation, and be a learner in our own right. The partner voice establishes the structure, safety, and container within which the coaching can take place, ensuring that the coaching process is jointly designed and responsive to the client's needs.

These seven distinct voices are integrated in a graceful architecture that invites the client into ongoing inquiry and action, while simultaneously challenging and supporting. In coach training retreats, participants with significant coaching mastery describe how powerful it is to be able to integrate a self-observation framework into their coaching. Participants with less experience find that the clear distinctions included in the road map make a strong coaching foundation.[1]

Self-Observation Using a Coaching Model

Most coaching models imply, or state explicitly, certain behaviors and actions. In presence-based coaching, these have mostly been described as moves to make. For this or any other coaching model, these behaviors can provide the basis for self-observation as a coach.

The critical questions to be constantly asking are, "In this moment, what is driving my choices? Am I present with my client? Who am I right now? What am I doing?" These questions bring us into self-awareness, accountability to our client, and sharp crystalline presence.

You can create a self-observation around one or two behaviors distinguished by your coaching model. Choose behaviors for which increased self-awareness on your part will have a direct benefit for your client. Use the template in Chapter Six to guide you.

Be rigorous about doing your self-observation over several weeks or sufficient repetitions that you begin to see the nature of the habit as it arises. Bring consistent, neutral, rigorous attention into this conditioned behavior over time. What happens? How is your coaching different? How are you different when you do this?

YOUR CLIENT

In coaching, it is primary to orient to our client. The view of our client that we hold can either limit or greatly expand the possibilities revealed in our coaching.

Any description or perception is limited and, by definition, reductionistic. Humans are miraculously complex. It is human nature to process information, seek patterns, and put them into our mental frameworks in order to be able to make decisions.

While it is useful to make efforts to understand our clients, we are in big trouble as soon as we think we know and understand them, however reassuring it is to us to believe we do so. To believe we understand someone is to stop seeing them. James Flaherty offers an eloquent description of the limitations of our interpretations of clients and concludes, "Human beings in every case will exist beyond the borders of whatever model is used to describe them. . . . A model is a well-focused snapshot; . . . humans are living, changing, adapting, and self-interpreting."[2]

It is critical to hold any assessment or view of our clients lightly, recognizing that any person will always be more complex than our description. If we focus too strongly on our reassuring but limited description, this will also affect the client and restrict her sense of possibility.

Constrictive Orienting

As a way of understanding the insidious nature of our limiting views, here are some unhelpful ways we can orient to our clients:

- *Profile:* We can see our client primarily through the lens of an "objective" assessment: a personality inventory, a 360 review, or performance feedback she has received. This description has uses, but it can also become ossified as a restrictive way of seeing her. When she then behaves differently than the assessment would predict, we are surprised because she broke the mold we had put her in!

- *Simplification:* We can view our client as a role player, seeing her capabilities and aspirations solely through the frame of reference of a company's competency model or her potential to contribute. The same client may also be a mother, an aspiring singer, an unhappy wife, a person of increasing age and declining health, an enthusiastic tennis player, or a grief counselor for hospice. Each of these descriptors represents an entire set of concerns and commitments that are real to this person. We diminish our view of our client tremendously if we fail to appreciate the larger landscape of her life.

- *Label:* We can see people as a collection of symptoms or as a cultural stereotype. We organize our response to them in relation to the behaviors that they are exhibiting, particularly the ones that cause problems for ourselves or others. In doing so, we lose touch with the client's subjective experience, structure of interpretation, and values and commitments.

- *Object:* We can orient to our client as an object to be changed through our carefully defined coaching process. Our process may be brilliantly designed to get results, and we may be very skilled and invested in using it. However, if it doesn't move our client, allow for creative joint design, and foster self-generation and new competencies, then it's not serving.

- *Source of income:* We can orient to keeping our client. For example, many coaches charge a monthly fee, and it's up to the client to say when the engagement should end. That's essentially asking the client to fire someone who has become established as a confidant, potentially with great intimacy. When there's no incentive for the coach to declare the engagement complete, it is easy to build dependency rather than self-generation.

- *Source of identity:* Perhaps the most subtle of these, we can orient to our clients as a source of our own gratification. In this, we engage our client in ways that will help us feel good about ourselves. We shape our conversations to affirm our own identity as coach and individual, perhaps teaching more than is useful for our client or making recommendations that establish our expertise. Coaching becomes about us, not about our client.

There are others. You get the idea. Each of these orientations provides a comfortable way to reduce something that is complex and multilayered. Our way of seeing makes us both more comfortable and less useful to our clients.

Generative Orienting

Here's the opposite list. We can also orient toward our client in a great number of ways that expand our view and make us a more useful resource:

- *Complex:* We orient toward our client as being more complex and mysterious than any assessment can possibly reveal. We do this by making observations and then holding them lightly, remembering that they are a partial truth and that any client always exists beyond our observations. We can allow ourselves to be curious, wondering in every moment what will be revealed in our client.

- *Whole:* We see the client as more than a contributor in a particular role with particular skills. We orient toward our client as a multidimensional human. We understand that given who this person is, there will be great similarities between how she is in the rest of her life and how she is in the job. We remember always that our client is a person in multiple commitments and that the commitments around which we are coaching her are only a portion of the landscape of her life. We see her as a whole person.

- *Emergent:* We see the client's behaviors as an expression of an underlying body of habits, defaults, and patterns of interpretation. These habits are evidence of what our client has been practicing for years and years. We invite our client into curiosity about the underlying patterns of conditioning and how they might be loosened to allow new possibilities to be revealed. We see our client as in the process of emerging.

- *Partner:* We organize the coaching process around the client. Coaching is a principle-guided partnership in which client and coach are constantly evolving, and the moves that are most helpful are shaped as we go, not determined in advance. The process is a container rather than a prescribed path.

- *Self-generating:* We orient toward the client's independence and capacity for self-generation. Well-done, coaching results in a client who doesn't need coaching. Orienting toward our client as a source of perpetual revenue creates perverse incentives and is likely to creep into the conversation in unhelpful ways. Orienting toward our client as self-generative and independent leads to better coaching. Strong, capable, successful former clients lead to more clients.

- *Opportunity for service:* The client's development should be the driver of our coaching. It is easy, and natural, for our conditioning to lead us to act in ways that are fulfilling and satisfying to us. At the same time, the uniquely human capacity for self-awareness and choice allows us to recognize and suspend our own attachments. Orienting to the client's development is a requirement to set aside our own identity needs and to become a servant.

GENERATIVE ORIENTING

- Complex
- Whole
- Emergent
- Partner
- Self-generating
- Opportunity for service

These fundamental orienting choices align awareness in a certain direction. This alignment largely determines what we are able to sense and how we interpret what we sense. It's like tuning the radio dial: the frequency that our receiver is tuned to determines whether we listen to country music or NPR.

Similarly, our orienting relative to our client shapes how we receive and interpret everything that she offers, the resources that are available to us, and ultimately what we're able to offer her. It is critical to set our internal radio dials to the stations that will best serve our client.

Too, our awareness influences the relational field and will shape how she experiences us, and how she will experience herself.

PRACTICE 4.1.

Distinguishing Constrictive and Generative Orienting

You can do this with anyone. For example, use a meeting as a practice opportunity. Shift your awareness from one way of orienting to another in relation to the leader of the meeting or to another participant.

Choose a person who has a significant influence in the meeting and sometimes irritates you. First, orient toward this person in his role, with specific behaviors that influence the meeting. See how he uses his influence. Consider how you might describe the behaviors he engages in and how you might coach him to act differently. Notice the behaviors that irritate you, and those that are effective and ineffective.

Now orient to him as a human who happens to be doing what he's doing, but who also has a life outside that activity: a wife, children, a mortgage, an ailing parent, commitments to support his family, a desire for a tropical vacation, and conflicting commitments in this meeting that are difficult for him to manage. Discern his intentions and what he cares about. See him with compassion and understanding that, in some sense, he's doing the only things that his history, habits, and interpretations of the situation allow.

Shift back and forth between these two very different ways of orienting. You'll find that with some practice, you can toggle back and forth with ease. This practice of shifting perspective is tremendously valuable.

PRACTICE 4.2.

Generative Orienting to Your Client

Before beginning a coaching conversation, orient to your client by reviewing notes from previous conversations, the actions she is committed to, and her desires and intentions. Consider how the generative distractions offered above apply to your client. At the same time, hold what you believe about her lightly, recognizing that she will be a different person this time than the last time. Bring into your awareness the landscape of her life.

When you enter the conversation, be curious about who your client is right now. "Who is this person?" "How might she surprise me today?" "What's different about her?" That's the openness and curiosity we want to be in as we orient to, and coach, this amazing, remarkable, miraculous person.

How was this conversation different as a result of your orienting?

Purpose

The question "For the sake of what?" lives constantly in us, whether we pay attention to it or not. Most often, we do not. We forget to ask the question and get so wrapped up in activity that we don't remember why we're doing something in the first place. Our purpose isn't so much about the activity that we're doing as about the reason we're doing it. It's our sense of purposefulness that imbues an activity with meaning. Orienting to purpose introduces spaciousness around the activity itself and places it in context.

Purpose is revealed rather than invented. We don't make up our purpose; we discover it through living our lives and discovering what is fulfilling and meaningful to us.

Purpose is within us rather than something "out there" to be pursued. It's as if we had an inner compass needle that allows us to orient ourselves and set a course in life. When our inner compass needle is aligned, we act in purposeful, directed, energized ways.

A purpose statement provides clear and succinct answers to three basic questions:

- What am I committed to?
- For whom will I do this?
- What value is created by this activity? What will be better as a result?

There's a well-known old story about three stonecutters. A man was walking down the street and happened on three stonecutters, each chipping away at a large block of granite. The man was curious and asked the first stonecutter what he was doing. The surly man grouched back, "I'm cutting this stone. It's my job! Let me work!"

He asked the second stonecutter the same question. "I'm building a wall," the stonecutter said, pointing to the long wall taking shape behind him. This helped a little, so the man turned to the third stonecutter and asked again.

The third replied, with a smile on his face, "I'm building a cathedral!" Sweeping his arm over the wall, he explained, "Decades from now, this will be complete, and my grandchildren will worship in the grandest cathedral in the land. And I will have played some small part in the building of it."

All were engaged in the same activity. But the third stonecutter was the happiest of the three. Oriented to purpose, he had an interpretation about his activity that gave it meaning. The drudgery of chipping away at granite six days a week seemed much less onerous because he was oriented to why he was doing it.

Purpose reminds us why we do what we do. It's the North Star by which we navigate in our conversations, a beacon for orienting.

Your Purpose

We can orient to our own purpose as a coach, educator, or leader. We can remember, for example, that working with this particular client at this particular time is an expression of our purpose of developing creative leaders.

Doing the work to recognize and clearly hold our purpose is an important piece of personal work. There are many ways to do this. If you haven't done this recently (or ever before) take some time to develop a life purpose statement for yourself. You can use the process in Appendix B or find guidance from other resources.[3]

On a more specialized level, we can also get clear on our purpose as a coach. This more specialized purpose is important to the subject of presence-based coaching, and a critical beacon for orienting ourselves as we coach.

PRACTICE 4.3.
Orienting to Your Purpose

Have a clear understanding of your own purpose in coaching. (One process for creating a purpose statement for your coaching is described in Appendix B.) Before a coaching conversation, review your statement.

Make this a different kind of experience from simply reading words. Remember the intention that you had when you wrote it. Consider how the conversation that you're about to have fits with your statement of purpose, and in fact provides an opportunity for you to fulfill that purpose. (If you do this, and the coaching conversation clearly does not fit with your purpose, that raises a whole different set of questions!)

Now begin the conversation oriented to your commitment. Maintain your awareness that the conversation is an opportunity for you to express your purpose, not as a theoretical future nice-to-have, but as living-in-the-moment truth.

The Client's Purpose

We can also orient to the client's sense of purpose. The client's clear statement of purpose provides a reference point to which we can orient. (The client, too, can orient to the range of commitments she is in by bringing them into her field of attention. We explore this later when we talk about centering in a commitment.)

Your client has a purpose for working with you. It is always there. For people not in touch with their purpose, it may take some exploration to discover it. It is enormously helpful to be clear about what the client's purpose is in her work and in her life and what the client's purpose is for coaching. If these are not clear, they may well be the essential starting point for the coaching conversation. For the former, the exercise in Appendix B can be slightly modified to support a client in discovering a sense of purpose in her life and work.

The latter, coming to an understanding about what purpose is being served by our work together, is a foundational coaching step. It is imperative that we understand what our client is committed to and why.

I strongly urge you to engage your coaching clients in early conversation about what they intend to accomplish through working

---

PRACTICE 4.4.

Orienting to Your Client's Purpose

Have your client's stated purpose written down clearly in an accessible place. (I keep it in a page on the personal website I set up for each client, where I can review it before each conversation.) Before each coaching conversation, bring your attention lightly to this statement of purpose and consider your client in the context of the statement. Allow yourself to orient to your client as being committed to fulfilling that purpose. Then recognize your role as a committed partner in supporting the client.

This is different from planning the conversation. It's connecting yourself, your client, and your client's purpose in your field of attention and inviting this purpose to be present in the conversation.

You can also remind the client of his purpose during the conversation. Reconnecting to purpose can be a strong orienting move that significantly shifts the context for a decision or an action. Seen in context of purpose, a decision may become abundantly clear. We'll talk more about this as a relational move in Chapter Ten.

---

with you. This conversation is part of the initial contracting in the coaching relationship. It results in clear understandings about the purpose for the coaching, which in turn becomes a touchstone for orienting in the coaching conversation and in taking action.

Here's an example. After some back and forth, a recent client recognized that his purpose for coaching was to "serve the organization as advocate for change and a mobilizer of people." This purpose invoked new possibilities for him. Although he was enormously capable, he had a tendency to withhold his convictions out of a conditioned notion that it was presumptuous to assert them. The mandate for change in his new executive role was a requirement for a different kind of leadership. Through our work together, orienting to that purpose became an important guide for him in making decisions and taking a stand for the change process.

COACHING OUTCOMES

Finally, the client's specific outcomes can be a basis for orienting at any point in the conversation. My leadership coaching work always begins with the development of purpose and outcomes. Outcomes are informed by, and serve, the purpose for coaching. Once developed and agreed on, the outcomes become a way of orienting myself before every coaching meeting.

Outcomes should matter to the client. Outcomes provide a hook for the client into a process that extends over time and will have its ups and downs. Whatever is going to happen begins with robust outcomes; they establish a field of commitment within which the coaching conversation can unfold. Consider: What is the problem that she is trying to solve? Why is it important to her? What are her real desires and potentials? If we are successful, what will she be able to do that is observable, behavioral, and lasting?

Orienting to outcomes provides the grounding for each conversation. Having them present in the field often reveals meaningful connections between the emerging conversation and the client's larger commitments.

Outcomes are most useful when they are:

- *Observable:* They can be witnessed by others or by oneself. There are lots of ways to measure even soft things. Be clear and specific about how success will be observed.

- *Behavioral:* Something that that client does, internally or externally, rather than a belief or good intention.
- *Lasting:* The behavior will be available to the client forever; it will become part of her well beyond the coaching engagement.

We return to our client from the previous section who defined his coaching purpose as "serving as an advocate for change and a catalyst for people." With that purpose clear, we worked together to develop outcomes that serve this purpose: "Observing your instinct to acquiesce, and replacing it with a strong, centered presence," "Leading efficient and energizing meetings with your staff," and several others. Each had specific conditions of satisfaction so that we could benchmark progress.

These agreed-on behavioral outcomes provided the road map for our coaching work. When he ran into difficult stretches, or taking a strong stand in a challenging work environment felt like too much, the purpose statement provided him with a North Star for orienting. The connection to his purpose animated our coaching work and contextualized the practices and new behaviors he was working with. While the outcomes all served the overarching purpose of leading change, several turned out to be good for his marriage as well.

Expanded Contexts

As we progress through life, we develop automatic habits to reinforce our identity in the world. We focus on immediate concerns that we habitually interpret as critical to our survival: the next meeting, the overdue report, the deluge of phone messages and e-mails. We see effective responses to these as measures of success. We organize ourselves around what is in front of our noses, living in a state of modern myopia. In this, we constrict our view and lose sight of what is often more important to real success.

The most difficult aspect of most problems isn't the problem itself but the stress, internal constriction, and reactivity that arise in us in relation to the problem. These reactions are a function of our thinking about the problem rather than the problem itself. They result from our interpretations and from obsessing about future consequences that may or may not occur.

As coaches, we can offer value because we live in a distinct world from that of our clients. Our world can be one in which the client's situation is seen in context, many possibilities exist, and the client's situation isn't nearly as threatening as he interprets it as being. When we orient to this view, we find spaciousness in ourselves by contextualizing the client and his situation. Our presence can ease the conditioned response our client is having to the problem. He then is likely to be able to be more resourceful and creative in responding to it. As well, he will be practicing the critical self-generative capacity of reorganizing himself from tightness and fear into resourcefulness and spaciousness. We saw this happen in the dialogue with Roger in Chapter Three, in which his constricted, defeated affect lightened, and he became much more resourceful.

There are many orienting moves that contextualize a situation and bring more spaciousness into the conversation. Each involves an internal move that brings the context into our field of awareness, thus relaxing the constricting grip of reaction. Here are four sample contexts that can orient us and provide greater spaciousness for ourselves:

- *Organizational:* We tend to focus on immediate needs, narrowing our interests to those of ourselves, our unit, team, department, division, or company, for example. There is always a wider view. Contextualizing any situation changes how we see the situation and the possibilities we can access. For example, orienting to the interests of a whole company places us in a very different perspective from seeing only the narrower interests of our department.

- *Temporal:* A narrow focus on the current situation means that it's all we can see. Any situation has a history and a future we can never fully know. The truth is that we've likely been in similar situations before and likely will be in similar situations in the future. Orienting ourselves within the passage of time reduces the inflated importance with which we imbue our current crises and allows us to breathe more easily.

- *Spatial:* We can orient to a more expansive view of our location. We can allow our sense of where we and our clients are to expand, our perception to become softer and more inclusive. We visualize our client sitting at his desk, we see the building he works in and the city in which he lives. We come to see our client as part of a much bigger picture. This can allow us to be more resourceful.

- *Spiritual:* For some, a spiritual orientation is of central importance. I've worked with many clients who saw their business role as an extension of their spiritual purpose and a venue in which to express their deepest values and concern for others. Orienting to this can catalyze an important perspective for people who recognize a connection to Spirit as important. The bumper sticker "What Would Jesus Do?" is a well-known popular example of this; for some people, it provides a powerful orienting move.

EXPANDED CONTEXTS

- Organizational
- Temporal
- Spatial
- Spiritual

It would be possible, and fun, to write a whole book of practices around these four contexts. Expanding our context is a powerful means of unhooking ourselves from the artificially high stakes that our conditioned survival tendencies attach to most situations in life.

Sharon Salzberg tells a wonderful story of being in a meditation retreat in Hawaii with seventy people and hearing that the largest tsunami in Hawaii's history was heading their way. There was no way to evacuate from their low-lying retreat center because the long coastal access road would be directly hit by the tsunami. The authorities informed them to get to the highest place possible.

The meditation hall was on the second floor, and there was little to be done. "We meditated as we waited for the tidal wave. . . . It was a tremendously profound sitting, as everyone faced the possibility of dying, engulfed in ferocious water. Some people prayed, others cried, some were silent." Later, after the tsunami missed the island, "We quietly gathered our things and went back downstairs. . . . We all had a radically different feeling about our knee pain and about the ordinary difficulties of our lives. For a while, everybody woke up to the things that mattered most to them."[4]

We don't need a tsunami or a brush with cancer to remind ourselves that life is fleeting and not to be wasted. The shift in perspective that illuminates what is most important to us is available to all of us in every moment. We access it through how we orient.

♨ PRESENCE PAUSE ♨

A CEO I worked with understood this well. A major, and necessary, change initiative was being launched. The organization of thirteen hundred people was already stressed and overwhelmed. She knew that there would be a lot of resistance to the changes and that it was critical that the key people involved in the implementation buy into the changes and enroll the wider organization.

In her launch presentation, she framed the reasons for the change and acknowledged the challenges that it would present. She reminded her people of their accomplishments in several previous major changes. And perhaps most important, she oriented people to a longer time frame, one in which they would look back, with pride,

---

PRACTICE 4.5.
Expanding the Context

Here are two short experiments that could easily become on-going practices. Play. See what happens.

1. Notice, right now, where you are. Allow your seeing to soften and broaden, taking in the environment as you read. Notice that the environment is just there, a backdrop to the activity of reading that you are engaged in. Even if there are people and conversations and activities, they can be seen as a backdrop. Allow yourself to continue reading, and simultaneously hold the sense of yourself in that context. Notice how your relationship to the activity of reading changes with the softening of your vision to include your environment.

2. Consider the flow of your life. Notice that you're reading this book at a particular moment in your life. Consider the experiences that led you to want to read this book at this time. And consider how what you're reading might affect what you do in the future. In your mind's eye, see a situation in which you are using these approaches, and with what positive result. Now bring your attention back to the reading, and simultaneously include this sense of a longer time span. How are you different?

---

on the time of change they were just entering. They would come to see this as a time in which they worked together on unprecedented challenges, supporting each other and moving the organization to a whole new level of performance. They would remember *these* as the "good old days."

Orienting is first an inner move that we make as a coach. It reminds us of the purpose and the context for what we're doing. Orienting lightens us and allows us to move more fluidly and creatively through our lives. It is a basis for reorganizing ourselves. Oriented in these ways, we find more spaciousness within us. We become a different kind of resource for clients because we have invited that which is most helpful into our field of awareness.

With practice, we build a level of mastery within ourselves. It is an obvious extension of inner orienting that we can coach clients to orient as well. The inner moves discussed in this chapter become the basis for similar relational moves with clients.

CHAPTER SUMMARY

- Orienting is an inner move of including specific elements in our awareness that allow us to be more resourceful, spacious, and effective.
- We can orient to our clients in ways that are constricting or generative. The latter means seeing our clients as complex, whole, creative, and miraculous.
- We can also orient to our own purpose as a coach, remembering why we are doing what we're doing.
- The client's purpose for coaching should be discussed in the early stages of the coaching conversation. When purpose is clear to both coach and client, specific coaching outcomes can be designed to support it. Both purpose and outcomes become fundamentals to which we can orient throughout our work together.
- We can orient to larger contexts, seeing the bigger picture of our client's situations. This alters our view and allows us to be a different kind of resource for our clients.
- Down the road, we can invite our clients to orient to these and many other elements as well.

CHAPTER 5

Holding

Believing in people before they have proved themselves is the key to motivating people to reach their potential.

John C. Maxwell

ORIENTING INVITES A DIFFERENT AND MORE RESOURCEFUL perspective and is conducive to presence. *Holding* maintains this presence, and extends it toward the client. We can establish and hold a relational field of awareness that includes the client.

This chapter derives from orienting and takes it a step further. It is through holding that we maintain our presence in the conversation and invite the client to experience presence as well.

HOLDING MOVES

The relational field
- Sensing the field
- Sensing qualities in the field
- Extending qualities into the field

Silence and possibility
- Holding the certainty of possibility
- Holding the client's potential
- Holding silence

THE RELATIONAL FIELD

Our way of being is evocative, distinct from what we actually do. Most of the impact of our coaching is in our presence; the rest is techniques. Yet many coach training programs focus on techniques, tools, and processes and pay only lip-service to the most critical part of what we bring to the table: our presence.

The strength of our presence has a direct influence on what we will call here the *relational field*. Relational field is a more precise description of what we usually describe as "atmosphere." You are welcome to think of this field as a useful metaphor or as a literal reality, as you wish. Either way, if you attend to the field, you will be different.

What Is a Relational Field?

Recall from Chapter Three that any relationship can be described as existing within a relational field. This field is shaped by the concerns and commitments that each person in the relationship holds. The field determines how we experience and interpret every interaction in this relationship. And in turn, every interaction shapes this field.

Fields are palpable and have real substance and power. Consider the tension between a boss and her subordinate during a difficult performance review. Consider a sweet and romantic candlelight dinner with a loved one, or the feeling of rousing excitement in the stands when the home team wins in a dramatic come-from-behind victory. These are felt experiences of fields. Unless we have the emotional depth of a fencepost, we can't help but experience something!

In the presence of such powerful fields, remaining unaffected demands a concerted effort. It is our nature as biological beings to respond to the pull of a relational field.

~⁎ PRESENCE PAUSE ⁎~

The Relational Field in Coaching

I am sitting at my desk in my retreat center in the mountains of North Carolina, writing this book with a clear purpose. Everything that is part of me, everything that is my history, shapes in some way

PRACTICE 5.1.
Sensing the Field

Practice sensing a field. The next time you're in a setting where a number of people are gathered for a shared purpose, allow yourself to experiment with sensing the field. A meeting, a sports event, a social gathering, a concert are great places.

In that situation, experiment. Relax. Allow your eyes to soften, so that your peripheral vision is more available. Imagine your skin as porous and sensitive; your whole body as a finely tuned antenna sensing what's around you: the mood, the feeling in the room, the excitement, resignation, anticipation, joy, anger. Notice changes and shifts in the field. Whatever is there, simply allow yourself to sense it.

What did you notice? And, how did you notice it?

what I write. You are reading this book in my future and your present. And everything that is part of you—your history and intentions and ways of interpreting your world—determines how you receive what you are reading.

You and I may never meet. Yet there is a palpable relational field that connects you and me. I am aware of your presence, in my awareness; it affects the words I write. These words are for you. I am, at this very moment, extending myself into the relational field that you and I share, with the intention of inviting you into a greater awareness of what might be possible for you. You can sense this intention, this possibility, in the field now. Realize, right now, that this book was written for you.

PRESENCE PAUSE

In coaching others, we greatly enhance our offer through being present. Our presence has a strong influence on the relational fields we are continuously creating with those around us. (So does our internal frenzy, our distractedness, our anger, or our resignation.) In coaching, we extend our presence toward the client. We intentionally hold a field that is likely to produce the experiences and results that we jointly wish to produce. We hold the field by (1) managing our own attention and awareness to become present, (2) extending that presence to include the client, and (3) stabilizing the relational field that connects us. This can happen in person or on the telephone.

Others may or may not experience the difference in the field that results. If our presence is strong and stable, our client may experience a significant pull or shift. Either way, it has the effect of releasing the coaching client from the default tendency to organize around identity preservation. Our presence means that we provide nothing to resist or defend against.

Even when we are fully present, clients have their own interpretive structures, and sometimes react and behave in unpredictable ways. But when we are present and that happens, it is clearly about the client herself. We extend a calm, supportive, resonant presence. This invites a sharp, unfiltered awareness of the unfolding moment in all its possibility. Holding the field provides an environment in which the client is more likely to let go of the conditioned tendencies that restrict the choices she is able to see and act on.

Experiencing and working intentionally with the field will greatly increase the depth of your coaching.

Qualities of the Relational Field

In maintaining and holding the field, we imbue it with certain qualities. The qualities are always there and available; orienting to them brings them into our awareness. Extending these qualities through our presence and attention affects the field.

You are invited to experiment with this yourself. Be curious; see what happens. Work with the field, doing so with the genuine intention to discover what might happen.

I consider the following qualities of the field to be extraordinarily useful in coaching. Each is a quality within us that can be distinctly sensed, developed through intention and practice, and extended to the client:

- *Spaciousness:* This quality is inherent in presence. There is spaciousness in the absence of conditioned habits, the recognition of a myriad of choices in the present moment, and a clearer view of the more expanded context in which we exist. Orienting to a larger context can invite more spaciousness into our inquiry.

- *Compassion:* This includes the recognition of how we and others create our own difficulties, the realization of the universality of these difficulties, and the desire to relieve them. Compassion is the recognition of our shared humanity and the basis for unconditional regard.

- *Unconditional positive regard:*[1] This quality represents an unshakable support and acceptance of our client. With unconditional regard, there is nothing coming from us that needs defending against. This does not mean that we automatically accept every behavior that the client exhibits. Discerning support differentiates between a person and his actions.

- *Resonance:* We experience a connection with our clients, and they sense that we see them and understand their concerns. In part this is accomplished through active listening and reflecting back what we hear. At a deeper level, resonance is an unspoken, felt connection in which both people know that there is mutual understanding.

- *Neutrality:* While we are passionate about our clients and their success, we are also absolutely clear about where we stop and our client begins. We care deeply. And we don't hinge our identity on our client's success, and we have no agendas for what she should do. We are free from attachment to, or investment in, a particular result.

QUALITIES OF THE FIELD

- Spaciousness
- Compassion
- Unconditional positive regard
- Resonance
- Neutrality

Sensing the Field

We may be skilled at noticing the tone of our conversations and the ebbing and flowing of connection and excitement as we communicate with others. However, it is a different matter to bring deep presence and intentionality to the relational field of our conversations; the difference is palpable. By sensing the field and experiencing ourselves within it, we stay much more connected to ourselves, the client, and the context within which the conversation is taking place.

PRACTICE 5.2.
Sensing Qualities in the Field

This practice will build your capacity to sense the field. While this can be done by visualizing another person, it is much richer to do it with a partner—someone you trust and who is willing to engage in an experiment with you. Familiarizing yourself with these distinctions will allow you to recognize and strengthen the qualities, and you will become much more able to work with them in your coaching.

This exercise can be quite intimate. Sit, facing each other, and simply be silent. Move through the following five qualities one at a time, speaking each out loud, and reading the prompts below. As you bring your attention to each quality, sense it in the field between you. Allow a minute or so for each quality, closing your eyes to better focus.

- *Spaciousness:* Sense that there's no urgency—that you could sit in silence and that it's possible to relax into that silence and feel each other, without any need to do anything. Sense the stillness.
- *Compassion:* Look at the other, and notice what you like and respect about this person. Appreciate the other's willingness to join you in this. See this person as simply another human being with many of the same concerns and flaws. See that like your own, this person's efforts and desires can be the source of great difficulties.
- *Unconditional positive regard:* See that this person is working hard at life and doing the best he or she can. See that this person's actions and behaviors are the inevitable result of how this person interprets his or her world.
- *Resonance:* Sense how this person is settling into the silence (or not). Allow yourself to be still and comfortable in the silence. Sense your connection to this person; sense the other sensing you.
- *Neutrality:* Notice that your experience is similar in some ways to the other person's and different in some ways. Allow the other person to have whatever experience arises, without any attachment from you. Recognize that you are you, and the other person is the other person. You are both connected and at the same time distinct.

Thank your partner. Now share with each other what you each noticed in relation to the different qualities.

Extending Qualities into the Field

Being able to recognize these qualities in ourselves and stabilize ourselves in those qualities is an important move. We also can strengthen those qualities in the field by sensing them, and then extending them, through our attention, toward our client and her concerns.

In orienting, we practiced inviting various elements into our awareness. Here we can practice extending particular qualities of the relational field. Because of the intimate connection that we have with our clients and the stable presence we become able to embody, the qualities of the field become something that the client can use as a resource in self-regulating herself.

We may have heard comments like, "Thanks for staying calm with that customer; it really made it easier for me to be nice to him." Here we're simply creating language for describing how we can do this in a more intentional way by extending particular qualities into the field to connect with, and support, our client in the conversation.[2]

This is not magical. It is simply an underappreciated fact that our experience directly results from how we direct our attention. With practice, we become masters at directing our attention. We learn to include in our awareness that which is helpful, and to exclude that which distracts and weakens us.

PRACTICE 5.3.

Extending Qualities into the Field with a Client

The next time you're in a coaching conversation, practice sensing these qualities in the field as well. It can be helpful to post the list of qualities as a reminder.

Realize that the qualities are already there and that the process of bringing your attention to them changes your awareness and therefore the field. Where you direct your attention changes what you experience. Said another way, the experience of a particular quality in the field changes as you look for it.

As you sense each quality, extend it toward your client. You can sense compassion, for example, or neutrality. Then imagine that this quality is extending out from you and wrapping around both of you. Imagine that both of you are breathing it in; it's in the atmosphere around you, enveloping both of you.

There is no need to inform your client of what you are doing. Experiment. Notice how the interaction changes as a result of this practice. How are you different? How was the conversation different?

Silence and Possibility

In addition to sensing the field and extending particular qualities into the field as described above, we also hold a fundamentally optimistic, forward-looking stance. We provide this for ourselves, and for our clients, who are sometimes distraught and overwhelmed as they enter their coaching conversations with us.

When we hold, for our clients, that there are solutions available that have not yet been discovered, or that they are capable of more than they know, we are a stand for them in significant new ways. And, when we are silent, we can, in that silence, convey confidence and faith that something useful can emerge.

The Certainty of Possibility

There's a big difference between knowing that there's an answer and knowing what the answer is. In a universe of possibilities, we can be very sure that there is an alternative pathway forward for our client yet very unsure about what that pathway might be.

Understanding the certainty of possibility provides a way to hold an optimistic stance. Remaining connected to that certainty, even when a conversation seems to be running dry, reintroduces spaciousness; we might not know what the best solution is now, but one will be revealed. Sometimes time and space or a different line of questioning unearths something that simply wasn't available to us earlier.

When we ask a question, we can do so with the belief and intention that the client will produce a useful, new, and generative response.

The Client's Potential

Taking the next logical step, we hold our client as whole, resourceful, and full of potential. From the perspective of our world, we are often able to see possibilities for them they cannot see for themselves in their world. Similarly, others can see our potential when we may not be able to. Standing for these possibilities is an enormous gift we offer.

In the early career example with which I opened the Introduction, my mentor saw me as being ready and capable of delivering a complex training to a group of high-performing Latin American Ph.D.s. At the time, I felt anxious and unsure, concerned that I would go to Costa Rica and not be able to deliver what I had committed to. My mentor's confidence in me allowed me to move into a challenging situation with what we might call "borrowed confidence." I didn't fully trust myself, but I trusted my mentor enough to enter the situation with a willingness to find out what I could do. Of course, my mentor was right; his experience allowed him to see potential in me that I hadn't yet seen or validated for myself.

As coaches, we embody a stand for the client for possibilities he may not yet be ready to recognize or claim.

Silence

In modern life, there is little silence. Our days are filled with meetings, phone calls, and other interruptions. Where external noise and distractions are lacking, our incessant internal chatter and thinking fill any available space.

Yet when we look closely, we see that thoughts, new ideas, and images emerge from silence. In the tumult of thoughts and activity in our lives, we come to notice brief, sometimes infinitesimal pauses between successive thoughts. We can think of silence as simply letting this pause expand. With sufficient expansion, instead of the brief

---

PRACTICE 5.4.
Holding the Client's Potential

Before your next coaching conversation, spend a few minutes considering the strengths of your client. You might write out a list of her skills, character traits, and experiences.

Now, let your creativity run. Allow yourself to imagine several practical possibilities, related to commitments she is working with, where she could use these assets in new and positive ways. Let yourself see and experience real possibilities for her that she could take action on now. Orient toward these possibilities; as you do so, they become part of the relational field.

In the coaching conversation, be aware of maintaining this sense of your client's potential, without getting personally attached to any specifics or even mentioning them to the client. You are simply holding them as symbols of the client's potential and as reminders to yourself of the invisible wealth of possibilities that exist for her.

moments of stillness being the background for thoughts, we rest in stillness, and the thoughts are interruptions to that stillness.

This deeper kind of silence, in which we are both inwardly and outwardly silent, can be experienced intentionally in meditation. We can also see silence as a resource in a coaching conversation. Rather than rushing to fill any silence with words, we settle ourselves. We let go of the moment-by-moment need to make things happen or to think of what to say next. We can simply be. In that silent being is the potential for new thoughts and ideas.

We can pose a question, and simply wait for that question to work in our client.

We can make a statement and allow it to land.

We can give the client all the time she needs to listen to herself and discover what is most important to say.

PRACTICE 5.5.
Holding Silence with a Partner

Find a partner who is willing to experiment with you. Agree on a period of time, perhaps five or ten minutes. Set a timer to go off at the agreed-on time.

Sit still together, as a shared sitting practice. This is not an eye-gazing exercise; your eyes can be closed or open, and you can sit either side-by-side or facing each other.

Notice any thoughts or urges to say anything, and just allow yourself to sit together in silence. Allow yourself to relax into it. It may be difficult to not say anything at first; the practice is simply to be together, without needing to make anything happen.

PRACTICE 5.6.
Holding Silence in Coaching

Now experiment with silence in coaching. When your client asks a question, allow a pause as you formulate your response. You might even say "Let me think about that for a minute" before responding.

Insert short pauses between sentences. When you ask a challenging question, let it sit there, even if the client is a little uncomfortable. Look for as many places to introduce moments of silence, a little space, into your conversation.

How does this practice change the pace and feel of your conversation? How did your client respond?

The inner coaching moves of holding the field, the client's potential, and silence create an atmosphere. The resulting sense of spaciousness and possibility provides room for both people's intuition to reveal things that a more constricted, linear process might not.

Here's an abbreviated example of a coaching conversation in which these elements were critical. My client is a senior executive with a military background, recently hired for a second career. His charge is to lead and revitalize a large nonprofit with lots of fiefdoms and antiquated performance standards. Neal is hard-driving, personable, impatient, and very ambitious. He is also rather discouraged.

It is six months into his tenure. Several key leaders are on board but many others have been resistant to the changes. He feels worn down by the unrelenting grind of meetings, crises, and the sheer volume of what needs to be done to build traction on the change objectives he has committed to achieving in the first year.

NEAL: Sometimes I wonder if this is worth it. I really didn't anticipate this being so exhausting.

COACH: Yes. You've got a lot going on.

NEAL: I question if my objectives are realistic. I worry that I'm asking them to move too far and too fast. I don't know if they can sustain this pace of change.

COACH: *Thinking, "He's got to give this some time. It's actually moving forward quite well, but he loses perspective." He locates his sense of compassion and unconditional regard, extending them toward the client.* Neal, what might be helpful to you right now? What different perspective might be available?

NEAL: I know it's easy for me to get overwhelmed and lose perspective. I knew this would take some time. We're just in the middle of it right now. Not everyone has my energy or my convictions that this is the right way to go.

COACH: (pausing, sensing resonance and compassion) I imagine it feels pretty lonely at times.

NEAL: Yes, it does. There's a lot on my shoulders right now.

COACH: Yes, Neal, there is. *Long silence. In this silence, both sense resonance, though Neal would articulate it as feeling understood. Neal's desire to explain more about how difficult it is seems to dissipate.* And now, tell me what makes it easier to carry that weight.

NEAL: (pausing) It's easier when I see people supporting this initiative. When I see people taking steps in the right direction on their own accord.

COACH: Does that happen often?

NEAL: Increasingly.

COACH: (sensing neutrality and unconditional regard) So, Neal, what happens in you that you stop seeing the support you do have? How do you lose sight of the need to give this time?

NEAL: (sounding irritated and defensive) Look, my reputation rides on the success of this. I was brought in to make something happen. I'm *totally* committed. If we succeed, I succeed. If we don't, I fail. It's that simple. And, I don't fail. *On one level, this is true. On another, this identity-based narrative, part of his habit, fuels his sense of being overwhelmed.*

COACH: *Extending neutrality and unconditional regard. Neal is testing the coach's support. The coach simply holds the possibility of a different view of this. The coach speaks clearly, and softly, at the same time.* Neal, I really see your commitment. No question. (pause) I'm simply curious about how you might negotiate with this in order to decrease your sense of being overwhelmed and discouraged. I'm curious about how you might work differently with the overwhelm.

NEAL: (a long silence; the coach waits, sensing that Neal is processing this) I suppose it's part of my drive. I know there's some part of me that feels defeated when we have setbacks. But really, I know we'll succeed. The negativity just makes it a lot harder than it needs to be.

COACH: *The coach is holding the possibility that Neal can articulate a more useful alternative perspective for himself.* So what's the possibility here? What perspective can you choose to be in?

NEAL: (pausing) I can choose the perspective that this is going to take time. That people are getting on board. That my team is coming together. There are a few people that won't come along and shouldn't stay. That's okay. I can have a longer view and not get so wrapped around the axle when I have a day like yesterday. *The conversation progresses to explore how to shift into this more spacious and productive perspective when Neal feels overwhelmed.*

Notice in this dialogue that Neal's inner state ranges widely. He starts rather discouraged and in turn feels burdened, defensive, and relieved, all in the course of a few minutes.

Notice, too, that the coach acknowledges each of these emotional places without trying to fix or convince him to be otherwise. The coach accesses certain qualities in the relational field and, staying present, becomes a stabilizing influence for Neal. Neal eventually becomes able to reorganize himself around a different possibility. With some additional work, Neal will begin to develop a new competency in self-regulation.

CHAPTER SUMMARY

- All conversations take place in what we might call a relational field of concerns, commitments, and possibilities. Each person in a conversation is influenced by this field; what each contributes or withholds also affects the field.
- We can influence and stabilize the relational field by extending our presence and attention toward our partner. Doing so establishes the most helpful possible atmosphere for generative conversation.
- Helpful qualities of the relational field are spaciousness, compassion, unconditional positive regard, resonance, and neutrality. These qualities are always available in the field. The more we are present and the more we are in contact with those qualities, the more stable the field becomes and the more the field becomes an invitation for the client.
- We also hold room for something new to emerge by remaining certain that unseen possibilities and solutions exist, by having an unshakable confidence in the client's potential, and by allowing silence.

PART
THREE

Generative Practices for Presence in Mind, Body, and Heart

What you are is what you have been,
and what you will be is what you do now.

The Buddha

Practice is the best of all instructors.

Publilius Syrus

A LONG-TIME FRIEND AND COLLEAGUE, REVIEWING A DRAFT OF THIS book, told me the story of his father, who took up golf in his late forties. By age sixty, he had become quite accomplished. Consistency at playing thirty-six holes of golf every week, hitting several buckets of balls weekly at a driving range, taking regular lessons from a pro, and lots of reading made him quite a good golfer, and he came to enjoy the game immensely. It was the consistent investment of ten to fifteen hours a week, every week, of time into practice and learning that led to his accomplishments. Ask any Olympic athlete, professional basketball player, concert pianist, dancer, or poet how they learned their art, and the answer will be, "Practice."

Ask any business leader how she became good at what she does, and you'll get a whole range of answers. Rarely, however, will you hear, "Practice."

Here's the deal. If you want to gain greater access to presence, if you want to become self-generative in your professional domain and in the rest of your life, if you want to gain mastery of your inner state, there's one and only one thing you must do: practice.

⚘ PRESENCE PAUSE ⚘

Practice is what we do in order to be able to make the inner moves described in the previous part of the book. Practice is how we become ready to make relational moves that are grounded in presence and invite clients into a new, more expanded, and resourceful inner state. Practice is how we come to a sufficient level of self-mastery to suspend our own filters, preconceptions, habits, and structures of interpretation in order to see our miraculous clients in the clearest and most undistorted ways possible. Practice is how we offer ourselves to our clients as the greatest possible resource.

When we practice, we are experienced by others as more available, resilient, calm, and settled in the midst of whatever is going on. We become able to extend these qualities into the field around us and become a stronger resource for ourselves and others.

Is that worth one to three hours a week of your time?

⚘ PRESENCE PAUSE ⚘

Part Three shows you how to go deeper. It is organized around a set of concrete practices that, repeated over time, build a solid foundation of self-awareness, presence, and mastery. Unlike exercises, practices are designed to be worked with for a lifetime.

These generative practices are the keys to the kingdom. There is sufficient material here for many years of developing your access to presence through the three doorways of mind, body, and heart. Through the doorway of mind, you will self-observe, be precisely aware of your habits, and let go of attachments as they arise. Through body, you will become centered, more fully alive, and able to stay present and resourceful no matter what is going on around you. Through heart, you will be compassionate, joyful, and grateful.

I strongly advocate doing some consistent generative practice every day. And it is wise to incorporate some regular practice for all three doorways. A starting point is to make a commitment to doing the three core practices from the next three chapters (sitting, centering, and touching your heart) daily. These are the foundational practices on which all others are built. Doing practices with the three doorways of mind, body, and heart will develop you in a faster and more integrated way than, for example, doing three mind practices. Ken Wilber speaks of this as "cross-training" and writes that regular practices in different domains reinforce each other.[1]

Set aside regular time, between fifteen minutes and an hour, at least five times a week. Morning is best for most people, and sets the tone for the day, but consistency is more important than timing. Commit to a consistent set of core practices, including additional practices as determined by your curiosity and the challenges you're facing at any given time. Find a committed partner or coach who knows the territory of self-generation and who can guide your unique development process, shaping practices for and with you. Visit the Presence-Based Coaching website at http://dougsilsbee.com/books/pbc for downloadable practices, practice tracking logs, and links to additional resources.

Experimenting with the practices described can lead to a rich and consistent lifelong commitment that is realistic to include in a busy schedule. Eventually you will recognize that you have decided to do this for the rest of your life.

My promise: practice will make you a different person.

CHAPTER 6

Mind

Watch your thoughts; they become words.
Watch your words; they become actions.
Watch your actions; they become habits.
Watch your habits; they become character.
Watch your character; it becomes your destiny.

Chinese proverb

Habit is habit and not to be flung out of the window by any man,
but coaxed downstairs a step at a time.

Mark Twain

BEGIN WITH MIND FOR SEVERAL REASONS. IT IS THE MOST FAMILIAR to me and the easiest place, given our cultural bias in the Western world, to plug into. As the son, grandson, nephew, and cousin of physicists, I presumed that the mind was the only thing that mattered. It's been through many years of self-exploration, and coming to understand better how humans really change, that I've come to see the body and heart as central to how we develop. For many readers, the mind will be the easiest place to discover this new territory; the body and heart represent relatively new areas for conscious exploration.

In order to be clear, available, and present for our clients, it is critical to be as unencumbered by our own conditioned habits as possible. Being constrained by our identity and driven by unrecognized attachments and aversions is the antithesis of being mindful, open, and resourceful. The ability to focus our attention and to recognize and let go of habitual behavioral drivers resides in the domain of mind. As coaches, this is critical for being present with our clients. On a larger scale, Weick and Sutcliffe describe the importance of mindfulness in high-reliability organizations such as aircraft carrier flight decks, where the ability to be fully present is essential.[1]

For thousands of years, Buddhists have mapped the workings of the mind in intricate detail. Based on their observations, a well-developed taxonomy of consciousness has been articulated, refined, and passed down through an extraordinary lineage of teachers. We are the beneficiaries of robust and proven practices that lead to presence, a focused clear mind, and great happiness. Perhaps surprisingly, or perhaps not, science is now mapping the neurological correlates of the precise experiences that Buddhists have identified, and cultivated through rigorous practice, for ages. There is no longer any question that the experiences of happiness, acceptance, and presence have direct and measurable correlates in brain functioning and that these experiences can be reliably produced through simple mindfulness practices that anyone can do.

Here, we are primarily interested in developing our ability to self-observe, focus our attention, recognize, and let go of conditioned attachments and aversions so that something new can open. This is foundational in the game of self-generation and is the basis for everything else.

You are invited to experiment and see what happens. In this, as in everything else in the book, I'm asking you to take nothing on faith. The proof of value will not come from the research that others have done or from claims that I make in this book, but rather from the evidence that you accumulate through the granular nature of your own experience.

Michael Slater, a biologist at a biotech company in Wisconsin, took part in a controlled study measuring the physiological effects of mindfulness practice. He put it this way: "I really am an empiricist in every aspect of my life. I doubt dogma, and I test it. I do it at the laboratory bench, but also in my personal life. So this appealed to me, because I could feel the reduction in stress. I could tell I was less irritable. I had more capacity to take on more stressors. My wife felt I was easier to be around. So there were tangible impacts. For an empiricist, that was enough."[2]

That's what we're after here. We want something that works for you, that allows you to be more effective and present in your role as a coach. Your assessments of the efficacy of what I am suggesting will come through your own experience and be validated by others who begin to experience you differently.

In this chapter, we focus first on building the observer. I offer a core sitting practice and build from there to describe what there is to notice. Then we move into other practices that address self-observation and working with habits and attachments.

MIND PRACTICES

- Core mind practice: Sitting
- Naming
- Self-observation of a habit
- Letting go of an attachment

BUILDING THE OBSERVER

At the core is our ability to self-observe, to notice what we are doing, when, and how. This generative practice increases our self-awareness and presence in any situation. We build it through repetition.

Self-observation results from an artificial splitting of our awareness into two parts: the acting mind and the observing mind. The acting mind is the mind that is running us. It manages our thinking, speech, movements, and behaviors. Everything that we do is an action taken by the acting self. The other is the observing mind, or the observer. When we are self-aware, the observer is watching the acting mind in practice. We cultivate the observer through practice. Self-awareness is the product of this self-observation.

Self-observation requires a neutral, accepting stance. Following our own gentle curiosity, we seek to build the most nuanced understanding of the workings of our own minds as possible. The human experience, continually arising moment by moment in our lives, provides limitless unique elements to observe.

PRACTICE 6.1.
Core Mind Practice: Sitting

Sit up straight in a chair that supports your back. Keeping your back straight, allow your feet to rest comfortably on the floor. Keep your head erect and over your shoulders, but don't strain. You may close your eyes or let your gaze rest softly on a blank wall several feet in front of you.

Bring your awareness to your breath. Depending on what's more noticeable for you, you might choose to attend to your abdomen rising and falling as you breathe. Or you might focus your attention in your nostrils, where the air moving in produces a certain coolness. Either location is fine. Simply bring your attention to the place you select.

Don't try to do anything in particular with your breathing. Begin to observe the sensation as the air moves in and out. To yourself, speak the words "breathing in" during your inhale and "breathing out" during your exhale. If you find your attention wandering (and you will—that's part of the game!), observe that your attention is elsewhere and bring your attention back to your breath. If you notice any self-criticism about not being good at this, notice that and bring your attention back to the breath.

Do this ten minutes a day. Twenty is better than ten, and five is better than none. If you can, sit twice a day: in the morning and again in the evening. Consistency is important. Just the act of sitting for some time each day has significant benefits: relaxing your body, slowing your pulse, letting go of stress, and training your attention.

While sitting, you're practicing the act of bringing your attention back to the present. Over time, you'll notice a significant difference in your ability to be present with others, with a task, and with yourself. This is mindfulness.

Now that you've tried this, let's talk about it a little. First, you may have noticed that your mind is pretty busy. We live in a revved-up world, and our minds normally keep pace with this by racing from one thought to another without pause.

It may seem, when you begin sitting, that your mind is racing more than usual. I suggest that, since you are not distracted by activity, you're probably just seeing more clearly what's been there all along.

⫘ PRESENCE PAUSE ⫘

Anyway, the "goal" is not necessarily to still the mind. Sitting is about noticing what is going on within you and increasing your ability to focus and hold your attention on something of your choosing. In this case, it's the breath. Having built the muscle of sustained attention, we can then focus it on listening to another person, on thinking through a project, on being present to our own experience, and so forth. We can generalize this capacity to hold attention on other activities as well.

Most Westerners are achievement-oriented. We can view sitting as yet another challenge in which to excel. The success-oriented overachiever who sets a performance standard of instant peace and serenity is likely to suffer immensely as she discovers the relentless distractibility of the human mind. Even (perhaps especially) smart people can't outthink sitting practice. Sitting reveals us to ourselves.

Our suffering diminishes, as in most other activities in life, when we remember that it's simply practice. We lower the stakes for ourselves, we relax, and we remember that success comes from simply bringing the busy mind back to the breath over and over and over.

What's to Observe?

When we become better able to bring our attention back from random streams of thought, there is much to see. Becoming present to the nuances of our own moment-by-moment inner life reveals multilayered and complex experiences.

So what is there to notice as we sit? Aren't we just watching our breath and trying to be calm and peaceful? Well, sort of. There's actually a lot to observe. As you continue with the core practice of sitting, you'll notice more and more of the rich tapestry of subtle experiences that make up our existence:

- *Mental activity:* The most obvious thing that we notice when we begin to become more mindful is the incessant, sometimes urgent, chattering of our own minds. Most of our racing thoughts focus on the future (planning action, anticipating problems) or the past (regrets, pride over a success, enjoyment of a memory). Obsessing over future and past leaves little attention for the present.

- *Emotions:* Humans are capable of a range of emotions: sadness, joy, anxiety, love, anger. These are most often subtle but can sometimes be rather intense. Emotions are relatively short-lasting phenomena that arise and pass countless times each day, typically unnoticed. Being able to observe our emotions provides us with a rich source of intelligence and allows us to experience the full range of our emotions without being overwhelmed by them.

- *Mood:* Mood is different from emotions. Mood represents a more persistent orientation in life that tends to bias us toward, or preclude, particular responses. For example, a mood of resignation means that we are less likely to take action or respond proactively to challenges.

- *Sensation:* Sensation is the input of your senses—the sound of someone's voice, light, the pulsing of your heartbeat, the pressure of the floor against your feet. There are countless sensory experiences going on all the time, disseminated throughout our bodies; they are complex and multilayered. Most of the time, we're in our heads and miss these.

- *Attachments:* Attachments are the pulls we experience toward something. They can be directly experienced and generally have components of sensation, emotion, and patterns of thought. For example, Janet's attachment to helping, from Chapter Two, would show up as a quickened heartbeat, a sense of energy in her chest, the emotion of eagerness, and thoughts of how she could arrange travel to the field location. The observer allows us to witness all of this in detail.

- *Aversions:* The opposite of attachments, aversions are a pull away from something that we resist or avoid, usually because we have learned at some point in our lives that it is unpleasant or harmful. Aversions too are revealed by a constellation of experiences in the sensory, emotional, and cognitive realms of our experience.

- *Stillness:* Last (but really first) is the stillness that lies underneath each of these phenomena. Each of the above arises and then passes. What they arise from is stillness, quiet, the undercurrent, the vast ground of possibility. When we begin to notice this stillness, we discover the stillness in ourselves as well. It is the source from which everything else arises. It's always there, always ready and waiting for our awareness to open to it. This is the field of presence, in which the future is unwritten, and all possibilities are available. You will notice it more and more.

Sitting is a practice. The resulting mindfulness means being present with all these elements of our experience. When we attune our awareness to notice all of this, there is much available to us that we miss in our normal, constricted, task-driven ways of organizing ourselves.

WHAT'S TO OBSERVE?

- Mental activity
- Emotions
- Mood
- Sensation
- Attachments
- Aversions
- Stillness

PRACTICE 6.2.

Naming

This is an enhancement of the basic sitting practice. Here, you name what you notice as you're sitting.

Sit with your attention on your breath. Most likely your attention will stay on your breath for five seconds, and then you'll be thinking about a potentially difficult meeting later in the day, planning your upcoming cruise, replaying what you wished you'd told your boss yesterday, feeling an emotion (like excitement), or sensing the itch on your left calf. The practice is to briefly name what you're noticing: "thinking," "feeling," or, "sensing." Then bring your attention back to the breath.

So, that's it. Sit. Breathe. Bring your attention to your breath. When you notice one of these other experiences arising, name it and bring your attention back to the breath. As you do this over and over, you are cultivating the "muscle of awareness."

Why do we do this? We sit as a means to know ourselves more intimately. We practice recognizing and suspending our habits in order to be more fully present and in service. We sit in order to contact the quiet space of possibility from which any new action arises. And we practice for the sake of experiencing our own aliveness.

For the first of these, we must build the capability of noticing and naming what is going on for us at any particular moment of time.

WORKING WITH HABITS

Recall that our personality is the aggregate of all the conditioned habits that make us uniquely who we are. Habits, by definition, narrow us. By defaulting to what has worked in the past, we prevent ourselves from seeing available possibilities that might be much more effective and satisfying.

As developers of people, we must become masterful at recognizing and suspending the habits of our personality that get in the way of our coaching. As an example, I come from a long line of teachers. Teaching is in my bones; it is a natural and sometimes unconscious part of how I see and relate to others. It's part of my identity, and I have come to recognize a significant and sometimes problematic attachment to being in the teacher role.

Because self-generation is fundamental to coaching, it is vital for clients to create their own solutions and solve their own problems. My habitual tendency to jump in and teach, rather than simply asking powerful questions and staying present, can get in the way. It requires self-awareness to notice when my attachment to teaching is about to take over. Then I can suspend that urge and be present with my client rather than telling him what he should do about his problem.

We each have unique habits and can't help but bring these with us into coaching relationships; they are part of the fiber of our being. Still, our commitment to efficacy requires us to do the ongoing inner work of recognizing and letting go of habits that don't serve our clients. (In my first book, *The Mindful Coach*, I go into depth on the nature of habits in relation to coaching and the ethical imperative to recognize and suspend them in service to our clients. That discussion is much more extensive than we have room for here.[3])

Here are some common habits that I see over and over in my coach training work:

- A tendency to teach or prescribe
- The tendency to avoid telling difficult truths
- The habit of seeing ourselves in our clients and projecting what we ideally hope we would do in their circumstance
- The tendency to follow predictable lines of inquiry or approaches to coaching that allow us to feel comfortable
- The need to feel competent or establish a perception of competence
- The desire to perpetuate the coaching relationship to earn fees or status
- Certain emotional triggers that tend to take us into impatience, judgment, sadness, or other unhelpful emotional states
- The habit of mistaking our client's success (or lack of it) with our own

These are not in and of themselves negative phenomena. They are simply historically rooted habits showing up in the present.

Habits become problematic when they drive us to the degree that our interaction with our client is distorted by our own needs rather than aligned to what the client needs from us. A subtle conditioned myopia sets in, in which we are organized around how our identity is affirmed or threatened. The consequence is a restriction in our ability to see and respond to possibilities in the relational field. For example, a common hurdle that I frequently see in mentoring and coach training retreats is the self-consciousness of the learner. Coaches are so intent on doing the right thing that they constrict themselves and become less present to the client.

In one retreat, I entered a room where two people were engaged in a coaching exercise. The person in the coaching role got nervous as I entered the room and missed an important cue from the client he was working with. The sudden self-consciousness when being observed by someone with greater competency was understandable. It also revealed his self-consciousness as a habit and the possibility of working with it in order to stay more present with himself and with his client. This became a significant learning theme for him and illustrates the essence of self-observation, the first component of self-generation.

It is critical to become skillful at recognizing and working with our own habits. Although nobody else can do this for us, skilled and honest colleagues, loved ones, and our own coaches and mentors can often help us see our own blind spots.

DESIGNING SELF-OBSERVATIONS

A central practice is that of self-observation. It is the first component of self-generation and invites present-moment realization. A self-observation is a designed structure that builds accountability for bringing conscious attention to a habit that is, by definition, automatic and unquestioned. We will likely be in the game of designing self-observations for and with our clients, so that they can observe the habits they have lived in for decades but that also may be impeding their efficacy. But mastery begins with ourselves.[4]

Self-observation is a development activity, not a performance activity. We are seeking to build awareness of the habit and choice about whether to engage in the habit. The self-observation is not designed to change the habit itself. This is counterintuitive for the majority of us who are accustomed to seeing a problem and going after the solution immediately.

Self-generative people tend to make positive, life-affirming choices that respond creatively to what is required. So behavior change generally results from self-observation anyway. However, the behavior change results through becoming more aware and self-generative rather than going after the habit itself.

Let's look at how to design the structure for a self-observation, which can be done in any number of ways. A basic approach has three elements; we'll explore them here, and how to develop a self-observation structure for a specific development situation.

1. A brief description of the behavior to be observed. *I'll use my tendency to offer prescriptive recommendations about how a client might proceed.*

2. The actual structure, consisting of an event, duration, frequency, and tickler:

   • The event consists of the circumstances in which the self-observation is to be conducted. *In my example, the event is every coaching conversation.*

- Duration is the time frame for the practice. Usually two to four weeks is a good period for a self-observation. Choose a duration that allows between ten and fifty repetitions of the self-observation. We're after an experiment of set duration, a finite end, and clear learning. *I'll commit to this self-observation for three weeks.*

- Frequency indicates how often we do the self-observation: hourly, daily, twice a day, weekly, or after every occurrence of the event, depending on what's being observed. *I'll do this after every coaching session for the three weeks.*

- The tickler is a way of embedding the self-observation into your systems so that you don't have to rely on your memory and good intentions. A timer that goes off hourly, a journal on a bedside table, or a computer reminder works well. Structure it for simplicity and accountability. *A simple way for me to remind myself will be to put the question on the template I use for writing session notes on my coaching conversations. This will automatically remind me to reflect on this particular habit after every coaching conversation.*

3. Questions that direct your attention to specific aspects of your experience and build your familiarity with the habit. The questions will be designed to fit the particular habit you're exploring.

- *When, with this client, was I prescriptive?*

- *What drove this tendency? Was it habit, or was this the best choice at the time?*

- *What did I do?*

- *What was the impact?*

- *What alternatives were there?*

The self-observation, then, consists of observing the named behavior, during the events described, for set duration and frequency, and responding briefly to the questions. Long responses to the questions are neither necessary nor desirable; very brief responses, in note form, are fine. The key is doing the observation rigorously and consistently over some period of time and bringing your full attention to it.

The following is a simple template that you can use for your own self-observations or, eventually, for your clients. (See Exhibit 6.1.)

EXHIBIT 6.1.

Self-Observation Template

Behavioral Description

I will observe my habitual tendency to offer prescriptive suggestions to clients when they don't specifically request a suggestion.

Structure

Event:	During my coaching sessions
Duration:	For three weeks
Frequency:	After every coaching conversation
Tickler:	Include the questions below in my session notes template as a reminder

Questions

1. When, with this client, was I prescriptive?

2. What drove this tendency . . . was it habit, or was this the best choice at the time?

3. What did I do?

4. What was the impact?

5. What alternatives were there?

I've put the example from above into this format as an illustration. Creating a structure that's easy to use, and embedding it in your system, ensures that you'll remember to do it. Use this structure, or design something else that works for you. (You may download a blank self-observation template from http://dougsilsbee .com/books/pbc/practices/soe.)

PRACTICE 6.3.

Self-Observation of a Habit

Identify a habit of yours that you suspect might at times limit your effectiveness or interfere with serving your client. This should be a behavior that (1) recurs relatively often in your coaching, (2) tends to "grab" you, in that there's a certain level of urge to it, and (3) you can see that there's a pattern to it. It gets triggered by something and you respond habitually.

Briefly describe the behavior. Then design a self-observation using the template shown above by re-creating it or downloading it from the website at http://dougsilsbee .com/books/pbc/practices/soe. Build an automatic reminder into your daily system rather than relying on good intentions to be successful. Then, commit to doing this self-observation for the duration you describe. Don't try to change the behavior. Simply observe it, and become intimately familiar with it.

At the end of the period of self-observation, respond to these questions:

- What patterns did you notice over the period of the self-observation?
- What evidence do you have of increased self-awareness in the moment?
- Did anything change about your actual use of the habit? If so, what?
- What new actions are available to you as a result of this?

ENGAGING IN SELF-OBSERVATION

Self-observing over time changes our relationship with the habit. Self-observation is inherently a learning activity focused on building self-generative capacity, as distinct from a way to change behavior. Still, it inevitably leads to greater self-awareness and choice.

Here's an example of how self-observation leads to behavior change. We use 20/20 hindsight to reflect at the end of our day. We remember that we actually did engage in some problematic behavior (for example, interrupting others) earlier in the day. We jot down notes about our experience and become curious. ("Hmm. I wonder why that seemed so urgent to me?") After several days, because we are collecting data, we become more attuned to the behavior and notice it closer to the actual occurrence. ("Oops! I just interrupted Joe!") This is still hindsight, but more proximate in time.

Soon the internal observer, which we've been cultivating, begins to notice what we're doing *as* we do it. ("I'm interrupting Joe right now!") This is a moment of realization. We may still interrupt, but present moment awareness is dawning. Then we begin to notice the driving impulse *before* the behavior. ("I feel my energy increasing and my back straightening. I feel impatient. I know what we should do. I'm about

---

PRACTICE 6.4.
Letting Go of an Attachment

Identify something that you are attached to—something that's routine, that you enjoy, that you have definite urges for, and that feels slightly indulgent. Perhaps your morning Starbucks visit, a glass of wine with dinner, or sweets. You get the idea. You choose.

Now give it up for one week.

So what reaction did you have to my suggestion that you give it up? What story did you tell yourself? You may have thought: "No, not that!" or, "I don't really need to do this exercise; I understand the point he's making!" If you are really honest with yourself, some experience of clinging arose at the mere suggestion that you give it up.

This is a way to practice making a conscious choice to let go of an attachment rather than indulging it, as our habits would have us do. This inner work of letting go of a morning coffee habit supports letting go of any attachment that drives us. On one level, it's about coffee. At a deeper level, it's about the generative practice of being able to witness and release any attachment. This is our ticket to freedom.

Try this experiment, using your habit to practice with for a week.

At the times when you would normally indulge this habit, self-observe around the urge itself. Let the desire or attachment arise. Let it be there. Be fully present with your desire. Realize that the desire is a phenomenon separate from you, the observer of the desire. Realize that you are at choice. And let the attachment go, recognizing that you don't need it.

This sounds simple but is decidedly not easy. All kinds of stories will arise to justify your indulging your habit. Depending on the strength of your attachment and your commitment to working with it, you may or may not find it easy to give up your habit for a week.

Don't set this up as a pass/fail test of character. This is really about being present with your urges, and then letting them go. Think of letting go of attachments as a competency in itself. There's much to discover, and, for sure, something of interest will be revealed if you stay in the practice.

---

to interrupt Joe. No, this time, I'm going to hear him out instead. Slow down, relax, breathe, listen.") This is reorganization. We've interrupted the habit and reorganized ourselves into a new behavior.

Through practice, the new behavior eventually becomes stabilized. We listen better, bringing our awareness to Joe. And it happened simply, easily, almost by itself.

This indirect approach is powerful and proceeds from the assumption that nothing is broken. We simply hold that there are always more choices, and some of the available choices will lead to more desirable results. As has been said, "You are perfect just as you are. And, you could use a little improvement!"[5]

A helpful view of self-observation is to be curious about our habits and to "make friends" with them. Habits served their purpose because we have learned well how to get along in the world.

Consider the nature of attachment as the underlying urge that drives our behavior. In self-observation, we witness, in real time, our urges and attachments arising and learn to be present with them. We come to recognize the urge itself as something that arises and passes. As we see our urges in their proper perspective, as a fleeting phenomenon, distinct from ourselves as observer, we are no longer controlled by the urge. To act on our attachment, or not, becomes an available choice.

We can also use self-observation to focus attention on a behavior that we want to develop and use more. We can develop a picture of the alternative behavior we want to nurture and observe our use of it over time. When we direct our attention to this new behavior, we'll begin to notice opportunities to use it and discover that we are using it regularly.

Coaching Implications

Presence in mind is essential to being effective as a coach. Through our minds, we are able to self-observe and notice when habits are arising that might get in the way of our work. We become able to see the possibility of different choices and of reorganizing in order to be a better resource for our clients. By mastering this in ourselves, we become more self-generative and fulfilled. We also earn the right to guide our clients through the same territory.

I'm sitting across from Bill, my client. Bill is pretty tightly wound generally, and particularly so this morning. He has a meeting the next day to present an exciting new proposal and wants to firm up some talking points before the meeting. He's very invested in having his presentation go well.

I notice my own racing thoughts about what's good about the proposal and my excitement about the opportunity Bill has in front of him. I recognize my strong urge to jump in with prescriptive suggestions on how to position his proposal. I notice my investment in his success and my vicarious attachment to having my ideas incorporated into his pitch.

I breathe, consciously letting go of my attachment. I ask myself what will be most useful for Bill right now. Relaxing, I see that Bill is so wrapped up in the details that he's lost his perspective. His anxiety is making it harder for him to identify with his audience.

I measure my voice, in order to be a balance to the whirlwind that is Bill. Rather than offering suggestions, I say, "Bill, let's step back. What's the most important implication for your audience? What must they understand in order to back it in the most informed way possible?"

Bill thinks for a minute, stepping back from his talking points in order to refocus on what's most important. He begins, "Well, really, the critical thing that they need to understand is that this opens up a whole new market that is going to require new ways of thinking."

Clearly Bill is accessing a strategic perspective that is far more important than the points I was attached to offering. My recognition and self-regulation around my old habit allowed me to be present with Bill and to provide what was needed.

CHAPTER SUMMARY

- Mind is the first doorway into presence. Through mind, we become astute observers of our inner world, including the nature of our own habits.
- A consistent daily core practice of sitting builds our capacity to witness the rich tapestry of thoughts, sensations, emotions, mood, attachments, aversions, and stillness that make up the full range of our experience.

- We each have default habits, internalized over decades of repetition. Being self-generative requires recognizing and suspending the habits that make us less effective leaders or coaches. Self-observation is a structured means for observing any habit or behavior that we wish to either change or cultivate.
- Through awareness, we learn to recognize and let go of the underlying urges that drive our behavior, discovering greater freedom of choice.
- Mastery in working with our own habits earns us the right to do the same with the leaders we coach.

Body

The body is incapable of not practicing. And what we practice we become. . . .
Even as you sit here reading . . . you are shaping yourself by your posture, the way
you're breathing, what you're thinking, feeling, and sensing. While this may seem
subtle and far below the level of our awareness, over time this has a powerful effect
in how we perceive the world and how the world perceives us.

Richard Strozzi-Heckler

We must learn to be still in the midst of activity and to be
vibrantly alive in repose.

Indira Gandhi

CHANGE IS FUNDAMENTALLY A BIOLOGICAL PROCESS. EVEN WHEN
we try to override an old behavior through a cognitive decision
(as in the classic New Year's resolution), we still need to have our
body cooperate in order to produce a new action.

Every action originates in the body. Thoughts are produced
by patterns of firing synapses in the brain; a speech act begins as a
thought and is then expressed through motions of our vocal cords,
modified by subtle movements of our tongue and mouth. We can neither conceive of nor produce an action without involving the body.

"The body is incapable of not practicing. And what we practice we become."[1] We are creatures of habit because at some point, a behavior got us what we wanted, and from that point on, we practiced it over and over. In order to replace what we've done for decades with something better, we have to practice new ways of doing until they are sufficiently stabilized in us to be available even when the worn grooves of old habits still call us. This is especially true and especially challenging when our habits have worked sufficiently well to produce a significant level of success.

To change, we have to engage the body.

PRESENCE PAUSE

This is new territory for many. Most of us, living firmly ensconced in our heads, are caught up in swirling thoughts about the futures we hope to either create or avoid, and we miss what is available to us now. At worst, we have difficult and contradictory relationships with our bodies, conditioned by marketers to crave a different body, or trained by unpleasant experiences to dislike our bodies. For many, our relationship with our body is reduced to caring for it as if it were a machine, so that it can carry our heads around through our ambitious lives as long as possible!

There's more. In the words of the poet:

> *The Church says: The body is a sin.*
> *Science says: The body is a machine.*
> *Advertising says: The body is a business.*
> *The body says: I am a fiesta![2]*

PRESENCE PAUSE

Our bodies offer a deep and rich treasure trove of information and experience that is readily available to us. Our bodies are the house of our aliveness, a repository of the universe's energy, a smorgasbord of sensation, and the source of pleasure, joy, and fulfillment. If we miss this, we're missing out indeed!

Recall the three products of coaching: competency, self-generation, and aliveness. Each of these requires a body. Trained bodies enable skillful, competent action, and enable us to experience presence and discover the possibility of self-generation. It is only through our bodies that we can experience what life is really offering us.

In this chapter, we explore the literacy of the body and establish a basis in language for working through the body. I'll offer practices for centering yourself in any situation and for increasing your awareness of the rich tapestry of sensation that is available to us in every moment. And we'll incorporate body awareness into the self-observation practices from the previous chapter, bringing great sensitivity to our "early warning system" about how our conditioned habits arise.

BODY PRACTICES

- Core body practice: Centering
- Observing versus sensing
- Body scan: Directing attention within the body
- Experiencing somatic responses to others
- Self-observation with somatic awareness
- Centering through a reaction
- Take on a body practice

ASSERTIONS OF SOMATIC LITERACY

The word *somatics* originally referred to "the body experienced from within, where we experience mind/body integration."[3] The experience of ourselves as a whole organism necessarily includes the body, mind, emotions, and spirit. Nothing is left out. Yet the body has often been relegated in our consciousness to the vehicle that transports our briefcase and brain to the next appointment, or an instrument of pleasure in sports, sex, and fine dining. As we begin to recognize that fully inhabiting all of these domains is essential for authenticity, effectiveness, and aliveness, reintegrating ourselves as a whole organism becomes a crucial element of the path.

Recognizing that the body is the seat of all action makes it important for anyone concerned with human development and change to have distinctions for observing and working through our own bodies and those of others. I offer a set of assertions that invite you to observe differently and to build your own somatic literacy.[4] Be curious about what these statements might open for you:

- *Our shape perfectly reflects our history.* The shape of our bodies is the inevitable and only possible product of our lifetime genetic, environmental, and experiential history. We store, in our tissues and nervous systems, the default habits that form our identities.

- *Our body determines our experience.* Our body determines, and limits, what we can see and respond to. The senses, reactions, and instincts of a highly trained soldier will respond differently to a perceived threat than those of a passive person. It follows that training and practice can change our bodies, and therefore the responses available to us.

- *A wealth of sensation is available through our bodies.* Our nervous system offers much richer and subtler experiences than most of us are trained to notice. Practice and attention training can attune us to the range of sensation that our own bodies offer. Sensation offers greater aliveness and a wealth of information on which to base creative responses.

- *Sensation provides an early warning system for our habits.* Our attachments and aversions always have a somatic component. Bringing awareness into our bodies reveals the earliest indicators that a habit is arising. Being present to the sensations associated with these habits allows realization and choice.

- *Practice through the body allows us to build, and stabilize, new competencies.* If we want to inspire others through authenticity, stay calm in conflict, or communicate difficult feedback with compassion, we must practice to build a body capable of producing the desired behaviors.

- *Joy and fulfillment are body experiences.* Happiness is an experience made possible by our nervous systems and can be practiced. It is not a function of external circumstances, of what we own, how much we make, or who we are with, although these external factors can be conducive. However, if we are not able to experience the sensations that our bodies offer, then no amount of questing will deliver us the happiness that we seek.

SOMATIC LITERACY

- Our shape perfectly reflects our history.
- Our body determines our experience.
- A wealth of sensation is available through our bodies.
- Sensation provides an early warning system for our habits.
- Practice through the body allows us to build, and stabilize, new competencies.
- Joy and fulfillment are body experiences.

With these assertions as context, let's explore practices that can open us to presence through the doorway of our bodies.

CENTERING

Centering is an internal process of bringing attention into our bodies, connecting with ourselves, and becoming aware and present. It is a living process of reorganization that shifts us from a state of being triggered or responding automatically into being self-generating, resourceful, and creative. When we are centered, we are alert, connected, present, and ready for whatever is next. Our actions are consistent with what we care about.

In the example in Chapter Three, Roger was discouraged. In that state, he was unable to deal effectively with the situation. When he centered himself, he became a different person with a much more resourceful view. In his centered body, he was more resourceful, and knew what to do next.

Centering is a practice that we can do over and over. Through repetition, we learn to reorganize ourselves from an unhelpful inner state into a centered, alert place from which we are able to respond in an appropriate way. Through practice, the inner state of center becomes familiar, and it is possible to move into it quickly and easily under any circumstances. Being centered, as you will see, makes it almost impossible to be anxious, stressed, or impulsive.

A quick online search will reveal many approaches to centering. All have to do with bringing attention into the body.

PRACTICE 7.1.

Core Body Practice: Centering

We can learn centering by organizing ourselves in relation to the three dimensions possessed by all physical objects, including your body:[5]

- *Length:* Stand up. Check out your posture, and organize yourself in relation to gravity so that you are supported effortlessly. Place your feet slightly apart, knees unlocked, and pelvis rocked forward slightly to straighten the spine. Sense the bottoms of your feet, where the floor presses against them. Relax your shoulders, letting them drop. Hold your eyes open, letting your gaze be soft and your peripheral vision be available to you. Allow your jaw to relax. Imagine that the top of your head is connected to the heavens as if by a string. Drop your attention to your center of gravity, two inches below your navel.
- *Width:* Gently rock your weight from right to left. Find the neutral balanced place in the center of this dimension. Sense the equal weighting on each of your feet. And be aware of your width, of the space you take up. It can be helpful to sense what it would be like to walk into a room and know that you fully belong, feeling an expansion in your chest that gives you the sense of taking up more space.
- *Depth:* Align yourself from front to back. Again, a gentle rocking back and forth from heel to toe can help us find the balance point. We are accustomed to focusing out in front of us, but there is also space behind us. Bring awareness to this, sensing the room behind you. Imagine weight and mass behind you, as if you had a giant, massive tail extending out along the ground. Allow yourself to feel supported by this mass and to let your belly soften and open.

This is scalable. By this, I mean that you can take five minutes or more on each of the three components, or you can quickly and easily shift into the centered place. Centering is an internal state rather than a specific body position, and you will soon find that you can center yourself sitting, walking, or brushing your teeth. With practice, centering yourself will feel like a quick and effortless "coming home" and be almost an instantaneous shift in awareness.

For now, use your time to explore and sense into the experience of each of the three dimensions. Center yourself at least ten times a day. Initially do this standing up. Then practice in different circumstances: sitting down, in meetings, before conversations, and in preparation for stressful events. See how you experience yourself differently, and what happens in your relationships.

Centering is the core practice for the body. I urge you to work with centering and discover what specific moves seem to make the biggest difference for you. Then practice frequently, so that centering first becomes a move that is readily available and then becomes embodied as part of who you are.

BUILDING SOMATIC AWARENESS

Sensation provides rich and direct information about how our conditioned habits are arising within our bodies. Our habitual reactions, triggered by people and information in our environments, generally show up first as a somatic reaction on the level of sensation. As our response gathers momentum, emotions, habitual patterns of interpretation, and ultimately predictable actions follow.

Sensation is the "early warning" component of this marvelously complex learned response. If we wish to be maximally engaged and creatively responsive in our world, we must begin with being attentive to the signals of our own nervous system.

Consider the following anecdote, told to me by a client I'll call Chris. She was working on a complex and stressful project that required specific actions from her boss with some key stakeholders. When we spoke, Chris had just been told by her boss that he had not followed through on a commitment that had set up a very humiliating situation for Chris. She felt set up and was furious. She described her reaction like this:

The moment he told me, I felt this wave of heat rising up in me. There was this massive energy in my chest and a tightness in my throat. I felt my hands shaking; it was as if I wanted to choke someone. I don't think most of this was visible to him, although I'm sure that I looked shaken. In fact, I was ready to kill! I felt all that in my body, and I felt totally justified in it! Then there was an instant moment of recognition that I was about to say something destructive. I stopped myself and took a minute to center and gather myself to speak. It took effort!

When I spoke, I was very clear and very direct. The energy was still there. But the destructive edge was gone, and I channeled it really well. He absolutely knew where I stood, but I didn't slay him. I think this was a great success.

Prior to this incident, Chris had worked with self-observation and centering. She was familiar with her own tendencies. And she could center herself quickly and easily. Chris was able to see her triggered reaction to her boss. Her detailed narrative of her internal process provides clear evidence of her growing competency at self-observation. She also describes the moment of realization (the present moment awareness of her reaction and the availability of choice) and the process of reorganization (observing the reaction, letting it go, and centering herself for more effective action).

In this case, the sensations were loud and dramatic; often they are much more subtle. When they're dramatic, of course, they are easier to observe. Nevertheless, a reaction that has that much energy behind it may be difficult to stop and can overwhelm our intentions to center ourselves unless we have practiced a lot. While subtler reactions are harder to spot in the first place, they are easier to self-regulate.

Somatic awareness is how we become centered, present, and capable of seeing and responding to opportunities for behavioral choice.

PRACTICE 7.2.
Observing Versus Sensing

The distinction between observing and sensing is important. To see this, run a bath or turn the shower on. As you're ready to step in, look at the bath or shower, and be an observer of yourself ready to step in. As you enter the water, allow the sensations of the water on your body to take over your awareness. Let your attention be fully in the sensation of it.

After a minute or two, as you're in the water, experiment with toggling your attention back and forth. Be in the observer mind, with your attention outside yourself, witnessing; disconnect from the sensation and observe yourself in the water. Then bring your awareness back into your body, feeling the sensations of the warmth of the water, of the tingling of the spray or the soft pressure of the tub against your skin. Let the observer disappear as you allow sensation to fill your awareness.

Toggle back and forth several times, making the distinction clear.

PRACTICE 7.3.
Body Scan: Directing Attention Within the Body

A body scan is a relaxing way to work with directing attention within the body. You can do it sitting or, preferably, lying down on your back on a comfortable surface.

As in the previous exercise, move your attention out of the observer and into your sensation. Begin with your breath, as in the sitting practice. Observe the various sensations, from the coolness of the air entering your nostrils to the rising and falling of your chest and abdomen as the breath moves in and out. Then allow your attention to slowly and systematically move through your entire body, beginning with your toes. Scan for sensation in your toes. Notice what there is to notice. If your attention wanders, gently bring it back to the sensations in your toes. Simply observe, without judgment, and without seeking to change or alter the experience.

Then slowly move up through your feet, ankles, lower legs, knees, thighs, and pelvic area, looking for sensation in each part of your body and experiencing it fully. Pause at each body part, simply noting any sensation, tension, or feeling of energy. Note which parts you can easily feel and which parts feel numb or unavailable. Then move to your belly, chest, back, shoulders, and arms. Finish with your neck, face, and head.

Notice any emotions or moods that are present. Sometimes these reside in a particular place. Other times they will be pervasive. Notice these elements of your experience.

This practice too is scalable. You can do a quick scan in a few seconds to identify where you are holding tension and bring your attention into your body. Or you can take thirty minutes or more for a detailed body scan—really a somatic meditation—that is deeply relaxing and builds the competency of inner focus and somatic attention.[6]

SOMATIC SELF-OBSERVATION

The previous practices build your somatic awareness and your ability to be present in your body. Since our habits include somatic, emotional, behavioral, and cognitive components, self-observation in its fullest sense must include sensation as well.

In the previous chapter, we developed a self-observation around a particular habit we tend to do as coaches. Let's expand this to include a somatic component. Some experience with centering and body scans will be important before doing this.

PRACTICE 7.4.
Experiencing Somatic Responses to Others

Your nervous system is constantly working as it anticipates what's coming next. With your new-found somatic awareness, you can tune into this and watch your somatic reactions to people in your environment. Jot down notes to help build the discipline of observation.

For example, notice the sensations in your body when you see someone with whom you have unresolved tension. Where do you tighten? Where is there increased energy? Where is there movement, or an urge for movement? What is triggered?

Now notice what happens in your body when someone you love enters the room. Notice what is going on in your body as you sit around a table waiting for a meeting to begin. Notice what happens in your body if you're the one who's late, and others are watching you arrive!

You can experiment while watching movies too. When the antagonist comes on screen and the dark music plays, what happens in your body? When there is a resolution of tension, where specifically do you relax? When the violins lead into a moment of intimacy, where do you feel that in your body?

Daily life gives you an extraordinary range of opportunities to notice your somatic reaction to people and events. Practice!

PRACTICE 7.5.
Self-Observation with Somatic Awareness

In Practice 6.3, "Self-Observation of a Habit," I invited you to do a self-observation of a habit that you engage in that you suspect interferes with serving your clients. For this practice, you can do either another round of the same self-observation or identify another habit around which to self-observe. Choose a habit that arises fairly frequently so that you'll have many iterations of the habit to observe.

Do a self-observation practice, similar to Practice 6.3, with the habit you've chosen. This time add the following questions to your self-observation:

- What were the earliest sensations that you noticed as this habit arose?
- How did those sensations change or evolve during the course of the experience?

Again, do the self-observation for a week or two, bringing particular attention to the subtle experience of sensation as a component of the habit. Notice that the sensation is part and parcel of the constellation of phenomena that comprises the anatomy of the habit. Familiarity with the subtleties of your habits can allow you to quickly recognize them as they arise.

You are cultivating your own behavioral early warning system.

WORKING WITH URGES

We have discussed extensively how attachments and aversions are the underlying drivers of our behaviors. We know these urges have a somatic component that shows up in the body as sensation and is directly observable.

When we get triggered, our tendency is to go into habit. Noticing this reaction is the first step toward working with it. We also need to be able to interrupt the momentum of responding to the urge in order to replace it with something else. This act of reorganization replaces the automatic conditioned response with a consciously chosen one.

There is evidence that our willingness to notice and stay present with our urges is tied to the ability to control addictive behaviors like smoking.[7] If we consider that any behavior that is driven by urges is, in some sense, addictive, then it follows that being able to stay present and work skillfully with our urges is pivotal to becoming more self-generative in our lives.

PRACTICE 7.6.
Centering Through a Reaction

Consider a difficult conversation that you need to have, or a conversation with someone to whom you often have a negative reaction. As you think about the coming interaction, consider your aversion. What aspect of this interaction is likely to be difficult? What aspect of your identity (the way you prefer to see yourself in the world) is confronted by this situation?

Plan the conversation. Before you begin the conversation and periodically during the interaction with the other person, center yourself frequently, bringing yourself into presence. Be rigorous about this, working with any reactions simply by centering, over and over.

What was different about the conversation as a result of centering?

BODY PRACTICES

All action originates in the body. What we have to draw on when the chips are down is what we have practiced.

A former client of mine was a quality engineer for a manufacturing company. Ken's role was to work with production units to ensure compliance with precision technical specifications, and he had the authority to require process changes when necessary. He was brilliant, passionate, and deeply committed. He was also abrasive; his brusque style had alienated both plant workers and production engineers. Although he had authority, he hadn't earned trust and cooperation; resistance to his style was creating a lot of tension and slowed necessary changes. Ken was in serious danger of career derailment.

In order to build a body able to work in partnership, he took on a practice of ballroom dancing. This may sound improbable, but Ken was highly motivated to change his situation, and he became persuaded of the relevance. In class, he learned to sense his partner, to lead gracefully, to have the somatic experience of partnership. He learned to relax and to move with, rather than against, another.

Ken was able to use the obvious metaphor as a cognitive reminder of what his role could be. On a deeper level, there was a new somatic sensibility available to him that enabled him to embody a fundamentally different approach to his relationships with operations. It took a while to earn back the trust he had squandered, but he was able to turn the situation around and go on to success and a promotion.

Of course, simply doing ballroom dancing was not a sufficient response to his situation. There were other, parallel coaching strategies that were also important as he turned his career around. However, the body practice turned out to be central to his success.

In fact, nearly every coaching client I work with engages with some form of body practice as a critical component of an integrated approach to development. A body practice can be designed to support almost any development objective.

Body practices can begin small, as with brief body scans, centering, and other simple practices that allow people to begin to become familiar with the world of sensation. Other practices take a higher level of commitment. Pilates, for example, builds core strength and, by extension, the ability to take a stand for something that is important to you. Other useful practices are yoga (for flexibility), rock climbing (for creativity under stress), breathing practices (for settling the nervous system), and aikido (for collaboration and working with conflict).

PRACTICE 7.7.
Take on a Body Practice

Identify a body practice that you can commit to doing consistently over a period of time. If you are working with a somatically informed coach, discuss what might be most relevant. If not, choose a body practice that builds competencies you need for your development outcomes. Commit to doing it for a period of time. Then do it.

When you practice, keep your attention in your body rather than entertaining yourself with reading, music, or TV. Staying present with your sensations fosters physiological changes as your nervous system rewires itself with new pathways.[8] Exercise without attention builds muscle mass; practice with attention changes who we are.

Dedicate your practice to a purpose that is important to you. For example, you could say to yourself before your morning run, "I am running to build the resilience and energy to lead others." Then be present, using the practice to build somatic awareness and a new way of being in the world.

Define success for yourself as doing the practice and being present in it. This is a learning activity, not a performance activity. Commit to it for the long haul.

A body practice is different from exercise. We are not working "on the body" with the objective of losing weight or toning our muscles. Rather, we are building a somatic capability that can be expressed "through the body" in every aspect of our lives.

Let's consider centering, our core body practice. Morihei Ueshiba, founder of the Japanese martial art aikido, was famous for always being centered, balanced, and ready, and he is considered by some to be the greatest martial artist in history. When Morihei was forty-two years old and unarmed, he defeated a renowned swordsman by deftly moving out of the way of every blow and thrust.[9]

A student asked Morihei, "It looks like you are always centered." Morihei responded, "No, I just come back quickly."[10] This is a useful lesson for all of us. When we ride a bike, it may seem stable, but our path down the road is actually a series of tiny corrections that we are always automatically making with subtle shifts in our bodies.

If a master like Morihei is unable to remain constantly centered, it's unreasonable for us to set this as a standard for ourselves. Rather, let's learn to bring ourselves back, quickly and easily. When we get triggered, we might momentarily be off balance, but we can quickly move into our state of centered presence, from which we can choose how we want to respond. It's the *move* of centering that we practice.

Bringing ourselves back, and constantly recentering in what we care about, is how we hold a course. A body practice makes this possible.

COACHING IMPLICATIONS

Being present through our bodies makes us much more available to ourselves and, by extension, our clients. In turn, helping our clients learn to center themselves in order to stay resilient and resourceful no matter what's going on, and to organize their bodies to take specific actions, is one of the most important things that we can offer.

I'm speaking on the phone with my client on the other side of the country. He has recently retired and is in the process of building a part-time business and making decisions about how to enjoy his well-earned retirement.

We're building a picture of his plans, both for his business and his retirement activities of volunteer work. As we talk, I notice myself feeling tired. My shoulders are sloping forward, and my chest feels narrower. My head is forward. I center myself and continue to sense my own body as he says, "I'm working really hard to let my network know about my consulting services." "I'm making a commitment to volunteer on several new boards." "I'm really disciplining myself to make several calls a day." "I'm having to hold myself accountable in new ways."

With each statement like that, I notice my own sense of burden returning. This might be important information. Though it's my body, not his, I'm curious about what it's revealing. I center myself again and speak.

"Larry, are you hearing the language you're using? A lot of it is about working hard at everything. Seems to me that you've already worked hard in your life to get to this time in your life. You've talked about looking forward to things being easier. Yet as you describe your actual activities, it sounds to me that you're approaching this in the way you've done everything else: like a challenge to be overcome. What do you make of this?"

Larry pauses. "Yeah. I see that. I'm getting tired listening to myself."

We explore this, and he has some sadness that his nose-to-the-grindstone approach is so internalized that he doesn't know how to do it differently. Through this discovery, a new possibility opens, and doing things with ease becomes a powerful theme for him.

CHAPTER SUMMARY

- The body is the second doorway into presence. Every action originates in the body. The body is the seat of our habits; to change these habits, we must engage it in a fundamentally biological process.

- In order to be self-generative, we must develop somatic literacy and awareness. Somatic awareness is fundamental to presence and allows us to access the wealth of information available through our bodies. We build this awareness by bringing our attention into our bodies.

- Centering is a core practice through which we become able to reorganize ourselves quickly and easily in order to be present, connected, responsive, and ready in any circumstance. Through our bodies, we become fully present and capable of taking generative action.

- Because our habits invariably include a somatic component, self-observation must include the realm of sensation. Our sensations provide an early warning system that a particular habit is arising, creating the opportunity to self-regulate and choose something different.

- Being able to stay present with our strongest urges gives us the freedom to choose not to follow their usual dictates.

- Body practices are a fundamental way to build new capacities through the body. By doing practices consistently over time, we become a body able to take actions consistent with what we care about.

CHAPTER 8

Heart

Love is the only way to grasp another human being . . . to see
the essential traits and features . . . [the] potential in him which is not
yet actualized but ought to be actualized. . . . By his love, the loving person
enables the beloved person to actualize these potentialities.

Viktor Frankl

There is no feeling in a human heart which exists in that heart alone—which is
not, in some form or degree, in every heart.

George MacDonald

THE THIRD DOORWAY INTO PRESENCE IS THE HEART. THIS CHAPTER explores the heart as the source of compassion and connection, and a means of accessing presence.

It is a telling symptom of the disconnect from what's most real and important to humans that words like *love, emotion,* and *feeling* are often deemed inappropriate in business settings. Yet Kouzes and Posner assert that "the best leaders want to get closer to others, want to be more intimate with others, than do the poorer performers. Recent research is also telling us that not only are these leaders more likely to be successful, they're also more likely to be healthy."[1]

We tend to reduce the heart to either the metaphorical seat of romantic love or a physical organ in the body that needs to be maintained for a healthy life. While the heart is both, it is also the center of a marvelously complex nervous system connected to, but distinct from, the brain.[2] This system endows us with rich sensations and experiences, and is a source of remarkable relational intelligence. "An open heart," writes Roxanne Howe-Murphy, "is the guiding force behind our ability to meet and engage in a fulfilling and healthy life. When the intelligence of the heart is lacking, there is an innate sense that something important is missing in life, even if the person cannot state what it is."[3]

It is through the heart that we have the deepest connections with other humans. It is the center of our relational being, compassion, human and spiritual connection. (Contrary to popular belief, the heart is not our emotional center, which actually resides in the limbic system of the brain.)[4]

In the relational activity of coaching, the heart provides a third doorway into presence and into a deeper and more resonant connection with our clients. In this chapter, we explore practices to access and develop the heart. We experience the heart as the seat of compassion and unconditional positive regard, and see how gratitude can lead us into the longing that is the root impulse for our development in the first place.

HEART PRACTICES

- Finding compassion for others
- Core heart practice: Touching your heart
- Kissing practice: Observing versus sensing 2.0
- Integrating three core practices in a quick self-regulation move
- Gratitude practices
- Connecting through the heart

Again, take nothing on faith. It is through your own experience that you will discover the relevance and the utility of what your heart offers. Open your heart, and see what is possible in this for you.

≈≈ PRESENCE PAUSE ≈≈

DEVELOPING COMPASSION
FOR SELF AND OTHERS

The heart is the seat of compassion. The word *compassion* derives from the Latin *com* (together) and *pati* (suffering.) Compassion speaks to the human condition and the universality of suffering. What causes us difficulty causes difficulty for others as well.

Compassion is not the same as pity. It is not feeling sorry for someone. Rather, it is the realization, or awareness, that we are in this together. We come to recognize that the suffering of others is not unlike our own experience. From this follow the recognitions that we share the human condition and we are all connected.

This realization can come in a flash. I recall a simulation we ran for a manufacturing company in the early years of my consulting practice when a plant manager finally recognized why his employees had a union after experiencing what it was like to try to solve a problem when blindfolded. Suddenly he saw the world through the eyes of his employees. He became more able to be compassionate with tough and often adversarial union leaders because he now understood better the common human experience that they shared.

Our particular suffering lessens with the understanding that it is only our version of something much deeper and more universal. We become less capable of isolating ourselves or hurting others. We become connected to the whole of humanity, and our actions are taken in the light of that connection.

With the recognition of our connectedness and the universality of suffering arises the desire to relieve that suffering, to help and support, to give care. In coaching, we offer unconditional positive regard, together with the desire to support our clients in whatever will relieve their suffering and bring joy and ease.

With attention, it becomes possible to recognize our own visceral aversion to a person or a situation and allow that reaction to dissolve into compassion. This compassion can be extended toward others. The Buddhist practice of *tonglen*, a powerful means to develop compassion, is about extending compassion to all beings. While relatively simple, it is not included here because of space considerations.[5]

Compassion for self is also a key quality to develop. Self-judgment, loneliness, and perfectionism are common causes of suffering among overachievers. When we are suffering about something—a frustrated

---

PRACTICE 8.1.
Finding Compassion for Others

There are a number of powerful ways of seeing how we are connected to people we resist. In fact, it has been argued that for us to see something in another that we resist or that bothers us, that same trait must be present in ourselves. Seeing this commonality moves us into compassion.

Choose a situation in which you are judging, labeling, or feeling irritated by another person. First, write down a description of what this person does that is difficult for you. Be as specific as possible about both the other person's behavior and your reaction.

Now temporarily suspend your judgments and irritations. Write as if you were the other person. Place yourself in her awareness, describing the behavior that you find irritating and speaking to the inherent positive aspects or possible motivations for the behavior. Write in the first person, using "I" statements, speaking as her. As you do so, let yourself feel what it is to be her.

Finally, consider how the other person is like you. What aspirations or concerns does she have that are not so different from your own? What attachments and aversions might be driving her behaviors? What do you have in common?

Let yourself sense this as compassion. Find the experience of compassion within yourself for the other person, letting your judgment or irritation soften. It is the felt experience of compassion that is the key.

---

desire, a relationship challenge, a sense of being overwhelmed—we can consider how our difficulties are really a surface indication of underlying attachments and aversions. When we see this and understand that those cravings are universal, we find commonality with others. Our own suffering begins to seem less unique and less onerous.

Compassion is the direct experience of our shared humanity with our clients. Through compassion, we discover both empathy and unconditional acceptance. However, our compassion must be rooted in a clear view of our client as a unique individual, not on our projection of our own unfinished business onto the silver screen of our clients and their situations, nor on a squishy desire for intimacy and emotional connection.

Compassion absolutely includes being direct, candid, and incisive when that is what is called for. When we are compassionate and accepting, even as we deliver challenging truths, we provide nothing to defend against or react to. Others experience our compassion and unconditional regard as a safe atmosphere.

EXPERIENCING THE HEART

The entire self-generative process is supported by compassionate acceptance, extended through the relational field. However, this requires the felt experience of the heart, as distinct from compassion as an idea or ethical imperative. Practice 8.2, Touching Your Heart, strengthens direct access to this experience.

Some people sense something the first time they try Touching Your Heart. Others, particularly brainy types, don't. If you didn't

---

PRACTICE 8.2.

Core Heart Practice: Touching Your Heart

Do this simple practice a few times a day consistently and over time. This is not a thinking practice, so any effort or attempts to think about what you're doing will just get in the way. In spite of my advocacy, self-observation is a brain activity and won't help you here. Nor am I asking you to look for, or to generate, emotions like joy or love. Rather, I'm inviting you to allow a different intelligence to emerge simply by sensing and feeling into your heart.

Sit comfortably, and close your eyes to decrease the input into your brain. Relax. Now, relax more. Hunch your shoulders up, then drop them. Relax. Center yourself to bring your attention into your body. Relax more.

Touch your heart, in the upper center of your chest, to direct your attention to your heart. . . . Smile, even if it seems artificial. Without thinking about what this means, simply connect your smile to your heart. Let your smile invite your heart to grow even stronger.

Keeping your eyes closed, relax, and smile to your heart. If you feel anything, let it expand. Follow the feeling, rather than observing or labeling what you feel.

Don't observe. And if you don't feel anything, don't try to feel. Just relax more, and keep smiling to your heart.

Consider that the feeling is already there, waiting; as you relax, it becomes available to you. Any effort, paradoxically, constricts the feeling and makes it less available. So simply keep relaxing, and smiling. Just feel.[6]

---

feel anything, don't worry. Here, observation only gets in the way. By letting go of all effort to observe or make something happen, most will begin to experience their heart.

Practice 7.2, Observing Versus Sensing, is designed to build access to sensation. Or, with a suitable partner, you can do the next practice. Either will support you in the Touching Your Heart core practice, and build the capacity to access sensation and aliveness directly.

Notice the difference between observing and experiencing. Practices 8.2 and 8.3 illustrate the distinction between the experience of sensation and aliveness, and being an observer. Self-observation is an important (mind) competency. However, observation also removes us from our actual (body and heart) experience. Both are relevant to our conversation about coaching, but they are very different. While the observer is highly useful, relying only on the observer can remove us from life, constrict our experience, and relegate us to the role of spectator in our own lives.

PRACTICE 8.3.
Kissing Practice: Observing Versus Sensing 2.0

This might not seem as if it belongs in a business book. Still, it's probably the most fun practice in the book! The practice requires having someone you want to kiss and who wants to kiss you. (If you don't have a willing partner, I recommend returning to Practice 7.2.)

Gaze into each other's eyes for a moment, embrace, and relax into a full, loving kiss. Feel each other, and feel the sensations in your lips and in your body. Relax and enjoy! Enjoy more! . . . Now separate.

Do the same thing again, except as you're kissing, observe. There will be a slight distancing in your awareness as the acting part of your awareness kisses and the observing part watches. . . . How is this different? Be curious as the observer, and watch and notice what is happening . . . Separate yourselves.

Now kiss a third time, this time with no observer, just sensation. Fall into it, being fully present in the kiss, with all that arises. . . . Nothing else exists—just this moment, this presence, this connection and aliveness and sensation.

This can easily become sexual. However, if we don't follow these urges, we simply experience greater sensation and aliveness that we can open to more and more.

By the way, I recommend doing this practice frequently!

PRACTICE 8.4.
*Integrating Three Core Practices in a Quick
Self-Regulation Move*

The three core practices that I have offered in this part of the book ("Sitting," "Centering," and "Touching Your Heart") can be combined in a quick move that can be enormously helpful when you are challenged or triggered. Of course, the benefit of the move in a pinch will be available to you only with considerable practice in easier circumstances.

When you're triggered, notice that you're having a reaction. Notice the quality and texture of it, how it arises in your storyline, your emotions, and your body. (Practice 6.1, "Sitting," builds your capacity to observe yourself through self-observation.)

Center yourself in your body. Organize your posture, scanning and aligning yourself. Breathe into your center. (Centering practice is described in Practice 7.1. With practice, center becomes a familiar state that you can move to quickly and easily.)

Touch your heart, and smile. Feel your heart, sensing your compassion. (Practice 8.2, "Touching Your Heart," quickly and easily puts you in contact with your heart and with a state of compassion.)

This quick scan, including core elements of mind, body, and heart practices, provides a simple, integrated, and, with practice, reliable way to soften your reaction to any circumstance, and reorganize your awareness into a broader, more present and compassionate state.

From there, you can consider how to respond creatively and appropriately to the requirements of the situation.

DECIDING THROUGH THE HEART

The heart has wisdom, knowledge, and guidance about life that is not available through our brains. Both are useful. They may, however, lead us to differing conclusions. For certain, the brain (and the corresponding value on analysis, objectivity, and rational decision making) is esteemed more highly in the world of business than is the heart (and the corresponding relational values of compassion, connectedness, and joy). It follows that if we value the principle of considering multiple perspectives in order to reach the best decisions, our own hearts provide a source of intelligence that we might do well to consider.

Most of us have made decisions from the heart. Here we are seeking to make this more visible as a decision-making modality and to cultivate heart-based decision making as an explicit competency that we can draw on when needed.

Heart decisions are not necessarily easy ones. I worked with a coaching client who was reluctant to make tough personnel decisions. He sought to find the best in people and was a nice guy who didn't want to hurt anyone. Through our work together, he came to realize that this reluctance to confront was actually protecting *him* from the unpleasant experience of giving tough feedback or letting a nonperformer go. He justified it in his own mind as taking care of others; in fact, he was taking care of himself.

One direct report, a manager with a lot of tenure, had been lackluster for years. He was unhappy in his job, and others frequently had to cover for him. My client came to recognize that the manager was suffering and that others resented him. As he learned to listen to his heart, he recognized that the compassionate decision was to let the manager go and support him in finding a job that suited him better. It was still a difficult conversation, but my client, the manager's colleagues, and even the fired manager were far happier after the move was made.

Accessing the intelligence of the heart takes a certain willingness to suspend judgment. I know this territory well; as a genetically inbred scientist and skeptic, it is easy for me to reside in the domain of the mind. And, consistently, as I'm able to suspend my own skepticism, I discover another intelligence awaiting within me—quiet, undemanding, yet always there. It's really a matter of my opening to it.

So how has your heart led you? When have you made a decision from your heart? What shifted in you as your heart told you what to do? What if most of your life decisions were made from the heart? What would you change?

✀ PRESENCE PAUSE ✀

GRATITUDE

Gratitude is a fast track into the heart. It is possible to be grateful for many things: the loved ones in our lives, the job that puts bread on our table (and for most readers of this book, provides great interest and satisfaction), the experiences that we've had in our lives, the growth opportunity presented to us by a difficult relationship, conversation, or situation, a moment of peace.

Herb Kelleher, then CEO of Southwest Airlines, famously testified in 1997, "Because I am unable to perform competently any meaningful function at Southwest, our 25,000 employees let me be CEO. That is one among many reasons why I love the people of Southwest Airlines."[7] Kelleher's comment, of course, was humorous. And it reveals a genuine attitude of humility and gratitude that contributed significantly to his legendary tenure and to the enormously successful culture of the company.

All of us have much to be grateful for; it's easy to forget about these things in the trials of daily life. Gratitude is a simple and effective way to become more present and appreciative of the fleeting gifts we have. Again, we access gratitude through feeling, through our hearts, not as a cognitive exercise.

PRACTICE 8.5.
Two Simple Gratitude Practices[8]

A simple gratitude practice is to keep a notepad next to your bed. Before going to bed, touch your heart. Then take a few minutes to write down three things that happened that day that you are genuinely grateful for. Do this over a period of time. This isn't just about recording data; take the time to really feel your gratitude for these things.

Another practice is to remember the vital few people who have profoundly influenced you in your life. These are the people without whom you would not be the person you are: grandparents or parents, teachers, bosses, a spouse, a child, or some iconic person you've never even met. Consider these people, speak their names aloud, and experience your gratitude that they lived their lives in a way that contributed to your having the life you have. Again, touch your heart before and during the experience.

CONNECTING THROUGH THE HEART

What we have been discussing in this chapter is similar to our conversation about the relational field. Through the heart, we are cultivating particular qualities within us, such as compassion and gratitude. Once accessed within ourselves, we can extend them to others.

These qualities are not intellectual constructs; they are palpable. We have all had experiences with wonderful people who light up a room on entering. Smiling, warm, even radiant, they seem to exude a feeling that others are immediately drawn to. They often bring out the best in others, and it feels good to be around them.

While this comes more naturally to some than others, we can all become more like the person described above. We can be an invitation. By touching and smiling to our hearts, we access that quality in us. When we extend it outward to others, their experience of us can change significantly. Kouzes and Posner put it like this: "We've found no better secret to becoming the best leader you can be than to stay in love. When you're in love with the people you lead, the products and services you offer, and the customers and clients you serve, you just pour your heart into it."[9]

PRACTICE 8.6.
Connecting Through the Heart

Identify a coaching conversation or another conversation with someone with whom you don't have a warm, easy relationship. This doesn't have to be a difficult conversation. At the same time, choose a situation that could clearly benefit from a heart connection.

Plan the conversation. Then, before you interact, take a few minutes and set aside your mental chatter. Touch your heart. Smile to your heart. Find your compassion for this person, and access the feeling of your heart. In your awareness, extend your compassion and your heart feeling toward the person. Sense the presence of these qualities in the relational field that includes you and the other person.

Now enter the conversation. Maintain a portion of your awareness in this feeling. Smiling to the other person will help you access your heart feeling and extend it toward the other. (Of course, a schmaltzy fake smile will only set you back. It's important to connect the smile to the feeling in your heart.) Enjoy the person, and your connection to the person, independent of whether they respond or not to your extension of these qualities into the field.

What happened in the conversation? How were you different because of your heart connection? What was unexpected or different?

Connecting to others through the heart is like being in love. We access this place within us, and we extend it to our colleagues, family, friends, and coaching clients. We change who we are from the inside, and by so doing, we change the world.

LONGING

Deciding from the heart. Compassion. Gratitude. Connecting to something greater. I'm suggesting that the experiences I'm inviting you into in this part of the book are ultimately spiritual. They lead us irresistibly toward the full human experience that is our birthright.

People throughout all times and all cultures have experienced similar phenomena; truly, the lineages from which these practices draw go back thousands of years. For now, you are invited to explore these phenomena through your own experiences. This is the alternative to accepting at face value what others have graciously described for us in their own enthusiasm. Do yourself a favor, and discover the territory for yourself.

Doing practices over time softens us and leads us to be more connected to ourselves, each other, and the flow of life. As you continue, you may be blessed to discover the experience of longing that lies underneath all of this. The longing isn't emotional, like grief or the sadness of loss. Nor is it the craving and attachment associated with our blind pursuit of happiness in places it is not to be found. Rather, this longing is deeper and more universal. It is in all of us and is similar to the memory of something familiar yet long lost: sweet, vague, and comforting. We find ourselves longing for vast connectedness, for the sense of returning home.

Heart practices, and being present with our own compassion and gratitude, move us toward this connection with our own inner longing. Longing, the source of the developmental impulse, while invisible, is at the root of all human aspiration and endeavor. Although it is often confused with the conditioned cravings that we interpret as ambition and drive for achievement, longing can be fulfilled only by meaningful contribution and spiritual connection.

Touching our longing is the inevitable result of sufficient practice and ever-deepening awareness. Longing calls us forward in our lives, toward contribution, toward surrendering into a fuller relationship with what matters, toward fulfillment and connectedness. As the poet Rilke says,

I yearn to be held
In the great hands of your heart—
Oh let them take me now.
Into them I place these fragments, my life.[10]

≈≈ PRESENCE PAUSE ≈≈

On Christmas day a few months ago, we spent hours at the hospital bedside of a dying friend. Being with her was the highlight of Christmas; she was radiant, accepting, peaceful, smiling. She could feel her longing, the pull to release into something greater.

We can experience this before it's time to go. We can learn to open to our own longing, to let the press and urgency of our lives fall away, and to become present with the very impulse for which our lives unfold. It is from this state—deeply present, in touch with our compassion, gratitude, and longing, accepting and radiant—that we best support others in their own journey.

Through practice and attention, we become guides in the territory of development. We become able to see how any learning opportunity that requires new actions, even something as mundane as learning a new technical procedure or holding a difficult conversation, is a step along the path for the people we are coaching.

As coaches, we meet our clients in their domain of concern. Most likely this will have little to do with universal longing and everything to do with competency, career, and current challenges. As we support them in their commitments, we also hold them in a bigger frame. We realize that beneath their immediate concerns resides a deep longing for connection, meaning, and contribution. We come to see our clients as not so different from ourselves: human beings on a lifelong quest that has brought them into relationship with us at this particular point in time. And we can be profoundly grateful that our own path has led us to the place where we can be of some assistance to these beings in their journey, knowing too that the opportunity to do so is a rare privilege, and is part of our own journey.

Coaching Implications

Presence through the heart allows us to access gratitude and unconditional positive regard and to extend them to our clients, allowing any protective tendencies in the client to relax. We become able to connect at a heart level.

I'm speaking on the phone with a client, a dean at a prominent business school. She is brilliant, a pioneer in her field, and rather abrasive. She has high standards. She doesn't mean to be intimidating, but people often find her so.

She's talking with me about a promising professor she really wants to keep at the university, but who has made noises about looking elsewhere. She's angry and states that she's bent over backward to accommodate the faculty member's requests for consulting time and other matters. She's angry about the professor's lack of loyalty.

I feel my body tighten as I speak with her and notice my growing irritation that she's so judgmental about her colleague. I touch my heart, smiling. I feel myself soften. I extend unconditional positive regard into the field. As I do so, it dawns on me how deeply committed she is to the university and how much she wants a high-caliber faculty. I feel compassion for her. I realize that her anger is rooted in how much she cares, and that underneath that anger lies suffering that the faculty member doesn't seem to notice how much she's tried to do to keep her.

As I feel myself settle, my appreciation for my client grows. I speak softly, aware of extending this heart feeling toward my client. "You are really deeply committed to the excellence of this faculty, aren't you?"

She pauses. She speaks more softly, "Yes, I am! I guess it shows, doesn't it?"

"Yes, it does."

We both pause. We explore how this commitment sometimes spills over into behaviors that alienate people. The conversation then moves in the direction of how she can open a more inviting conversation with the professor she so wants to retain.

CHAPTER SUMMARY

- Heart, the third doorway into presence, is the source of our compassion and relational being, of our human connection.
- Cultivating compassion for ourselves and for others dissolves our judgments and allows us to be more fully present.
- The heart's intelligence, like somatic awareness, is not accessed through observation, but rather through feeling and sensing. Again, practice is necessary to bypass the observer mind and move directly into the aliveness that the heart offers us.
- Touching your heart is a core practice. With time, we become increasingly able to contact the heart's unique intelligence quickly and easily.
- The heart's intelligence can inform our decisions and can sometimes lead to a very different course of action from that of our analytical brain.
- Connecting to others through the heart provides intimacy and resonance. These qualities contribute to a conducive atmosphere for self-generation and learning.
- Practices in compassion and gratitude often lead to an experience of longing. This longing is the very root of the developmental impulse and leads inexorably to a greater sense of connectedness to the whole.

PART
FOUR

Relational Moves
for Presence-Based Coaching

*The true worth of a man is not to be found in man himself,
but in the colors and textures that come alive in others.*

Albert Schweitzer

PART FOUR TIES EVERYTHING IN THIS BOOK TOGETHER. WE'VE SEEN some of the inner moves that the coach makes in order to be present and resourceful. We've explored the practices that build the mastery from which we can make both the inner moves previously described and the relational moves that follow in this part. Now let's see what presence-based coaching conversations look like.

I present these moves primarily through one sample coaching case, that of Carly. Carly is an actual client, although I have altered specifics and included several elements of work with other clients. In some sense, Carly is a composite. This approach can best illustrate the wide range of relational coaching moves that are the topic of the next three chapters.

We'll assume that Carly has been working with her coach over several conversations and has begun developing basic competency in self-observation, centering, and somatic awareness. She is also considering putting her hat in the ring for a promotion to regional vice president of another division. Support from her vice president and direct boss, Gary, will be crucial if she does this.

Chapters Nine through Eleven are organized around the components of self-generation; each of the relational moves generally supports one of those components. This line is a bit arbitrary at times, but the distinctions are useful. I grouped self-observation and realization together in Chapter Nine for reasons that are explained below. Chapter Ten includes a range of reorganization moves, and Chapter Eleven illustrates stabilization. I'll illuminate some of the coach's inner process as well.

Carly's case illustrates a range of coaching moves but isn't representative of all coaching clients. In Chapter Twelve, I show how a few similar moves can be applied with very different clients.

In everything that follows, it is foundational that:

- As coaches, we do our own practices prior to engaging with our clients, so that we know the territory of self-generation for ourselves.

- Coaching moves invite presence. Paradoxically, they also require presence in order to be received as authentic, genuine, and relational. Our own presence precedes making the relational moves described here.

- During the coaching conversation itself, we continually work with ourselves, accessing the wisdom of our mind, body, and heart in order to stay present and resourceful in the shifting dynamics of a lively conversation.

- We can offer to our clients any practice or inner move that has been helpful to us in our own learning. Everything in this book is designed to support development; presumably we learn from our own exploration of the territory. Offering what has been helpful to us can be a great gift for our clients.

CHAPTER 9

Coach for
Self-Observation and Realization

*To live is so startling it leaves little time
for anything else.*

Emily Dickinson

*In the world to come, I shall not be asked,
"Why were you not Moses?"
I shall be asked, "Why were you not Zusya?"*

Rabbi Zusya

W E BEGIN OUR DISCUSSION OF RELATIONAL COACHING MOVES with self-observation, since self-awareness is the basis for everything that follows. There are specific coaching moves that encourage self-observation, and we can design practices for it.

I've lumped realization with self-observation into one chapter, even though it's a distinct component. Realization is simply something that happens in us. It arises from self-observation; we don't have realization moves.

What follows is a range of relational moves that invite self-observation and make realization and self-awareness more likely.

MOVES FOR SELF-OBSERVATION
AND REALIZATION

Reflect
- Name our own experience
- Reflecting observations
- Reflect what is produced in us by our client

Invite internal awareness
- Invite self-observation
- Invite presence
- Track sensation
- Access the intelligence of the body and heart

Focus the field
- Bring relevant factors into the conversation
- Create immediacy
- Spotlight habits in real time
- Spotlight aliveness

Challenge identity

REFLECT

We begin by reflecting our own experience to our clients. Because we live in a separate and distinct world, anything offered from our world that is not already accessible in our client's world will necessarily expand his view. Sharing our experience expands the information available to our client in that moment, and models competency in self-observation.

Naming Our Own Experience

Disclosing what we are noticing in ourselves provides valuable information on how another human experiences the field. Simple statements do a lot: "As you describe that situation, I'm aware of a tightness in my chest, and my shoulders are hunched up." Or "I notice that my mind is racing to think of a solution." These statements model self-awareness. By sharing our experience, we show someone else what it looks like to be aware of these distinctions.

Let's listen to the conversation with Carly. As we begin the story, Carly had e-mailed her coach, asking for a meeting, after a difficult presentation in which she felt attacked by members of the audience and unsupported by her boss, Gary. This meeting was planned on short notice and is therefore taking place on the phone. (I want to emphasize that presence-based coaching, and working somatically, can happen over the phone as well as in person.)

After reconnecting, the coach opens the conversation.

COACH: So tell me about what happened with Gary. *Carly goes into some detail about the meeting and what she perceives as predictable attacks from a couple of participants. She talks about frustration with Gary and that this has happened before. The coach asks a couple of questions; Carly is mostly talking, and talking fast, about what happened.*

COACH: *The coach is monitoring his own internal experience during her description, and pauses before responding.* I'm noticing a lot of tension in my neck and shoulders as you talk about this. And I'm noticing my emotions . . . anger and maybe a little self-righteousness. . . . I'm thinking, "How could he DO that?"

So far Carly has been describing what happened; her focus is "out there." Presence-based coaching seeks to move attention inward. The coach's simple move of describing his inner experience implicitly invites Carly to reflect on her own. Also, sharing details of our own experience may illuminate some nuance of the client's that she may not have recognized. This is different from empathy, in which we communicate understanding of the other person's feelings and experience. Here, we are speaking authentically about our own internal experience.

Sharing our experience makes possible a different kind of response for the client. In the business culture in which she resides, there is likely little precedent for awareness of somatic or emotional experiences. Grounded in our own self-awareness, cultivated through practice, we can name the somatic and emotional levels of our experience. This makes it more legitimate for the client to discover these richer layers of her own experience, or at least to become curious about whether they might be there.

Reflecting Observations

Reflecting to our client what we observe in her is like holding up a mirror. We can increase the client's self-awareness by pointing out phenomena that she may not at all be aware of. These too may be on cognitive, somatic, and emotional levels.

> COACH: May I offer an observation? (pausing for permission) I notice that, as you describe this, your voice is speeding up.

Notice, first, that we asked permission to share our observations. It's important to do so, especially early in a relationship when we are building trust and establishing the grounding for our conversation. Notice, too, that these statements can be in part assessment and in part interpretation. To say "your voice is speeding up" is objective; "your voice sounds sad" is interpretation. It's important to ground these reflections so that we're not simply making things up, and so the reflection is a useful and accurate piece of information for our client.

The client, of course, may judge for herself whether these assessments or interpretations are accurate. Our reflection simply invites the client to explore whether the observation is true. To explore, the client must self-observe.

This move can lead not only to self-observation but also directly into realization.

Reflect What Is Produced in Us by Our Client

We provide our client with priceless information when we reflect to her what is produced in us by her actions or way of being. The more powerful our client is, the less likely she is to receive the unvarnished truth that is so critical for making good decisions and correcting ineffective leadership behaviors that may greatly impede her effectiveness.

As coach, we have many opportunities to help our clients become informed about their impact on others. Formal feedback processes like 360-degree reviews provide useful information, but in a sometimes complex and heady fashion that can be overwhelming and is no substitute for real-time feedback from a trusted and candid ally. Providing reflections in the moment offers an instantaneous opportunity for self-observation and realization, which are much more likely to lead to real change than piles of data.

The conversation between June and Rick in Chapter One provides a good example of this move in action. Here's another:

> COACH: Carly, I noticed that you raised your voice as you were talking about the presentation, and I notice myself feeling a little tense, a little tightness in my stomach as you talk.

Any of these three moves—naming our own experience, reflecting observations, and reflecting what is produced in us by the client—implicitly invite the client to self-observe. They provide an opening into presence by directing attention into what is happening right now.

INVITE INTERNAL AWARENESS

We can also invite a client into self-observation explicitly through asking a direct question. If a client is new to self-observation, the inquiry is often made easier if it's preceded by one of the previous reflecting moves. The reflection provides an example, and the client can then check in with herself to see if what she notices is similar or different.

Invite Self-Observation

Asking questions about our client's cognitive, somatic, or emotional experience invites her into the present moment. We may notice a shift in the client: a lull in a stream of conversation, a shift in tone, a physical shift, a sense that something is different in the relational field. We can ask, "What was that?" Or, "What is happening in you right now?" We are curious, and we're inviting the client to express her internal experience. Mostly likely, she is not fully aware of her internal experience; asking becomes a requirement to self-observe and then articulate what she observes.

> COACH: So, as you talk about the presentation, what do you notice going on inside you?

CARLY: I notice tightness in my chest. And I feel some anxiety. And frankly, I'm angry. Look, I'm pretty strong. Those people were hostile, but I can deal just fine with them. At the same time, I deserve better support from my boss!

Carly has self-observed on three levels of experience: somatic (tightness), emotion (anger), and cognitive (story about her strength and what she deserves). These represent three distinct yet interrelated elements of her reaction. Being able to observe these phenomena is the first step in familiarity and skill in working with the habit.

Each level of experience offers an entry point into greater depth. Talking about the story can sometimes be useful. Inquiring further into the emotion (where does she feel this in her body, what is the quality of it, or where does the urge lead, for example) can be important for someone who is unfamiliar with her own emotional range. Other people tend to have strong emotions, and their inner work may be to learn to stay present with those emotions without being overwhelmed by them. The somatic experience is often a powerful way into deeper presence and understanding, as we shall see.

As coaches, we are receptive, holding ourselves as "soft clay." Our attunement with our own cognitive, emotional, and somatic experience allows us to sense our client, be affected by her, and allow the most useful openings to be revealed.

Invite Presence

If we have been working with our client for some time and she has worked with some of the practices in Part Three, we can invite her directly into the experience of presence at any point in our conversation. We do so through a touchstone that connects her into the practice she has been doing.

"Touch your heart," "Center," and "Notice what's going on with you right now" are simple and powerful reminders for (respectively) heart, body, and mind. When someone has been practicing to any extent, these reminders usually bring her immediately into a more resourceful state.

Our capacity to be present as we do so makes an enormous difference as well. If we are present through our own inner work, these brief reminders will be received as invitations, not techniques.

Track Sensation

Asking the client to track her sensation is an invitation to stay present with her experience. We invite her to watch and see what changes. Let's follow the above opening and see where it goes:

CARLY: Gary didn't back me up when the questions became hostile. It shouldn't have been a surprise, but for some reason I'm always stunned when he doesn't support me.

COACH: I know you've struggled with that in the past. So, is it okay if we explore this a little? *This is a choice point. Traditional coaching would likely explore options for dealing with Gary. Presence-based coaching explores present moment experience. The coach asks permission to work with this in more depth.*

CARLY: Yes, I'd like to be able to deal better with it. I'm pretty angry still.

COACH: Okay. Let's work with this for a while. Stay with your experience. Where are you experiencing the tension?

CARLY: In my chest and shoulders. I'm tight. I feel angry and set up.

COACH: So notice that there's a lot going on in you right now as you consider what happened. There's a somatic experience of tightness and tension. There's the emotion of anger. And your cognitive interpretation of being set up. See all those layers? *The coach is training Carly as an observer by naming the three layers of experience so she can see them.*

CARLY: Yes, quite a show, isn't it?

COACH: *Normalizing Carly's reactions.* Yes, we all are a show! Now I want to invite you to stay present with your experience, particularly your somatic experience. Tell me more about the quality of that tightness. Where is it more intense? Where less so? Is there movement in it? *Carly is being asked to track her sensation.*

CARLY: Movement? Let's see. Well, not really. I do feel a little less tension in my shoulders than a minute ago. My chest is really tight, though, and hot. Feels like I could hit someone.

COACH: Good noticing. What else?

CARLY: There's a lot of energy in my arms. They feel impatient, almost itchy. That's kind of funny. There's a little sense of movement, like something moving down my arms from my neck and shoulders.

COACH: Great. Just let that move. Nothing to do with it, just enjoy it and watch what happens.

Sometimes simply staying with the sensation and asking the client to report out what she's noticing will lead to a change in what's going on.

Access the Intelligence of the Body and Heart

We can also ask questions of her body that might add some perspective. Since behavioral patterns and interpretations are inextricably linked to patterns of armoring and energy in the body, questions that move attention and inquiry into the body sometimes produce surprising answers.[1] "What do your neck and shoulders have to say about this?" might evoke the response, "I'm protecting myself; I can't count on my boss," or, "I'm really angry about this and my instinct is to hurt someone!" Or perhaps we'll ask her to connect to her heart and see how this shifts her sense of the situation:

COACH: Carly, you've practiced accessing your heart. Take a moment to touch your heart and feel it.

CARLY: (taking a few moments to touch, and feel, her heart, and to feel how things are different) I'm peaceful, calmer. When I touch my heart, I feel different, more relaxed. I feel more acceptance of Gary.

COACH: That's great. How is this helpful to you? *Accessing her heart changes her state. The coach is exploring how things look different in that state.*

CARLY: Well, I know that I actually did a great job on the presentation. Even though I was attacked, I stayed calm and provided good answers. That's useful to remember! I still think that he should have jumped in; it's his credibility that was on the line. At the same time, I can find some compassion that he didn't want to take the hits; some of those guys are tough! I think he was more scared than I was.

COACH: What do you notice in your body now? *Inviting Carly back into presence.*

CARLY: Well, I feel lighter. The tension in my chest is a lot lighter; I feel some warmth and lightness in there. And the movement in my arms is stronger. My arms feel pretty lively!

COACH: And how is that lightness helpful to you?

CARLY: I can imagine having a different conversation with Gary. Five minutes ago, I was ready to slay him. Now I can see having a constructive conversation. And I'm clear I need to have one. *By being more present, Carly has naturally shifted from the previous state of anger into a more compassionate and resourceful state. She sees different action possibilities.*

Notice the shifts in attention throughout this dialogue. Carly's body and heart are informing the conversation. We'll come back to Carly in a few paragraphs.

For now, let's summarize by remarking that directing a client's attention into her own internal experience doesn't lead her to predetermined answers already known to us. Rather it's an inquiry driven by genuine curiosity, with unknown results. With some development of somatic self-observation skills and more openness through the heart, sensation can be very powerful. We access a deeper level of inner experience that can lead to significant discoveries and reorganization.

FOCUS THE FIELD

The field provides a rich backdrop of connections and meaning that are available to us. Connecting elements in the field explicitly to the client's present moment experience brings relevance and meaning to the coaching conversation. We can think of this as focusing the field.

Bring Relevant Factors into the Conversation

We focus the relational field by naming what's already present in it, thus bringing something from the background to the foreground. We bring into the room the realities that are relevant to the topic at hand.

COACH: Carly, let's make a connection here. When we talked last week, you had just spoken with Gary about supporting you for a promotion. So that's context for the presentation where you felt unsupported. How does that affect your reaction?

CARLY: (her voice rising and speeding up) It's huge! I need his support for this promotion! If I can't count on him in a stupid meeting, how can I count on him for a promotion?

COACH: Yes, that is huge. Did you notice your voice just then? *A request for self-observation.*

CARLY: Yeah. I started winding up more. I think I'm pretty anxious about this. *Carly notices her reaction and immediately connects it to the context of the support she needs from Gary.*

Carly is having a habitual reaction in the present moment, triggered by the belief she holds about the support she needs from Gary and the high-stakes situation that she's entering. Because Carly is a strong leader, quite capable of handling errant and hostile participants, it is likely that her strong reaction has more to do with being able to count on Gary for her promotion than with what happened in the meeting. It's also possible that this is a pattern for Carly and that she is often sensitive to lack of support. Some therapies would explore the roots of this. However, in presence-based coaching, we work with what's showing up in the moment. This reaction to being unsupported, then, is an opening for our work with Carly.

Create Immediacy

We create immediacy by spotlighting when a behavior or habit important to the client's outcomes is showing up in the moment.[2]

I've seen a well-meaning but intimidating CEO get what others had unsuccessfully been trying to tell him for years. It happened in a moment when I was able to identify and reflect an intimidating behavior that I noticed during our conversation, share the impact that behavior had on me, and speculate that others might experience being intimidated as well. In that moment, he had a realization based on a microcosm of a daily occurrence. He had been well aware of the implications but not the genesis.

Creating immediacy connects what was "out there" to what's showing up right now. Seeing that our issues are arising in the present is the opening to realization.

> COACH: *Contextualizing.* Carly, I don't know your boss, and I can't interpret his motives. However, it seems important to me to keep the whole landscape in mind. You've asked for his support on a promotion, he's been unsupportive in other situations in the past, and you had a pretty strong reaction to his lack of support here. What do you make of that in terms of what there is to do here?

> CARLY: Yeah. (pauses) Seems a time for me to be paying close attention to this relationship. It certainly raises the stakes on how I talk about this with him. I think I need to be careful. (Carly's voice gets quieter.)

> COACH: Maybe. Feel that, Carly. Feel what you're doing with that internally. *Traditional coaching would likely explore whether to be careful, or strategies for talking with Gary. Presence-based coaching hones directly into present moment experience.*

> CARLY: Yes, I'm getting anxious again. Thinking about the promotion triggered it. I can feel it in my chest again, but it's different from the tension. More an energized feeling, but not in a good way. There's a sense of collapse. I'm not safe. Careful. It's as if my body were saying, "Get small. If I blow this, I'll never get this promotion." *The coach notices tightness in Carly's voice. Carly is self-observing both her somatic reaction and the associated story. This is another habit—a collapse, playing it safe.*

> COACH: Feel that. *Validating and emphasizing Carly's direct, present moment experience.*

> CARLY: Yes. I get it. (pause) It's a pretty strong shift! *Carly's energy is increasing again; her voice gets stronger and more upbeat.*

When Carly considers her career risk, an immediate reaction, characterized by anxiety and carefulness, is triggered. This is an internal experience that likely happens frequently in her professional world. Normally strong and direct, she becomes tight, small, and careful when the habit grabs her. It is showing up right now. Because it is happening in a laboratory setting, it can be observed, studied, and worked with.

This is realization, a powerful moment for Carly. In realization, the habit loses its grip.

Spotlight Habits in Real Time

It is important to normalize these observations. A reaction may be strong, even overwhelming. By seeing it as a simple phenomenon, by observing and distancing ourselves from it, we learn to work with it rather than being hijacked by it. Naming it as a habit is the first move in this.

COACH: That's great. You're noticing your somatic reaction to a thought process. First, you said that the stakes were high. And then your body did what it knows how to do: hunker down, circle the wagons, play it safe! *Notice that the coach is describing this as a phenomenon separate from Carly. This helps with the dis-identification and self-observation.*

CARLY: Yes, it was instantaneous! "Hey, we're on dicey ground! Play small, tread lightly, don't invite attack."

COACH: Practiced that before, have you? (laughs) *A little humor is helpful in disidentifying from the habit. The coach wants Carly to see that this habit is just something that happens, not as fundamentally who she is.*

CARLY: (laughing) Just once or twice!

COACH: So you saw yourself going into habit?

CARLY: Yes, that was my habit. That's what I do.

COACH: So there's the habit, right now, in this moment. It's helpful to see it so clearly, isn't it?

CARLY: Yes, I can feel how familiar this is.

COACH: Now, let's pretend, in this moment, that you have the choice to stay out of habit. *Carly is in realization, and the coach introduces the possibility of reorganization. This will diverge from self-observation moves for a moment; coaching conversations never follow the script.*

CARLY: What do you mean?

COACH: Well, consider that you can do anything you want. It's a new moment. You might have practiced that old habit a lot, but you can write a new script at any moment.

CARLY: (pauses) Yes, I see that. That's a little scary.

COACH: Yeah. It's shifting out of an old identity into the new, more powerful identity that you're building. *The coach is connecting the present moment to Carly's narrative about her identity.*

CARLY: Yes, I can feel that. It's a little scary, but it's good.

COACH: So step into this, Carly. What's a new and creative way to frame this opportunity? *The coach pushes Carly toward a new perspective.*

CARLY: Well . . . Good question. This conversation with Gary could be an opportunity to practice something different! I can talk to him from a strong, centered place rather than bending over backward to not make him mad when his support is critical.

Carly recognized the habitual reaction and chose the possibility of a new response. She could feel the difference in her body. We can see, in this snippet of conversation, the potential to begin to focus the conversation into mobilizing energy and commitment for a different kind of conversation with her boss. This is reorganization in action.

Spotlight Aliveness

Normally we push through life and miss what's available to us in every moment. When we're present, we sense much more than when we're caught up in our heads. It's the difference between slamming down a plate of macaroni and cheese on the way out the door and slowly letting a dark chocolate truffle dissolve on our tongue, filling our mouth with rich sensation.

Being in the present moment is the only place in which we can sense all that is available to us. When a client is experiencing this aliveness, it is very useful to spotlight it and enhance presence.

COACH: You are seeing the possibility of talking to him from a strong, centered place. What does that feel like right now? How is your body responding to that possibility?

CARLY: That feels great! I've got lots of energy now. It's all over. Not the anxious feeling, but more readiness, aliveness. I feel awake. There's anticipation.

COACH: Do you like it?

CARLY: Yes! Actually, the sensation is quite enjoyable! Who could have thought that thinking about a conversation with my boss could be so much fun!

Notice Carly's aliveness. When we bring our attention fully into the present, into our bodies, we begin to notice the wealth of sensation that most of the time is beneath our awareness. Sensing this is what it means to be alive, to be awake. While work provides the content, aliveness is an inevitable product of coaching. This is how it happens.

CHALLENGE IDENTITY

Self-generation is built in part by loosening the grip of the habits that make up our client's identities. We can ask questions that challenge our client's identity or expose the gap between what a client holds herself to be (identity) and what she actually does (behavior). We can explore how the client contributed to the situation and how this contribution might be in conflict with who she has held herself to be in the world.

Exposed, this gap reveals that her identity isn't the whole story. Her sense of herself has to expand to include this bigger picture. This can be difficult at times but also quite liberating. It's important for the coach to be neutral and compassionate.

COACH: Carly, seems to me that we're likely to end this conversation with a plan for you to talk with Gary about what happened. But, first, I'm wondering how you contributed to the situation. What is there for you to see in this?

CARLY: Well, not to be so naive as to assume he's going to support me. I should have known better.

COACH: It's happened before, right?

CARLY: In every possible way!

COACH: So what part of you is unable to see or act on the knowledge that Gary is unlikely to back you up? What does this blindness reveal about you? *This is an identity question, and cuts to how Carly perceives and interprets the world.*

CARLY: Yecch! I feel like a kid here! (pause) You know, there's this naive part of me that thinks everybody just ought to be nice and support each other. I look at people through these rose-colored glasses. I assume that everyone is as hard-wired to take care of people as I am. It's just what I do. And I guess I assume that everyone else is like that too. When they aren't, I'm shocked! *Carly has identified a piece of her structure of interpretation. This is how she sees the world; it's a part of her identity.*

COACH: Say more about being shocked.

CARLY: Well, there's a disconnect. When Gary didn't back me up, I was floored. Like, how could he do that? When he didn't act like my world expected him to act, I was livid! So, why was I so surprised? I have plenty of evidence that this is exactly what would happen. It's just the way he is. Gary was just being Gary!

COACH: Feel that disconnect. Sense the gap between what you think the world should be and what it is.

CARLY: (pause) Yeah. It's pretty big! I feel pretty naive, and even a little ashamed. (voice quivers with emotion)

COACH: Yes, there's that self-judgment piece again. Recognize it? *Carly is a hard driver; previous conversations have revealed her tendency to be self-critical. The coach's observation of the arising of the self-judgment and shame allows Carly to simply observe it and not either fight it or get caught up in it.*

CARLY: Yes. I go right there.

COACH: So let go of the self-judgment. It doesn't serve you; it's just another habit. *Pause. The coach neither indulges Carly's emotions nor asks her to deny them. There is a choice point here. If Carly had little access to her emotions, staying present with this feeling might be important and useful. Here the coach is assessing that it's more a distraction and encourages Carly to self-observe and let it go.* Just allow yourself to see clearly and feel how strongly you are invested in this ideal world. And, how that investment keeps you from seeing the real world.

CARLY: (long pause) Yes, I get it. That's a pretty big gap, isn't it?

COACH: So stay in this realization. *There is a long pause. Carly experiences a sense of relief, a powerful feeling of expansion in her body, and a deep acceptance of both herself and Gary. This is realization, and is very different from the emotional state that she was in a minute ago.*

CARLY: When I stopped being self-judgmental, it actually became kind of funny! Then it was just poignant. We all work so hard to prop up our particular world. And it's just not a big deal. *At times, there can be a lightness and acceptance of it all. This acceptance, really of the human condition, gives us enormous freedom of action.*

COACH: You're right! It's not a big deal. So what do you make of this?

CARLY: Maybe I just need to deal with the world as it is and not get so out of whack when it's different from the world that I expect. Gary was just being Gary.

COACH: What would you have done differently?

CARLY: I would have anticipated the attacks and the need for Gary to jump in. I would have made very clear requests of him in advance and asked him to commit to our playing specific roles. I can see that I colluded in setting this up. *Realization leads to new possibilities. The requesting piece is new in this conversation and becomes an actionable theme.*

In the presentation situation, Carly proceeded in the way most of us do: within the world produced by our interpretations and untested assumptions. The coaching conversation placed her directly in the incongruity between her identity (including both her behavior and her interpretations) and the world as it actually is. The simultaneous experience of both of these provided a powerful realization of how she contributed to the situation.

Out of this realization emerged alternative possibilities, more grounded in the reality of the situation and more skillful than what actually happened. So does a self-generative moment allow us to reorganize toward more effective action.

CHAPTER SUMMARY

- We coach for self-observation and realization by continually directing our clients' attention into their present moment experience. We invite self-observation, reflect our own experience as a model, and continually invite clients to explore their own experience.
- We encourage clients to pay attention to sensation throughout the body, legitimizing it as a valuable source of information.
- Simultaneously we keep the conversation relevant by bringing the outside context into the conversation and creating immediacy by spotlighting when what's showing up right now reveals something that might be important "out there."
- We focus the field by spotlighting habits as they arise and the experience of aliveness. The recognition of these in real time greatly increases self-awareness and resourcefulness.
- Challenging identity happens when we expose the gap between the identity someone holds up to the world and what they actually are doing. When our clients are able to see this gap clearly, their understanding of themselves necessarily expands.

CHAPTER 10

Coach for Reorganization

There are risks and costs to a program of action. But they are far less than the long-range risks and costs of comfortable inaction.

John Fitzgerald Kennedy

The real act of discovery consists not in finding new lands but seeing with new eyes.

Marcel Proust

THE MOMENT OF REALIZATION WIPES THE SLATE clean, dissipating the grip of our habits, and allowing a new possibility to emerge around which we can mobilize energies and commitment. Sustainable change is produced by an internal reorganization, rehearsed over and over until it becomes a new way of being.

With Carly, several previous moments of realization could have provided a take-off point for reorganization toward a new course of action. The most recent was Carly's realization of how unrealistic her automatic expectation of support is and the possibility of making very clear requests when she needs something.

Let's follow this conversation further as we explore relational moves for reorganization. The coach is supporting Carly in becoming capable of significant new actions that are generative of the future that she wants. The new, emerging Carly will be *cognitively* clear about her course of action, *emotionally* flexible and able to work with what arises, and *somatically* energized and organized toward courageous and committed action.

MOVES FOR REORGANIZATION

Shift perspective
- Shift frame of reference
- Access future possibilities now

Reorganize around center
- Center
- Center in a commitment

Build competency in self-regulation
- Extend what's needed
- Identify internal somatic resources
- Make internal processes explicit
- Connect with the heart

Mobilize commitment

SHIFT PERSPECTIVE

We can invite our client into a perspective shift that dislodges her from her comfortable (and limiting) structure of interpretation. This is simultaneously disorienting and liberating. A human can see only so much from within her world. By freeing her from the constraints of her current view, a new view is possible that can lead to dramatic new insights and possible actions. (In Chapter Four, we had a lengthy conversation about orienting; this is similar. Perspective shifts change what is included in our attention, the connections we will make, and the resources we can access.)

Shift Frame of Reference

We can invite a client into a new perspective by changing her frame of reference. For example, we can ask a salesperson, "Place your-self in the perspective of an engineer. What concerns might you have about this deal?" Or, we can ask our client, "Imagine that it is five years in the future. Describe what your career looks like now!" Each of these disorients and then reorients the client into a new perspective in which solutions may be available that previously were inaccessible.

I once found a solution to an intractable problem that I had been unable to solve by asking myself, "If I were Donald Trump, what would I do?" (This led to my chartering a small aircraft to retrieve a forgotten passport to catch an international flight to meet my first head of state.)

It's important to place the client as fully as possible into the new frame. Using present-tense language, providing as vivid a picture as possible, and using sensory language all help with the immediate felt sense of the perspective. Let's invite Carly into a useful perspective shift:

COACH: Let's try something here. Are you willing to experiment with a shift in perspective? *Checking for willingness.*

CARLY: Sure.

COACH: Okay. Imagine it's a year from now. You've received the promotion, and are now a regional vice president. You're looking back over this past year and considering what led to this significant career breakthrough. From this perspective, can you describe what has transpired in your relationship with Gary and how you are different as a result? *The coach reorients Carly into a different future perspective, using present-tense language, as if she were already there.*

CARLY: Well, I would have overcome my concerns and had a direct conversation with Gary.

COACH: (interrupting) Carly, let me interrupt you for a minute. I want you to place yourself in the future. You're describing it in the conditional. Listen to the difference: "I would have" is tentative and dependent on some possible event. Try, "I used that incident with Gary to . . ." Hear the difference? Place yourself in the perspective that it already happened. *The coach isn't just a stickler for syntax. Carly was introducing psychological distance between herself and the future perspective. The coach is after immediacy and wants Carly to make it as real as possible.*

CARLY: Okay, I get it. Let me try that again. (pauses) Remember that painful incident with Gary? I really used that as a wakeup call. I learned that I couldn't just expect people to jump in to support me. I had to learn to be proactive in managing my relationships to get the support I needed. Now I'm much clearer with people around me about what I want from them. *Hear the immediacy in Carly's description this time?*

COACH: Great. Feel how different that is? Let's explore this more. What is different for you now?

CARLY: Now I really focus on this business of making requests. I used to be the good girl so that everyone would jump up and race to support me. Now I act skillfully in my own interests. Of course, that doesn't mean I'm Attila the Hun! I'm still a nice person. And I'm much better at letting people know what I need, so that they can provide it.

COACH: How has this helped others? *The coach is aware of Carly's tendency to take care of others' concerns; seeing how her requests actually help others could neutralize a key driver of Carly's conditioned habit.*

CARLY: People want to be supportive. Making requests shows them how. It makes it easier for people to do what they want to do anyway.

COACH: How has this been useful in your career?

CARLY: There are lots of ways. I've always known that I needed to be a better advocate for myself; I just felt that asking people for things was demanding. I now see that making clear requests helps me, but it also helps others. This is big for me and was really important for me in being seen by others as ready for the promotion. I'm a much stronger leader now in the regional vice president role.

The coach's move provided Carly with a new perspective. The breakdown with Gary in fact revealed the opportunity to be more direct in requesting what she needed. The new perspective is a reorganization in awareness and enables the client to see and choose new possible actions.

Access Future Possibilities Now

In this shifted perspective, we can access specific possibilities that might normally be unavailable. We work in the present to make that future possibility a stronger reality.

COACH: What can you do now that is consistent with this future picture of you as a leader?

CARLY: I can start with Gary. I can be very clear and direct with Gary in requesting the support I want. I actually think he'll respond pretty well. He's not a bad guy; he's just timid and political.

COACH: From the future perspective again, how will you reflect back on this specific conversation? *The coach is inviting a perspective shift again, this time about a specific action.*

CARLY: From the future? (pause) When I was clear and direct in spelling out what I needed and asked him for a commitment, it actually made it easier for him because he didn't have to take the risk of deciding. He supported me in a couple of dicey situations and went to bat for me on the promotion in ways I didn't expect. And it was because I chose to see it as an opportunity to develop this skill.

COACH: Great. What do you notice as you describe this?

CARLY: Well, it's liberating. It is very clear what there is to do. And it places the current challenge in a larger perspective. I'm kind of breathing a sigh of relief. I can see that there might be a way through this, and even some benefits. *Carly now sees the Gary issue in a larger context. This reduces the stakes; Carly finds it "liberating."*

COACH: So what are the benefits?

CARLY: Well, I can choose to view this as an opportunity. I can choose to see Gary as a teacher of sorts. He's my practice partner for being a better advocate for myself!

COACH: So what action will you take?

CARLY: I can have a clear conversation with Gary. I can tell him, really specifically, what I expect from him in the next meeting. And I can request that he commit in advance to backing me up.

This new perspective frames this as not just a difficult conversation that has to be navigated, but an opportunity to develop a competency that has real long-term pay-offs for her career and satisfaction.

An uncomfortable situation now offers an opportunity to practice the generative skill of bringing herself more fully into relationships. Seeing it this way recontextualizes the conversation, lowers the stakes, and provides renewed energy and purposefulness. Carly has moved past the reaction she was in earlier, sees the opportunity to practice making requests, and sees the situation, and Gary, in a much more accepting and empowered way.

Carly's request is likely to be received very differently by Gary if it is made from Carly's energized, clear, congruent body than if it originates in her careful, self-protective body, even if the words are identical. This is an example of two very different inner states producing very different results. Learning to reorganize our inner state and our bodies so that actions are taken with congruence and authenticity is central to effectiveness. Making requests is simply the relevant domain in which Carly can practice this.

REORGANIZE AROUND CENTER

Centering, the core practice from Chapter Seven, is a fundamental skill for self-generative leaders. Centering is a reorganization move. It's a shift into presence, into openness, into a relaxed readiness for whatever's next.

Center

We can invite our client to center herself at any point in the conversation. This is particularly useful when a client shows up to our meeting frazzled and carrying the frenzy of the day in her body or when something comes up in the course of our conversation that triggers a reaction.

I strongly suggest centering for nearly every client. If the client has been doing this generative practice for a while, it may be sufficient to simply remind her to center, as the state of centeredness will be familiar. I often ask a client, whether on the phone or in person, to talk out loud about what she's doing as she centers herself. By doing this, we both get a sense of what she does to make this reorganization happen. The clearer these distinctions are to the client, the more available and embodied becomes the experience; articulating the particular steps she goes through helps.

If the client is not familiar with the practice, I provide instructions and center myself with her as she does it.

Center in a Commitment

Recall that the first product of coaching is observable competency in fulfilling on commitments. It is not sufficient to simply be able to see great new action possibilities. Our client needs to be able to actually take these new actions with the people and situations that trigger her habits in the first place.

Presence-based coaching supports clients in the internal reorganization necessary to take these actions in an authentic and committed way. Beyond centering, we can invite our client to center herself in a specific commitment.[1]

We all live in multiple commitments. We can orient to a commitment by stating it out loud. Then we can center ourselves in the field of that commitment. Experiencing ourselves as a centered body totally organized toward a commitment provides a reference experience that can be drawn on later.

Recall the example from the Introduction in which an early mentor gave me a level of self-confidence through his presence. I then drew on this experience a few days later when I discovered that I would be delivering my ten-day training in Spanish. I was able to draw on that confidence in the clutch. It was a familiar state that I could return to, rather than something that I had to generate in the clutch.

Let's see how the coach works with Carly on centering in a commitment:

COACH: So what are you committed to with Gary?

CARLY: I'm committed to holding a different conversation with Gary. I'm committed to telling him that I had counted on his support in this meeting. And I'm also going to own that I didn't make my expectation explicit.

COACH: Sounds like a good opening. As you said, however, this is an opportunity for you to practice making requests. What particular request do you have of him? *The coach is asking Carly to get clear on her commitment.*

CARLY: My request is really for very specific support. We have a follow-up meeting coming up, and I'm bringing data that a couple of people aren't going to like because the information reflects poorly on their judgment. I want Gary to say that the data are the consequences of a decision that everyone supported at the time. I'm willing to explain anything about the data. But he was there when the decision was made; I wasn't.

COACH: (noticing a little tension in his own body as Carly speaks) So, what do you notice as you speak that?

CARLY: I feel a little defensive, vigilant.

COACH: And in your body? *The coach is directing Carly's attention to her body, inviting her into presence and accessing an important source of information.*

CARLY: My energy is high, my arms are energized, and I feel a little tense. Ready for action!

COACH: Okay, now center yourself. Stay clear about your commitment to making this request. And tell me what you're doing as you center. *She is having a habitual reaction; the coach is asking her to center herself in her commitment.*

CARLY: Okay. I'm straightening my posture. I'm sensing the floor under my feet and the chair holding me up. Actually I'm standing up now. Letting my shoulders go. Following my breath. *Carly is reporting how she reorganizes herself; speaking the words makes it more explicit to both herself and the coach.* I feel myself settling. I'm more relaxed. More present.

COACH: Now, tell me, in that centered body, what is your request of Gary? *Notice that the coach is working back and forth from somatic awareness to the external context, and that Carly's body is a constant source of information about the situation and her response to it.*

CARLY: (pauses) I'm requesting that he hold the group accountable for the decision they made and to back me up when I present data they don't want to look at.

COACH: How does that feel when you say it?

CARLY: That's pretty different. I feel much more settled with it. It's a clear request, and I don't feel defensive. It's his job. I'm just asking him to do his job.

COACH: Okay, good. Now let's pretend I'm Gary. Be in that centered body. Make the request. Speak to me. *The coach is turning it into a role play. This ups the ante for Carly on staying centered.*

CARLY: (pauses) "Gary . . ." Okay, let me try that again. It's sure harder to keep that center when I'm talking directly to you!

COACH: Good. How do you notice that? Where are you getting off center?

CARLY: I'm tightening up. I can feel my shoulders hunch up, and my chest contract.

COACH: Great. That's the game, Carly, notice how quickly you're able to notice how and where you get off center. Now work with it. Be rigorous. Recenter yourself. Take your time. When you're ready, make the request. *The coach is working with Carly on reorganization in real time. This is Carly's edge. She is preparing herself somatically for embodied, authentic action with her boss. This internal reorganization is crucial to self-generation and differentiates what we're doing here from much performance coaching.*

CARLY: (takes time to recenter) Okay. Here goes. "Gary, I'm requesting that in next week's meeting, you back me up if they jump on me again. Jeff and Rick are not going to like the data. I want you to stand up and tell them that it's accurate, that it reflects the decision the whole group made last year, and that we need to make a decision based on these facts. I'm requesting that you actively support me in this."

COACH: That was different! How did that feel to you?

CARLY: Well, I could feel a lot of energy. There was a trace of anxiety, but it was just there in the background. It didn't take over. I feel very clear, very centered.

COACH: Great. It impressed me as clear and congruent. *The conversation continues, refining the request, working with staying centered and asking Gary for an explicit commitment.*

We can see the constant presence in this dialogue. We can see Carly bringing her attention into her body, recentering, over and over. We can see her accessing her somatic experience. We can see her reorganizing herself around her commitment, moving toward a point where there's no dissonance within her as she speaks it.

With practice, Carly will be able to hold this conversation in a calm, centered, direct way. She is building the self-generative capacities of an authentic leader.

BUILD COMPETENCY IN
SELF-REGULATION

Reorganization is sometimes dramatic and sometimes more like a moment-by-moment working with our internal state. In presence-based coaching, we seek to build our client's competence at this ongoing reorganization. On this more subtle and iterative scale, we can also refer to reorganization as self-regulation.[2]

Extend What's Needed

Recall our discussions of the relational field. Based in our own process of self-regulation, we extend our presence toward our client. Our inner state invites her into an internal state that is relevant and useful for the actions that she wishes to take.[3]

The stability of our presence is a powerful support for the client as she learns to self-regulate. We extend a particular quality into the relational field, embodying and stabilizing a quality within ourselves that she is not yet able to readily access for herself. We become a resource for the client.

For example, if the client is internally chaotic, we settle ourselves and extend settledness toward the client like a lifeline. If the client is in a mood of resignation, we access our optimism and extend this toward our client. If the client is anxious and distracted, we move into a deep presence and extend this. This doesn't automatically change the client's experience. However, the change in the field is often palpable, and a client might say something afterward like, "You were so calm; it helped me to calm myself as well."

Identify Internal Somatic Resources

Building on the previous section, we can learn to identify resources within our own bodies. If I ask you to tell me where in your body you can find compassion or love, you are likely to say, "In my heart." Similarly, if we are sensitive and we practice, we can learn to discern the locus, within our bodies, of calm, of strength, of courage. These are internal resources, and, unlike a book or a CD or a coach, our internal resources are always available to us.

Let's listen in as Carly discovers this:

COACH: So we've been practicing this conversation with Gary. You're making your request in a direct, authentic way, and you're staying centered while doing so. I'm curious: When you get pulled off center, like when you assume that your current actions could lose you the promotion, what's the first place you notice that in your body? The very first twinge of losing it?

CARLY: It's my chest. I feel this rising sensation in my chest, a tightening. It's anxiety.

COACH: Okay, great. Now where's the place in your body that's the least anxious? Where in your body can you direct your attention to access calm when you feel that early indicator in your chest? *The coach is inviting Carly to locate an internal resource.*

CARLY: (pausing and sensing) It's my legs. My feet. They feel calm, rooted, supported.

COACH: Okay. Let your attention be in your feet.

CARLY: Yes, I like my feet!

COACH: Good. They're a great resource for you. I want you to experiment with this. Try touching that anxiety. Picture a situation, like Jeff and Rick criticizing your data, that triggers that anxious feeling. Sense your reaction. (pauses) Can you sense it? *The coach is setting up an experiment.*

CARLY: Yeah, it's right there. I can feel the tightening in my chest. Definitely there.

COACH: Okay, now just notice that. No need to do anything with it. Just notice it, and then drop your attention to your feet and legs. Use your feet as a resource to access your calmness, your settledness. Orient to them, and to that quality in you. (long pause)

CARLY: Yes, I feel myself settling again. It's a definite shift.

COACH: Okay, now check in with your chest again. Is the tightening still there?

CARLY: (pausing) Just a trace. It's almost gone. That's great!

Carly experienced self-regulation by shifting her attention to a different place in the body. This is the beginning of a competency that could be built through practice.

Make Internal Processes Explicit

If the client experiences a shift, we ask her how she did it. After all, it is *her* nervous system that shifted, and it is *her* self-generation that we are committed to supporting. Our egos might want to claim that we made something happen. However, it is far more helpful to the client to tease apart her self-regulatory process so that she can continue to develop her personal self-generation technology. So we ask, "A few minutes ago, you seemed rather pessimistic. Now you're energized and positive. What happened? How did you *do* that?"

Asking the client to repeat the steps she just took anchors them and provides a reference experience that may be useful the next time a similar self-regulation is needed.

> COACH: So that's a self-regulation move, Carly. How did you do that? *The coach asks Carly to anchor the move for herself, making explicit a process that she can replicate.*

> CARLY: Well, it was actually pretty easy. I noticed the tightness in my chest and that rising sensation. Then I shifted my attention to my feet. I let myself feel them, and I even moved them around on the rug to get more sensation there. And I don't know if I'm making this up or not, but I let myself feel calmness in them. But all of me got calmer. It's like there was a quality there that the rest of me could use. And when I checked in, the tightness was almost gone. *Carly has become a skillful observer, and articulates her internal process well.*

> COACH: Nice going! Think you could use that?

> CARLY: Like every day? I'm not quite sure I believe it yet. I need to experiment a bit more before I really trust that this is real!

> COACH: Have at it. Do the experiments, but really do them. If you're trying to disprove it, your mind will be successful. If you're simply curious, and really allow your attention to shift, you'll find out for yourself if it works for you. *The coach is asking Carly to verify for herself if it works.*

Carly is practicing self-regulation, which can only happen in the present moment. We can see that the skill of shifting from anxiety into centered presence is relevant to many areas of Carly's life.

While it may be specifically useful in her conversation with Gary and in her presentation of the data to a critical audience, it's also likely to be helpful in her marriage, with her teenagers, and in her interviews for a potential promotion.

Carly is becoming a more self-generative leader. The challenges and breakdowns that arise in her life provide her with limitless opportunities for practicing these moves.

Connect with the Heart

Connecting to the intelligence of the heart is a reorganization move because it produces a palpable inner state. The heart is a continually available resource. Rather than reorganizing toward a commitment, this is more about softening and moving into compassion; in this heart state, we often see things from a different perspective.

COACH: Carly, touch your heart. Smile, and feel your heart. *This draws from the core heart practice, with which Carly is now familiar.*

CARLY: (touching her heart) Okay.

COACH: What do you feel?

CARLY: I feel that nice feeling in my heart. It's pleasant!

COACH: Let it become stronger. Then tell me how things look different from that state.

CARLY: It all feels gentler. I can be kind to Gary in this; I see how he's doing the best he can do.

COACH: Now, in that place, in touch with your compassion, go back to what you were saying earlier. Do you believe that Gary *wants* to support you?

CARLY: (pausing, then smiling) Actually he does! He can be a pretty nice guy. He wants to support me. He just doesn't know how. If I script it for him, he'll try.

Because Carly's been doing the heart practice, this heart state is readily available to her. It may not always work, especially if she is strongly triggered. However, in many situations, it can be quite easy to touch into the compassionate heart intelligence. Self-regulation through connecting to the heart brings us into this desirable state, in which it's very difficult to be angry or resentful toward others.

MOBILIZE COMMITMENT

As the saying goes, "The road to hell is paved with good intentions." In the rarified presence of a coaching conversation, it is easier to see things clearly, including new actions that we can take, than when we return to the demands and fragmentation of our work environments. Good intentions don't carry us very far in that environment.

It is critical, in furthering development, to mobilize and maintain commitment. We work with this in coaching so that commitment is more available "out there." We can connect a future action (like Carly's conversation with Gary) to both purpose and the felt somatic experience of mobilized energy. And we ask for a firm commitment. This mobilization of commitment is a type of reorganization. By doing it in the coaching session, the same move becomes more available to the client in the real situation where it's needed. It might look like this:

COACH: So we've done a lot of work around this conversation with Gary. Are you ready to commit to holding that conversation?

CARLY: Yes. I know it's the right thing to do.

COACH: Knowing something is the right thing to do isn't the same as being committed to doing it. Knowing is in the mind; commitment is in the body. It's your body that has to take the action.

CARLY: Hmm. Yes, my mind is clear about this. My body? Tell me what you mean.

COACH: Well, all action originates in your body. A conversation has to be mobilized from somewhere within your body. We all have good intentions. But when push comes to shove, our body does what it's ready to do, regardless of our intentions. Put a glass of wine in front of an alcoholic, and intentions are out the window. Make sense? I want to know if your body is committed to holding this conversation or if you're going to go out of here with good intentions and then collapse in front of Gary.

CARLY: Well, that's different, isn't it? (pause) How do I know? I think I'm committed. I'm not afraid of difficult conversations once I'm clear about them. It's just when I link it to the promotion, my body tells me to be careful!

COACH: Exactly. So, where do you feel commitment in your body? Stand up, center yourself, and find the source of your commitment. *This is a request for presence. It's a disorienting question, and Carly has to look differently to answer.*

CARLY: (standing and reorganizing herself) Okay, I'm starting to get this. I can feel what you're talking about. I feel more alive. I feel my length, my width. I feel energy in my gut. There's a strength there. (pause) My commitment is in my gut, isn't it?

COACH: Is it? *The coach turns the question back on Carly, wanting her to be her own authority on this.*

CARLY: Yes, it's in my gut.

COACH: Carly. Take a minute and anchor your commitment in your body. (long pause) What do you notice now?

CARLY: Well, I'm energized, but it's very grounded and settled. There's no doubt about it.

COACH: Why are you having this conversation? *Commitment is mobilized through orienting to purpose.*

CARLY: I'm having the conversation because I deserve Gary's support. More important, I'm having the conversation for the sake of being a leader who can mobilize people toward something. And making requests is how that happens. The conversation with Gary is practice for that.

COACH: Now feel that in your body. Connect the purpose to the action, in your gut. *Commitment is mobilized in the body.*

CARLY: (pausing, sensing) That's it. I can feel the power of that. (long pause)

COACH: Got it?

CARLY: Got it.

COACH: Okay, now tell me what you just did. Tell me the move so that when you need to mobilize your commitment, you know how. *The coach is asking Carly to make her move explicit.*

CARLY: Well, I got clear about my intention. Then I centered myself and found the source of my commitment. I connected the action to my purpose. And then it all sort of came together. The action, the somatic sense of commitment, the purpose: it was all one experience.

COACH: That's it, Carly. (pause) Now, when are you going to have the conversation? *The coach asks for a specific time line for the commitment.*

CARLY: We meet every Tuesday morning for an hour. I have an agenda item around this next presentation anyway. I'll do it then.

COACH: Great. I'll ask you how it went next time.

We mobilize commitment in the body. The future is being created, moment by moment, in the present. So the energy we need to create a different future is necessary now. Doing what Carly just did sets a firm course toward this desired action. Of course, there will sometimes be breakdowns. Things happen, and our body's conditioned responses get triggered. Our bodies don't let us take the actions that we had intended to take. When this happens, Carly's opportunity is to self-observe to see what is happening and then reorganize herself on the spot to take the intended action. With practice, this mobilization will become more and more available to Carly.

If there's a breakdown and Carly finds herself unable to take the action, that simply reveals that more work is needed on either the requisite skills or mobilizing commitment.

CHAPTER SUMMARY

- Reorganization can be spotlighted and practiced in real time during the coaching conversation. This makes it much more likely that the client will be able to repeat the reorganization move in actual situations where the stakes may seem much higher.
- Shifting perspective is a relational move that is really a reorganization of awareness. This often reveals new ways of seeing or acting in a situation.
- Centering in a commitment is a reorganizing move that aligns the entire somatic self with a commitment. Doing this repeatedly is, in itself, an important self-generative practice.

- Self-regulation results from making moment-by-moment adjustments to our inner state. This is a form of minor reorganization and allows us to maintain a chosen state. We can support our clients in self-regulation by extending needed qualities in the field, making internal processes explicit, helping the client discover internal somatic resources, and connecting to the heart.
- Mobilizing commitment takes place in the body. It can be practiced in the coaching conversation so that it's an inner move available to the client "out there." Commitment to a future action can be mobilized in the present.

CHAPTER 11

Coach for Stabilization

If you have built castles in the air, your work need not be lost; that is where they should be. Now put the foundations under them.

Henry David Thoreau

Success is not the key to happiness. Happiness is the key to success. If you love what you are doing, you will be successful.

Albert Schweitzer

OUR CLIENTS ARE BUILDING OBSERVABLE COMPETENCIES FOR fulfilling commitments. These competencies can include anything from technical skills to the rather intangible elements of an authentic leadership presence.

Coaching for stabilization primarily means jointly designing fieldwork (self-observations, practices, experiments, and complementary learning activities) through which clients build these competencies. More important, through this fieldwork, our clients open to a radically new perspective on their lives as a whole. They come to see that everything is an opportunity for self-generation and that they can conduct their entire lives as an experiment in learning. Work, career, marriage, community, and parenting are the practice fields in which they develop self-generation and an ever-expanding capacity for creative engagement with their world.

The coaching moves in this chapter are intended to address both of these levels. First, they help stabilize specific, often job-related, competencies. Second, by learning to design fieldwork themselves, clients learn to translate insight and intentions into the concrete, rigorous practices required to stabilize any new skill. This leads to the self-generation that can inform every area of our clients' lives.

MOVES FOR STABILIZATION

Design fieldwork
- Design self-observations around conditioned tendencies
- Design self-observations around a new behavior or action
- Design relevant practices
- Invite clients to take on generative practices
- Identify relevant body practices
- Design complementary learning actions

Work jointly

Create new "facts on the ground"

DESIGN FIELDWORK

The opportunities for fieldwork are limitless. Because coaching is about the way we approach our lives, almost any experience can provide relevant learning. We'll explore several distinct areas of fieldwork. The result is a set of mutually reinforcing learning activities that weave a rich, multifaceted development framework that keeps our clients actively engaged in learning between coaching conversations.

Development demands rigor and commitment; as coaches, we cannot deliver on our promises of particular coaching outcomes if the client doesn't take action. At the same time, fieldwork must fit into the context of the client's life without adding too much to an already full plate. Clients will find fieldwork energizing if it has relevance, is interesting, stimulates curiosity, and engenders results. Missing these elements, fieldwork becomes yet another task to be checked off the list or an onerous responsibility that requires disciplined, nose-to-the-grindstone tenacity.

Let's return to Carly, whose fieldwork will end up including self-observations as well as a conversation with Gary and other things. Because she has a demanding high-level job, a working husband, three teenage children, church commitments, and two frisky dalmatians, it is important for success that coaching fieldwork be designed to fit into this busy life.

Carly's coach is aware that the meeting will soon come to a close. It's time to move toward defining the fieldwork that will keep Carly engaged in her learning process between now and their next meeting in two weeks. To recapitulate, Carly has:

- A cognitive recognition of her tendencies to assume that others will support her if she's a "good girl."
- A felt experience of collapsing and playing safe when she feels the stakes are high.
- A commitment to have a conversation with Gary in which she makes specific requests for support.
- The perspective that this situation provides an opportunity to develop important leadership skills.
- An experience of recentering around her commitment and reorganizing herself using a place of calm in her body as a resource.

While Carly is a composite of real clients, the conversational tendrils that follow from this point are illustrative. I'm going to take some artistic license and offer several possible dialogues that diverge from the point in the conversation where we left off. This is analogous to the choice points that arise in any conversation. My intent is to illustrate how several fieldwork possibilities could be developed; clearly, not all of these would happen in the same conversation.

Design Self-Observations Around Conditioned Tendencies

This is a way to bring rigorous attention to a particular area of developmental interest. As discussed in Chapter Six, we are in the business of training attention to observe the arising of a habit. We saw that the moment in which we default into a well-rehearsed but possibly self-defeating behavior can actually be a moment of choice. Granular self-observation is what allows this to happen.

In some ways, this move belongs in the previous chapters on self-observation and realization. However, I chose to put it here because, as fieldwork, this is really designed for stabilization of increased self-awareness. Self-observation as fieldwork builds on the realization that takes place during coaching.

Carly's coaching session will show us how we translate this realization into fieldwork.

COACH: Let's focus on the moment of collapse. It gets triggered when you consider making a request, and particularly when the backdrop is that a promotion is on the line, right?

CARLY: Right!

COACH: You described that rising sensation in your chest, the tightening. How many times a day does that happen?

CARLY: Well, perhaps a lot. Sometimes I'm sure it's subtle, and I don't see it. But I noticeably get tight several times a day. It's a very stressful environment right now.

COACH: Yes, I know it is. It's important to remember that the environment is difficult and to recognize that elements in the environment trigger particular responses in you. *The coach supports Carly's assessment, then pauses for emphasis.* Carly, the way through this is to recognize that the reaction, the stress, is in you. You can learn to self-regulate in a way that you don't take on what's around you.

CARLY: That feels pretty far off right now.

COACH: Yes. And every single time you practice the moves you've been learning, you carry less of that environmental tension. Do you see that?

CARLY: Yes. Definitely. Just in moments, but in those moments, it's really clear.

COACH: That's the work. Moment by moment. Over and over. And one day you'll look up and see that you're really different. That your relationship with the difficult environment has changed. It hasn't changed. You have. *The coach is orienting Carly to a purpose, a desirable future state.*

CARLY: I see that in principle. In practice, it feels very difficult!

COACH: You'll be surprised. If you stay rigorous in your practices, you'll be surprised at how quickly you become different. That's your work, though, to stay in the practices. (pause) We're getting short on time. I have a suggestion for fieldwork. Would you like to hear it?

CARLY: Yes.

COACH: I'm requesting that you do a self-observation. I want you to practice observing the very moment when that habit gets triggered. To bring awareness into the precise moment when you begin to hunch up, tighten your chest and shoulders, feel that anxiety coming on. You don't have to change anything. I'm just asking you to be curious about what happens. *The coach is suggesting a self-observation practice and appealing to Carly's curiosity. This is a learning activity, not a performance activity.*

CARLY: Tell me more.

COACH: I'm requesting that you keep a log. Twice a day, say at noon and again at the end of the day, you'll look back over the previous few hours and find two examples of when this reaction got triggered. Then jot quick notes about what triggered it, what happened, and what choice you made. I'll write out some specific questions for you. You're observing yourself: you're the scientist *and* the lab rat!

CARLY: Okay; I think I understand.

COACH: Remember, Carly, you're not trying to change anything. You're just being curious, bringing attention into this phenomenon. The subplot, of course, is that by tracking it, you bring your attention to it. With attention comes choice. A sharp awareness of the moment your habit arises allows you to self-regulate. If you can't spot it, you can't self-regulate. *The coach provides sufficient explanation of how this works to help with buy-in.*

The coach can create a set of specific questions to guide this self-observation. A sample set is shown in Exhibit 11.1. More on how self-observations produce behavior change can be found in Chapter Six.

Carly will do this self-observation for several weeks, at the end of which she will discuss with her coach what she discovered. Most often, this practice results in a much greater familiarity with the nature of the habit and an ability to spot it arising very early.

EXHIBIT 11.1.
Carly's Self-Observation Example

Behavioral Description

I will observe my habit of having my "careful" state triggered. In particular, I'll look for feelings of tightness, assumptions that others will support me, and the behavior of not making clear requests.

Structure

Event:	My anxiety/careful habit
Duration:	For three weeks
Frequency:	Twice a day, at end of morning and before leaving work
Tickler:	Include the questions below in my session notes template as a reminder

Questions

1. What was going on when the habit arose?

2. What was the first evidence, in my body, that I was acting habitually?

3. What did I do?

4. What was the impact?

5. What alternatives were there?

Design Self-Observations Around a New Behavior or Action

These self-observations train our attention on particular moves designed to produce different results. The neuroscience literature increasingly suggests that frequent repetition of a particular action, coupled with directed attention and presence as the action is being taken, leads to the establishment of new neural pathways in the body.[1] Literally, our physiology changes over time to produce a new default.

Here, a useful behavior is to make requests of others or to reorganize herself from the anxious state to a centered, ready state. A conversation with Carly about the former might go like this:

COACH: Seems to me that an important thing to be practicing is making requests. How do you see this?

CARLY: I agree. It's especially hard to do this when I think it's just something that someone should do anyway. It feels rude to tell someone what their job is.

COACH: I hear that you have a bit of a story going on about this. Do you hear a story in that? *The coach is exposing Carly's practiced interpretation.*

CARLY: Yes. It's part of my "good girl" view of the world.

COACH: Yet you've also said that making requests can make it easier for someone to know what's required of them, right?

CARLY: Yeah. The story is just what I tell myself in order to not make the request.

COACH: May I suggest some fieldwork?

CARLY: Of course.

COACH: I'm requesting that you do a self-observation around making requests. *Presenting this as a request gives Carly the experience of being on the receiving end of requests; this is relevant to her practice.* Every day you reflect on the requests that you've made of your management team, of Gary, of the server at lunch, of your kids. Choose two or three. They don't have to be big deals; little ones are fine. Then track what the request was, what you noticed in your body right before and right after making the request, any story you told yourself about why you shouldn't make it, and the story that eventually enabled you to make it. I want you to become intimately familiar with how you make requests and what enables you to do so. How does this sound?

CARLY: Interesting. I suspect I'm going to notice some tension before I make each request, and what I feel afterward will depend on how the person responds.

COACH: Seems likely. But be a good scientist and don't predispose your observations. Just be a neutral observer and see what you learn. Are you willing to do this as a daily practice for three weeks? *The coach asks for a clear commitment and a time line. These are key components for a request.*

CARLY: Yes, this is interesting. This makes sense to me.

COACH: I predict that because you're paying attention to this, you'll begin to notice this more and more and will find opportunities to make requests that you've never seen before.

Making requests is a fundamental competency, observable by others, that is useful in all relationships and many situations. Carly's self-observation will increase her presence as she takes this action. Because of this, it will become more available to her.

The same conversation could also explore an internal action, like centering, that others might not notice at all. Self-observation builds awareness and choicefulness and develops new competencies through practice with attention.

Design Relevant Practices

We can design practices that the client can do over and over that develop familiary and competence in a particular action. Like working out a particular muscle, this action becomes more and more available to us.

We intentionally commit to embodying, through repetition, an action or behavior that is important to us. We can intend to respond to a difficult conversation in a particular way, just as my son, Nathan, can plan a particular kayaking move before he gets to the river. However, when we sit down for the difficult conversation, or Nathan approaches the lip of a waterfall, there's no place to hide. That's the moment in which our bodies either perform, or don't.

In these raw moments we rise (or sink) to our level of practice. Intentions don't carry us very far. However, if we have practiced and have encoded the necessary moves into our body over and over and over again, we are far more likely to perform under pressure. I've watched Nathan watch kayaking videos ad infinitum, kinesthetically rehearsing a difficult move in his body. Then when he gets on the water, it's already hard-wired in him.

So may we, in our own endeavors, single out specific moves that are critical to our success and practice them until they are embodied. Whether our business requires making requests, kayaking, delegation, staying centered in a difficult conversation, or committing to a specific bold future, the more we practice, the more available the critical moves are when we need them. We did this extensively throughout Part Three with practices that develop presence and self-generation. Too, we can design specific practices to develop the behaviors on which our commitments depend.

Carly took on a practice of making requests. She practiced at restaurants, where if she preferred blue cheese on her salad instead of the feta proffered by the menu, she requested it. She practiced at the dry cleaners. She practiced making very specific requests of her managers, of her executive assistant, and of her boss. She asked several trusted colleagues to pay attention to her requests, and if she was less than crystal clear, to point that out to her.

Carly discovered that formulating these requests actually helped her become clear about what she wanted in the first place. When making requests, Carly was always kind and courteous, and she found that she was helping other people deliver on their commitment to satisfying her. She began to shift her unquestioned story, a relic from childhood, that making clear requests was pushy. Making requests became a win-win.

After several weeks of intensive practice in various situations, making big requests of Gary seemed much easier. This was true around specific support in tough situations and also in relation to asking Gary's advocacy for her promotion. The content was different from in a restaurant. However, organizing herself around making requests had become significantly easier, even in high-stakes situations. And she was increasingly perceived by others as a clear, direct, and authentic leader.

Invite Clients to Take on Generative Practices

Recall the three structures of development: engagement with a competent partner, generative practices, and outcome-specific fieldwork. Any of the generative practices in Part Three can be included in a coaching program. Generative practices, by their very nature, will enhance the client's ability to learn more specific competencies.

All of my coaching programs include some generative practices, most often sitting, centering, and touching the heart. These practices are foundational and inform every area of a client's life. They also greatly expand a client's ability to learn and take new actions. As our work together progresses, we overlay more specific practices around particular competencies.

Identify Relevant Body Practices

We can invite a client to commit to a body practice designed to nourish an underdeveloped quality in the client that is relevant to the desired outcomes from coaching. Many of my coaching programs also include this element. The instruction is to do the body practice with presence and full attention and with a clear connection to the purpose for which the practice is being done.

A body practice that might be relevant for Carly is the martial art of Push Hands. This draws from tai chi and involves coordinated movement with a partner that requires responsiveness, sensing how the partner is moving, and staying centered no matter what the partner is doing.

As in Push Hands, Carly's boss will not always do what she might want; her ability to stay centered, present, and resourceful no matter what Gary does or doesn't do is important. Push Hands provides an experience, and a powerful felt sense, of this ability to move flexibly with someone else while remaining fully balanced and centered in herself.

Let's see how a coach might present this to a skeptical Carly. This will be described as a telephone conversation, because people are often dubious about whether we can work with bodies over the phone. My answer is an emphatic *yes*. If we were meeting in person, it would be easy to do this experiment with each other as partners.

For your own learning, I recommend that you try this yourself as you read this. Imagine that you're Carly.

> COACH: I have a suggestion that I think will really be helpful to you in this. I want to invite you to take several private lessons with a tai chi teacher. I'll recommend a teacher near your office, so it will be easy for you to arrange sessions.
>
> CARLY: I need to understand this one better. Frankly, I don't think I can commit to this right now.

COACH: I know it's a really busy time. But I think you'll be amazed at what this will do. Let's try an experiment. Okay?

CARLY: Okay.

COACH: Thanks, Carly, for being willing to try this. Now, stand up, and move away from the furniture so you have a little space around you. Let me know when you're ready.

CARLY: (after a short pause) Okay. I'm facing the window, in the middle of my office. The view is great!

COACH: Okay, good. Now I want you to stand with your right foot slightly forward, and your left foot back. Face your torso toward the window. Does that make sense? *The coach checks in frequently, since there is no visual feedback.*

CARLY: Got it.

COACH: Now extend your right arm out toward the window, and shift your weight so that 80 percent of your weight is on your right foot and you're reaching toward something out the window. Let your knees be slightly bent and lean forward, reaching. Imagine that you're really wanting something that's out there. Feel a sense of reaching, of grasping, of leaning on something like an imaginary post that's supporting your arm and your weight. (pause) Can you sense that? *The coach is setting up a somatic distinction that Carly can sense in her body.*

CARLY: (pause, experimenting) Okay. I can feel that.

COACH: Feel the leaning, and sense your reliance on the post.

CARLY: Okay. I got it.

COACH: Now feel what happens in you if the pole collapses. If it just disappears.

CARLY: Well, I feel off balance, like I'm falling forward. I was counting on it, and when it's gone, I'm off balance. I lost my center.

COACH: Good. Now, really feel that.

CARLY: It takes a little imagination, but I can get that sense in my body.

COACH: Yes. Now how does this experience relate to what we've been talking about? *The coach is inviting Carly to create relevance by connecting the experience to the context.*

CARLY: Oh, I get it. It's like Gary. Gary's the post. And I was acting as if he was there, but he wasn't. Some part of me really counted on him, and when he didn't support me, I felt betrayed and off balance.

COACH: Yes. How does that land in you?

CARLY: Well, I can see more clearly in this metaphor how I set myself up to count on someone I couldn't count on.

COACH: Yes. It's a metaphor. It's also a real, present moment experience in your body.

CARLY: Yes, I see that. *There will often be a similar somatic sensibility in the experiment as in the real-world situation.*

COACH: So let's play with an alternative. Take the same stance. Now take a minute and center yourself. Tell me what you're doing.

CARLY: I'm dropping my attention, relaxing my shoulders. I feel the floor under my feet. I'm relaxing my jaw, opening my chest. I feel myself settling.

COACH: Good. Now let your knees bend a little with that settling. Imagine yourself like a tree, rooting into the ground. Feel your weight, your solidity. Got that?

CARLY: Like a rock.

COACH: Like a rock! Great. (pause) Now feel behind you, as if there were a massive dinosaur tail attached to your back. Put most of your weight on your front foot again, but keep your center, your groundedness, your balance. Feel that. (pause) Now extend your right arm again, extending your energy out. Imagine that you're making a request and your right arm extended out is that request. And your weight isn't committed. Whether the post is there or not, you're still in balance, still centered. Sense that, and tell me what you notice.

CARLY: This is really different. I have the sense that I can move freely without losing my balance. I can connect to something out there and interact with it, but I'm not dependent on it. I'm committed, but not overcommitted. I'm in relationship and contained within myself at the same time. *Carly has experienced a somatic distinction; this was clearly different from the previous experiment. She is experiencing in her body being connected and centered at the same time.*

COACH: So, sense that for a minute. (long pause) Anything else?

CARLY: Yes. This is great. It feels strong and liberating at the same time.

COACH: How does this experience inform your relationship with Gary?

CARLY: Well, I can make requests of Gary, be in relationship with him. But if he's not there, says "no," or says "yes" but hides when the chips are down, I don't have to get knocked off balance. I'm still centered and able to respond in any number of ways. I'm still flexible.

COACH: Bingo. You got it. (pause) So the tai chi teacher will do this with you—except as a real person, not a post. It's a practice called Push Hands, where you move with another person, but the person isn't predictable. Sometimes your partner will be there, sometimes not. And sometimes your partner will try to throw you off balance. You get to practice being centered and in relationship at the same time! It's fun. And it's very relevant to what we've been working with here. Are you willing to try this out? *The coach is testing for commitment.*

CARLY: Yes, I'll try it. At least I'll try it once.

COACH: Great. Try it once, and we'll talk about it. I'll work with you to get the teacher lined up. Meanwhile, you can do this practice. Do it ten times a day; it doesn't take long. Simply take the stance, feel it, and extend from that stance, keeping your center. Connect it to the business of making requests, so that in your awareness, you are asking somebody for something.

Now you try it. Sense what Carly sensed in her body. Feel the distinction between leaning forward and counting on something that's not there and centering yourself and extending from center. Sense how the latter stand allows you to extend into relationship without giving yourself up, or being dependent on the other.

～ PRESENCE PAUSE ～

What if this were really true? What if, in a short period of time each day, we could really practice and internalize specific competencies that have a tremendous impact in our lives? What if, for example, doing Push Hands could develop in us a felt sense of engagement from center that we could then access during the most testy, difficult workplace conversations we can imagine? What would this mean for how we develop ourselves? Our clients?

Are you willing to test this for yourself? Really? How would you do so?

ஃ PRESENCE PAUSE ௸

The body practice outlined is specific to the coaching outcomes that Carly is committed to. She is practicing something that is both a metaphor and an actual way of being. She is having a reference experience of centeredness that she can draw on in any circumstance. She is embodying something that with time will become part of who she is in relationship.

As a creative, presence-based coach, you can, with your clients, identify body practices that are relevant to your clients' specific leadership development needs. Push Hands for staying centered in challenging relationships. Pilates for building core strength for taking a stand. Yoga for building more flexibility for rigid leaders. Rock climbing for accessing creative solutions under pressure. Ballroom dancing for practicing building collaborative partnerships. Sky-diving for a client who is contemplating a major career change.

Depending on the client and the circumstances, body practices can take the form of a short practice done ten times a day (centering), to a weekly class (tai chi), to a one-off experience (sky-diving), to a practice done at home to a DVD four or five times a week (yoga).

There's no formula for choosing an appropriate body practice. At the same time, there is a way of practicing, in the body, almost any leadership trait or competency that you or your clients need. The key is establishing relevance, in the client's mind, so that she is clearly practicing something in her body that will support her in her commitments.

This is totally different from parking the body on the treadmill, fixing the gaze on the TV, and sweating for thirty minutes. That may be good for the mechanical body, but it doesn't build leadership. Rather, we are:

- Committing to a body/mind practice in which we are fully present to our experience
- Practicing something new through our bodies
- Sensing our body
- Creating relevance to our larger context
- Dedicating the practice to a particular purpose to which we are committed
- Rewiring our bodies to become a different person

If this sounds like a big claim, it is! We are shifting the ground of our being. This is self-generative, developmental, and central to the enterprise of developing more authentic, grounded leaders capable of responding to the enormous challenges of our modern world.

Design Complementary Learning Actions

Finally, we can design actions that provide complementary perspectives and experiences relative to what Carly is working on. These can include a wide range of possibilities. Let's explore what other kinds of creative actions could support Carly as she develops her "centered requesting muscles":

- *Activator:* Submitting her résumé for the promotion is taking a stand for something and raises the stakes in her conversations with Gary. An activator is a bold act that adds impetus and energy to a commitment.[2]
- *Conversations:* Holding a specific conversation with Gary will provide a practice opportunity, allow Gary to respond to Carly's clear requests, and shift the relational field that includes both of them.
- *Experiment:* Carly can try experiments in making requests in different circumstances or staying centered in challenging conversations. In an experiment, it is impossible to not discover something.
- *Feedback:* Carly can invite someone to observe her in a meeting and provide feedback, or request that people tell her when she is not clear about asking for what she needs.

- *Interviewing:* Talking to others who demonstrate a proficiency can be useful in learning how they do it.

- *Journaling:* Daily or frequent writing, sometimes with guiding questions, provides reflection. A self-observation (described above) is a special example of this.

- *Movies:* Specific movies that demonstrate competencies or a relevant way of being can be very powerful. The film *Gandhi*, for example, provides many examples of authentic, centered leadership.

- *Music and poetry:* Art can sometimes reach parts of our brain that logical thought cannot. Mary Oliver's "Wild Geese," for example, is a poem that might speak to Carly's sense of belonging and help her relax; the third movement of Mozart's Fortieth Symphony might have some of the feel of measured, centered, graceful action.

- *Observe others:* Observing someone who is proficient at a particular skill to be developed is a powerful means to get a picture of the competency in action.

- *Reading:* A book or article or web reference that provides insight or perspective on the competency. Matthew Budd and Larry Rothstein's book *You Are What You Say*, for example, has wonderful material on making requests.[3]

- *Tasks:* Doing a particular task that requires extensive use of the competency to be developed. For example, Carly could volunteer to lead a cross-functional team where she will need to coordinate action without line authority. This will be putting herself in a situation made to order for making requests.

- *Training:* Classroom, online, or CD-based training or retreats can provide a particular experience or foster a skill that supports the coaching outcomes.

- *Writing:* Responding to specific questions, developing a purpose statement or vision, journaling daily, and writing creatively all provide a means of organizing and expressing something new.

Clearly, coaching can include many different activities. The key is ensuring that the activity is relevant and meaningful.

Because we all live in interpretation, this meaning can be created. For example, I suspect that Mozart did not have Carly in mind as he wrote his brilliant Fortieth Symphony! However, if there is a feeling in the third movement that evokes the felt sense of the optimistic, self-assured act of making a request from center, why not connect these explicitly and use the music as a catalyst for the internal reorganization needed to make requests in a certain way?

WORK JOINTLY

We bring transparency through joint design of the coaching conversation, revealing what we are thinking and doing to connect the client to a view outside her own. As coaches, it is tempting to be prescriptive. We can think, "Well, my client needs to be more forceful in his assertion of leadership, so I'll have him take kick-boxing!" Might work, might not. We must be very careful of our own attachment to what we believe is right for the client.

We can also ask the client to generate her own action possibilities. Often, the client will be more able to identify what needs to be done than the coach. In other situations, the coach as resource will likely be able to offer relevant and powerful learning actions.

When we do so, it is helpful to think of our fieldwork suggestions as invitations. We can offer something; it is up to the client to accept or decline. We owe the client an explanation of why we believe the offer to be relevant. The client can then assess how it fits and if she's willing to commit.

In the dialogue above about Push Hands, a skeptical Carly became willing to commit to trying it because of a felt, present moment experience that established immediacy and relevance. Here's another example of a fieldwork invitation:

COACH: Carly, who's a person in your company who is really good at making clear requests?

CARLY: Well, Rudy is. He's my counterpart in the other division. People always know where he stands. He's very direct, and people trust him a lot.

COACH: Would you be willing to have a conversation with him and talk about how he does it? *Coach is checking for willingness for this action step.*

CARLY: Maybe. I don't know that he even thinks about it.

COACH: What might you gain from the conversation?

CARLY: Well, I don't know. I might learn ways to think about this differently. Or ways to prepare myself for making a request. And if he's not thought about it, it might be interesting to him as well.

COACH: Yes, I see that as well. Seems to me that part of your internal work is to first consider what you want. And then make clear, centered requests so that it's easy for people to support you and so that you're not bowled over when they don't. It's kind of a two-step process. Does that make sense?

CARLY: Yes. I do think that once I'm clear, I can ask. My tendency is to not think of it until it's too late. That's what happened with Gary. I just assumed. I was so blind.

COACH: Yes, and now you see more about how that happens. And by practicing both, you'll be a different leader. *Coach connects this action to purpose and context.*

CARLY: Yes. I think so too.

COACH: So recognize that in this moment, you could choose to commit to a conversation with Rudy, or a different person, or none. (pause) What feels right to you? *Coach extends unconditional regard and neutrality in the field.*

CARLY: (pausing to check in with herself) Feels right to try it with Rudy. I don't know what I'll learn. Still, it's a relationship that I need to strengthen anyway. If I get the regional vice president job, I'll actually be his boss. We're pretty open with each other, and I think he'd be interested in the conversation. I'll do it.

COACH: Great. By when?

CARLY: I'll contact him by next Friday and set it up. He's in Europe, so I don't know what his schedule will be like, but I'll at least get on his calendar.

Ownership by the client is paramount. Note that the coach put Carly clearly in the driver's seat. The coach asked her to check in with herself about what felt right. There is no wrong answer. Carly is simply invited to make a choice, right now, that puts the action of talking to Rudy either in motion or to rest.

Actions are taken in the future, but they are committed to in the present. The energy and congruence with which we commit to something make a big difference in how likely we are to be successful.

The moment of deciding is a practice in itself. Carly is checking in with herself and discerning what she wants to do. While it's not a major decision, it is a practice opportunity. Carly takes a moment to be present to her own experience and the choice she faces. In that moment, she is developing the competency of self-generation itself.

Do you see any relevance, in the process of deciding what she wants, to the competency of requesting that Carly is building in her work?

How would this conversation have been different if the coach had pushed Carly into talking to Rudy? What would have been lost?

⚯ PRESENCE PAUSE ⚮

When we design fieldwork, we are choosing specific actions that are developmentally focused and invoke a future. They are determinative of who we will become. It greatly accelerates the client's development of self-generation to be integrally involved in this process. Failing to do so is treating her as an object that we are developing. Inviting her into making present-moment choices that build a future is the very essence of coaching.

CREATE NEW "FACTS ON THE GROUND"

Coaches encourage clients to take actions that will have a visible impact in the human system that surrounds them. Development is not simply a matter of building skills to navigate an unchanging world. Rather, the fieldwork changes the client, and the client changes the system around her. Changes in the system in turn require new responses from the client. This dynamic interaction between client and system provides constantly shifting realities that keep the coaching process alive and interesting.

Consider Carly. Speaking to Rudy about how he organizes himself to make clear requests may surprise him. Conventional business thinking might hold that there's too much vulnerability asking a potential direct report for ideas on leading more effectively. However, thinking systemically, Carly might also consider that this is an opening for a more candid relationship with a strong leader she might be managing and that the move sets an expectation that clear requests (and, implicitly, candor and self-development) are of value to her.

Since requesting is also apparently important to Rudy, it's a good opening for a stronger relationship.

Bold clients take actions that raise the bar for themselves. Carly could talk to her current direct reports and explain that she is committed to making clearer requests. This will create an expectation that she will behave differently. Consider how success in making requests will build a perception among her managers of Carly as a clear, direct leader. Consider how her increased clarity might increase cohesiveness and productivity in her team.

Consider how Carly's applying for the regional vice president position in the other division could shift the way people perceive and respond to her, as well as the energy and sense of possibility that she too would experience.

All of these are effects in the system around her, catalyzed by relatively simple acts that Carly has taken. These effects have the consequence of changing the context within which Carly is making choices. For example, with a new expectation for consistent, clear requests from Carly, her staff might be reluctant to take the initiative when the request is not forthcoming. This might lead her to need to do work around setting expectations for her staff to take initiative. Or someone else interested in the same regional vice president position might be threatened by Carly's visible new assertiveness and seek to undermine her. She may be required to address this new situation proactively, with integrity and clarity. This requires a new competency.

While our coaching efforts are investing in the development of an authentic, self-generative leader, the leader is simultaneously changing the system around her. We can see both the iterative nature of the coaching process and the way in which coaching (and the resulting accelerated development of the client) produces ripple effects within the organization.

Coaching, then, alternates between focused conversations that shift how the client interprets and acts on possibilities, and generative actions that produce new facts on the ground. The evolving coaching conversation must always keep the development of the client relevant to the emerging context.

These conversations with Carly are building the three products of coaching. First, Carly is acquiring specific competencies that are relevant to her commitments. In this particular conversation, she is developing the competency of making requests, which is critical to being an effective leader and strengthens her as a candidate for the regional vice president position.

Second, Carly is becoming increasingly self-generative. She is increasingly able to self-observe, work with her inner state, and center herself in order to respond creatively and authentically.

Finally, she is more present to her own aliveness, her emotional range, and the sensations within her body. This contributes directly to experiencing greater joy and fulfillment.

CHAPTER SUMMARY

- Stabilization of new competencies requires specific fieldwork in which the client goes out from the coaching conversation and engages in self-observations, exercises, body practices, and other learning activities.
- Practices, through repetition, are instrumental in building specific competencies that the client needs. These practices can include both generative practices, such as centering and sitting, and practices directed at a specific competency. Body practices can contribute significantly to a client's capacity to take new actions.
- We design self-observations that the client can do as fieldwork. These can include self-observations around habits a client wants to change or new behavior a client wants to cultivate more.
- Creative, well-designed fieldwork should integrate different modalities, be relevant to the client's outcomes, provide interest, and fit into a busy life.
- Joint design provides a higher level of client ownership and also supports the client in understanding the principles and approaches that make coaching work. The client's thorough understanding of the coaching process supports her in becoming independent and self-generative.
- Fieldwork changes things "out there." A client's actions often produce reactions in others or create expectations. These facts on the ground change the requirements for the coach and the context within which coaching is taking place. This iterative dynamism allows, and requires, great creativity in the process.

Milestones:
Entry, Continuation, Completion

All men should strive to learn before they die,
what they are running from, and to, and why.

James Thurber

Impart as much as you can of your spiritual being to those
who are on the road with you, and accept as something
precious what comes back to you from them.

Albert Schweitzer

W E HAVE EXPLORED IN DEPTH THE PROCESS OF presence-based coaching. We've looked at the inner moves the coach makes in staying present, orienting to what is generative and useful, and holding a relational field that can evoke presence and new possibilities. We've discovered how a coaching conversation, with the intimacy that only the present moment can produce, can support the components of self-generation. Most of the book, in fact, has been about moments and about how those moments collectively produce competence, self-generation, and aliveness.

Now it's time to step back and look at presence-based coaching from a longer time perspective. It's useful to talk about entry points, continuations, and completions. These, of course, are still moments; however, they are moments that represent significant milestones in the flow of a coaching relationship. Engaging with them intentionally and consciously builds the architecture within which coaching conversations derive meaning and context.

MOVES FOR ENTRY, CONTINUATION, AND COMPLETION

This is not intended as a complete description of moves for entry, contracting, and so on. Rather, they are points of emphasis, explored through the rest of this chapter, that clarify how presence-based coaching principles apply in these particular milestones.

Entry
- Invite the client into presence
- Establish relevance of present moment to larger concerns
- Reveal client's habits gently
- Jointly develop purpose and outcomes

Continuation
- Invite clients to self-assess progress
- Validate and benchmark progress
- Share assessments and possible next steps
- Renegotiate purpose, outcomes, and structure

Completion
- Jointly share assessments
- Address outstanding issues
- Jointly design ongoing self-generative actions for client
- Declare completion

ENTRY

Carly's case illustrates a range of coaching moves. Carly is an ideal client: motivated, self-aware, reasonably competent at self-observation. She is a great partner for a coach and a great case for a book.

Many coaching clients will be less ready, willing, and able to enter skillfully into presence-based coaching than Carly. It would take another book to explore, for example, client resistance, negotiating substantive outcomes with self-assured people who aren't convinced they need to change anything, and working with the breakdowns that inevitably occur in coaching. Those topics are beyond our scope here.

However, it will be useful to look briefly at two other cases. These too are real cases with changed particulars. These brief snapshots of initial conversations with prospective clients will give a sense of how we might initially enter a conversation with a client and how a presence-based coaching conversation, drawing from the principles already articulated here, can begin to respond to the concerns of very different clients. As you read, keep in mind that these are edited, so the moves may strike you as slightly abrupt. In reality, the moves unfolded over the course of a longer conversation.

The Alpha Male Executive

Ron is a chief operating officer in a large bank. He has been in his current position for eight years and at the bank for twenty-five. He is very competent in financial and legal areas and has successfully kept the bank profitable and in solid regulatory compliance for years. However, he is a technocrat, not a leader. Turnover in Ron's area of responsibility is high, profits and the company's stock price are falling, and there are intractable delays on making some changes that the CEO had initiated some time ago. The CEO has told Ron that his leadership style and certain performance indicators really need to change and "strongly suggested" that he get coaching. He gave Ron the feedback that he often intimidated others, who found him unapproachable and distant, and that this was interfering with progress on key initiatives.

This is an initial face-to-face conversation with a prospective coach:

RON: So why should I work with you?

COACH: I don't know, Ron. Tell me a little about why you think we're in this conversation.

RON: We're here because my CEO told me to look into coaching. Look, I know there are problems. But we're superstars in other areas. Three weeks ago, I got the riot act from Stan. My performance has been great for twenty-five years. And now he's telling me that I need coaching?

COACH: Sounds like you feel you're being treated unfairly. Is that true?

RON: Yes. I'm doing a good job. We can all get better; I've got to tighten down on some things. But I don't need remedial help.

COACH: So coaching is remedial help?

RON: Isn't it? Aren't you like a shrink for people who need hand holding to manage their jobs? Look, I know you're only doing your job. I just don't need remedial help. I'm successful. I know what I'm doing. *Although Ron sounds confident, he was shaken by the CEO's feedback. He has no prior experience of asking for, or receiving, this kind of support. Ron is defensive and likely projecting anger at his boss onto the coach. The coach is ready to change the game.*

COACH: So let's stop here for just a moment. I want to ask you a different kind of question. Is that okay? *Asking permission may increase Ron's willingness.*

RON: Sure. (shrugs) *The coach senses Ron is resigning himself and briefly wonders what else Ron resigns himself to.*

COACH: What other way of seeing this meeting might be available to you? How could this meeting, maybe, work to your benefit? *The coach is inviting a perspective shift.*

RON: Well, we could end it sooner so that I could get back to work! (glances at his enormous gold watch)

COACH: Yes, we could. (chuckles, not rising to the bait) And maybe we'd both be missing a unique opportunity. That would really be unfortunate! (smiles broadly) *The coach is extending compassion and unconditional positive regard in the relational field.*

RON: (hesitates, taken a bit off guard, glances at the coach, and momentarily softens his face toward the hint of a smile, then resets; when he speaks some of the edge is gone from his voice) Maybe.

COACH: (providing a different perspective) So, let's assume for a moment that we're both well-intentioned, competent professionals, and we have about forty-five minutes to make a joint decision on whether there's anything more for us to do together. Fair assumption?

RON: Okay. Fair enough. *The coach's proposal is hard to argue with, even for Ron, who ostensibly asked for the meeting. However minute, they have a point of agreement.*

COACH: So, first, I really don't know if I can be helpful to you or not. *Neutrality.* Determining if I can be useful is my purpose for this conversation. So, Ron, what's your purpose for this conversation? *The coach is orienting himself to a purpose, and inviting Ron to do the same.*

RON: Well, I'm assuming that you can't help me.

COACH: Yes, Ron, I agree with you. You're assuming that I'm remedial help for losers. We can agree that you are a competent, successful professional. So, Ron, consider this: What if I actually could be enormously helpful to you, but because of the assumptions you're making about what coaching is and who I am, you never let yourself see that possibility?

RON: (pauses) Well, I suppose it's worth forty-five minutes to find out.

COACH: (smiles) Well, thanks for giving me the benefit of the doubt!

RON: (semi-smiles) I'm not at all convinced, but I'll listen.

COACH: Okay. I'm not here to pitch you; I'm sure you get enough pitches. Now it seems to me from what I've seen that you're really good at knowing how to say *no* to coaching. Your body posture, your language, your assumptions about coaching. All of those worked together as an integrated "no." Basically you entered this meeting with the door closed pretty tightly. Would you agree?

RON: Yes, I'd agree.

COACH: So, here's the question for you. How could you do this conversation differently? I mean, if you buy the assumption that we're two competent successful professionals, how would you go about determining for yourself whether I could be useful to you?

RON: Well, I'd ask you about what coaching is. And how you think it might be helpful to me.

COACH: Is that an exchange you're genuinely willing to have?

RON: Yes, I'm willing.

COACH: Great! That's a conversation that I'd also be interested in having. That strikes me as an invitation. Earlier, I felt resented.

Now, we're meeting each other differently. Do you feel that? *The coach is asking Ron to self-observe.*

RON: Yes, it's different.

COACH: So here's the first answer to your question. As a coach, I can help you become more aware of what happens inside you in specific situations. Of how you affect others. In the first few minutes of this conversation, I experienced you as pretty tough and inaccessible. And now you've invited me to a real conversation. You were competent [*a value of Ron's*] at doing something inside yourself to shift from tough to more open. (pause, extending resonance toward Ron) So, Ron, what did you do?

RON: (feeling both complimented and unsure) Well, I decided that I was here, and I might as well see what you had to say. I decided to be more open. When I decide something, it happens.

COACH: I see that. So in my language, I say that you reorganized yourself to be in a different kind of relationship with me. You started out rather adversarial, and you made a choice to change that. It's a critical leadership skill to be able to self-manage in order to connect with people, motivate them, and enroll them in what's important. You just showed me that you can do that. And it's something that we can all become more skillful at. (pause) What do you think about that?

RON: (a bit tentatively) Yes, I see it's useful. *Ron clearly sees the distinction but isn't skilled enough to know quite how it happened. At the same time, he sees the relevance of what just transpired to the feedback that his CEO gave him. The coach has invited Ron into self-observation and made it relevant to Ron's larger context.*

COACH: So one place that coaching could support you in being an even stronger leader is by helping you discover how to be more intentional and skillful at building relationships with people in order to lead and motivate them.

The conversation continues. By the end of their time together, the coach has built trust with Ron, defused Ron's concerns about "remedial help," and revealed several distinctions relevant to Ron's concerns. Being present with Ron, using moves that invite Ron out of his story and into the present, and offering an experience of coaching as safe and interesting allowed Ron to accept the help that his boss was suggesting.

Ron is not an easy client. He's out of touch with himself, insulated, and well protected by strong defense mechanisms. Presence-based coaching has created an opening. There is more to do before there is a viable agreement for coaching, but the door is at least open.

The Fast-Tracker

Barbara is a sales director, considered a high potential to be a vice president within the next several years. As part of a larger group of up-and-coming leaders in a telecommunications company, she has been offered coaching. She is eager to begin though knows little about coaching. Barbara is a fast climber and has had several promotions with significantly increased responsibility in short succession.

This conversation is an initial interview between Barbara and one of three prospective coaches she is interviewing:

COACH: So, help me understand where you are in your work, what excites you, and the challenges you face. That can lead us into conversation about how coaching might be helpful.

BARBARA: I've made several really nice advancements in the last few years. They've given me an opportunity to gain experience in several important areas. And I'm expecting a VP job in the next two years. I'm not ready right now, but I will be ready soon, and I think coaching could help with this. *The coach notices that she speaks in a very polished way and slightly fast. He has a fleeting impression that she is positioning herself.*

COACH: So what will it take to be ready for the VP job, in your mind?

BARBARA: I need to be better at selling my ideas and being collaborative at the same time. I'm great at selling, but sometimes I don't listen very well. I'm a strategic thinker, for both the company and for myself. But sometimes I get feedback that I'm too sharp or aggressive and that I intimidate people. I want to be the kind of leader people want to follow. *Based on this, the coach assesses Barbara as having some level of self-awareness and at least a tacit commitment to self-development.*

COACH: So, you've heard this feedback from others? What seems . . .

BARBARA: (interrupting) Well, I've heard it several times. And it showed up on a performance review a couple of years ago. It kind of stung.

COACH: So, it bothered you? Have you heard . . .

BARBARA: (interrupts again, and doesn't respond to the coach's question) I do think there's some truth in it. I get excited. I have a lot of energy, and sometimes that spills out, especially when I'm stressed.

COACH: (pauses, curious) Are you excited now?

BARBARA: (surprised) Well, a little . . . Why?

COACH: *Very neutral, extending unconditional positive regard.* Well, I noticed you interrupted me twice. I'm just curious and wondering if this might relate to how others experience you. What do you think?

BARBARA: (composes herself quickly, and appears to draw herself up slightly, pulling back; there's a hint of a smile, but there's little warmth in it) Sorry. I did interrupt you.

COACH: No problem. (smiles slightly, extending unconditional positive regard) I like your energy. I just think there might be something to see here. Are you willing to work with this a little? If we do a little actual coaching, then you can see better how it can help you.

BARBARA: (tentatively) Okay. That makes sense.

COACH: Thanks. So, a minute ago, I asked if you were excited and you said, "A little." Right?

BARBARA: Yes.

COACH: And that was right after you interrupted me twice when I was asking you questions.

BARBARA: Yes.

COACH: So I'm curious about what your inner experience was at that point in the conversation.

BARBARA: (pauses, then speaks with energy) I was feeling enthusiastic! I like that the company offered me coaching. I'm hopeful that it can help me get to a goal I've had for some time. I'm energized.

COACH: And you said earlier that you wanted to be a better listener and not be seen as "sharp" or "aggressive."

BARBARA: Right.

COACH: I could see how, if you interrupt a lot when you feel enthusiastic, people might describe that as aggressive. Does that make sense?

BARBARA: Yes, I can see that. (pauses, then speaks more slowly; her eyes seem more animated, she draws herself slightly taller, and her voice drops in pitch) But I don't want to give up my enthusiasm. It's my lifeline. I've been in very challenging jobs, and it's my energy and optimism that keeps me at it. Really, it's survival for me.

COACH: I like your enthusiasm! *Extending compassion; the coach also notes this "survival" interpretation of enthusiasm.* Barbara, I noticed that your tone changed slightly when you talked about how important your enthusiasm was. Did you notice that? *The coach is reflecting and asking her to self-observe.*

BARBARA: Well, it feels defeating to be told that I'm aggressive when I just see myself as energetic. It's discouraging. I wouldn't be where I am without it. *Her identity is very linked with this enthusiastic energy, even though it clearly creates problems in some situations.*

COACH: Yes, I see that this is really important. You don't have to give it up, you know.

BARBARA: Well, people read my enthusiasm as being aggressive. I don't know how to be enthusiastic and not aggressive at the same time.

COACH: Great. I think you just hit the nail on the head. Let's try it right now. I want you to be enthusiastic and connected to me at the same time. Can you do that?

BARBARA: I think so, but say more.

COACH: Well, when you interrupted me, you were connected to your enthusiasm but disconnected from me. I think you can be connected to both. I think you can be connected to your sources of energy and power and to the people you have to influence at the same time. What do you think?

BARBARA: Yes, that's the challenge!

COACH: Okay, let's practice right now. Talk to me about why you are excited about the VP position. Feel your enthusiasm and energy for it. And at the same time, stay connected to me. Make eye contact with me. And rather than selling yourself, imagine that you are revealing something precious to someone who really cares about you. Be enthusiastic, and at the same time slow yourself down and be in relationship.

BARBARA: Okay, I get it. (slows down her words and makes better contact with the coach) Well, as a VP, I'll finally have real influence on our strategic marketing. I'll have major responsibility in a world-class company and will work as a peer with some of the best in the business. I know it will be a challenge, and I have a lot of energy for it. *The coach has a sense that Barbara is with him rather than talking over him. Her voice is more measured, her eye contact strong, her face more expressive. There's more life in her eyes.*

COACH: Can you sense your enthusiasm?

BARBARA: Definitely. Can you?

COACH: Yes, I can.

BARBARA: And do you understand why it's hard to suppress my enthusiasm?

COACH: Yes, I see that. I like your enthusiasm. I just wouldn't want to feel run over by it. (pause) That felt different. What was your experience? How were you aware of me as you talked?

BARBARA: Yes, it was different. I was more aware of you.

COACH: I sensed that as well. How can you tell?

BARBARA: Well, I was noticing your eye contact and aware of you listening. And I was open to your questions rather than running off down a track in my mind.

COACH: (speaks gently, extending positive regard) So, how might coaching support you around this?

BARBARA: Well, given what just happened, I'm suspecting that you might be quite helpful in learning to not run people over with my enthusiasm. I'm seeing that I can be enthusiastic and connected to others at the same time. I think that's a tough balancing act for me.

COACH: Yes, it can be tough when the culture says that you're supposed to be strong and aggressive to get ahead, but when you do it, you're not acting like you're supposed to act.

BARBARA: Yes, that's exactly it.

COACH: So, this is that edge: being powerful and energetic, and at the same time being relational and authentic, both of which the culture requires. So right now, how did you do that? How did you simultaneously speak enthusiastically and be in relationship with me? *The coach directs Barbara to reflect on the current conversation in the context of her larger concern. As in the previous example, the coach asks the client to articulate for herself the move she made. This makes the beginning competency explicit, and helps Barbara take something practical from their first conversation.*

The coach and Barbara have some additional conversation about this, then move on to other topics. Without naming these explicitly, the conversation has required Barbara to self-observe (her enthusiasm when she interrupted) and to reorganize (in order to be enthusiastic and connected at the same time). It is easy to see, based on even these few minutes of conversation, how we could construct an experiment or a rich practice that Barbara could do as fieldwork.

The coach may or may not take a few minutes to reveal some of the principles of change that underlie the moves that he made in the conversation. He also has curiosity about the habitual nature of Barbara's energy and enthusiasm and what else she might disconnect from when she gets enthusiastic. The initial conversation is likely not the place to open these topics, but over the course of coaching, they will make for rich exploration.

At this early point, Barbara can sense that something shifted in her and has connected it meaningfully to the larger context of her concerns. Further conversation will make these distinctions more and more explicit. In the first conversation, the coach is simply staying present with Barbara and exploring where an opening might lie. There are lots of places to go from here.

Both of these conversations address the immediate concerns of the potential client. The work of coach and client will lead to substantially deeper territory than what was explored in the opening conversation.

At this point, the purpose of the conversation is to build trust, ascertain if there is an opening for coaching, and have a conversation of relevance from which both people can make an assessment about whether to move forward.

This may seem a modest starting point given the promises in this book about the significant and sustainable products of coaching. However, it is critical to see these first tentative steps toward engagement in the larger perspective of human development and the process of presence-based coaching. Every incremental step toward greater awareness and efficacy is, for Ron and Barbara, a step toward greater presence and contribution.

If client and prospective coach decide to work together (and this must be a joint decision), the next item of business will be to begin to shape the purpose and outcomes of the engagement. The coach already has some assessments of Ron and Barbara that may be useful to explore. If they work together, the iterative process of coaching will accelerate their development as professionals and humans while, of course, always keeping the client in charge of how fast, how deep, and in what direction.

In starting, we meet clients in their swirling world of ambitions and concerns. At the same time, we remember to always see them from our world, where they are, like ourselves, simply diamonds in the rough.

CONTINUATION

A coaching engagement is best done for a specific period of time and in service to the particular outcomes that were agreed on at the outset. This produces more accountability for both coach and client than open-ended engagements, in which it is up to the client to declare completion with a partner with whom there is likely great intimacy and trust. I advocate for assessing progress against these outcomes periodically throughout the engagement and when nearing the end of the contracted engagement.

One way that works well is to invite the client to review the coaching outcomes and assess his progress against each. We can request specific evidence to support this assessment. The search for this evidence, especially for behavioral outcomes that provide the core of most developmental coaching programs, is in itself an act of self-observation. The assessment process requires the client to self-observe, furthering self-generation. The resulting conversation often provides opportunities for the client to own the new competencies at a new level, backed by evidence.

Renegotiating and recommitting to a continuation of coaching is in itself a practice for clients in sensing, clarifying, and requesting what they need. As always, the way in which we conduct the process is, in itself, a practice in self-generation.

Let's eavesdrop on a continuation conversation. Jean is a manager at a medical laboratory; she has completed six months of work with her coach. She came into coaching with a general need for "better management skills," and they worked together to develop specific coaching outcomes.

The coach asked Jean, before this conversation, to assess her own competency in each of the outcomes and to find specific evidence to support the assessment. One outcome was "Increased competency in planning and completing important priorities on a monthly, weekly and daily basis." They are talking in person.

JEAN: I'm actually quite pleased with how I did on that outcome.

COACH: So what's the evidence? *Evidence grounds an assessment. It's great to be pleased. It's even better to be pleased if there's something substantive to base it on.*

JEAN: I really stick to my planning process. Sometimes things get in the way of execution. It's not perfect. At the same time, I am religious about my monthly, weekly, and daily planning time. You know I tracked it thoroughly. I haven't missed a weekly session since September and hit 92 percent of my days in January. I think that's terrific.

COACH: What enabled that to happen, Jean? *The coach is asking Jean to look underneath the observation for the underlying enabling process; by making it explicit, she'll be able to access it better in other situations.*

JEAN: I really made it a practice. You know, you talked a lot at the beginning about practices, and it didn't make much sense to me at first. But I really see how the body practices made a difference.

COACH: How did the body practices inform your planning?

JEAN: Well, I saw how I would just make it complicated for myself, and how I could just decide to act instead of thinking about it. I learned how to move easily into action with my morning walking practice. Once I could easily make the move into walking, then it was simple to apply the same move to my planning sessions. *Jean is describing a self-generative competency, acquired through a body practice, that enabled competency in a completely different domain.*

COACH: So it became easier, right?

JEAN: Yeah. It's just what I do. Every Friday afternoon before I leave the office. Every morning when I come in. Five minutes. No big deal. (pauses) You know, it happens in other areas of my life as well. I move more easily into tough conversations with my teenager. And with someone on a committee at church whom I really disagree with. I just face into things better. I'm not quite sure how it happened, but it's very clear.

COACH: Can you feel the normalcy of that in your body right now? Can you feel the "no big deal"? *The coach is asking about the somatic experience of having embodied this new habit. This is a self-observation and an inquiry into evidence of the stabilization of a new competency.*

JEAN: Yes. Six months ago I wouldn't have even understood that question! But, yes, it's just no big deal that I do this planning practice. And at the same time, the results are huge! I'm so much better organized, but it doesn't take any effort. That seems almost odd when I think about it!

COACH: You know, it just means you're a different person! The old Jean didn't know how to do this. The new Jean does!

JEAN: I like the new Jean!

This brief dialogue illustrates some of the elements of self-assessment. We are consistently directing our attention back into our own experience. What's the evidence out there for a competency? What's the evidence inside? How did it happen? And what's the breakdown? On the journey of development, where's the next emerging piece of work?

We can notice the greatly increased self-awareness that Jean has developed as a client over six months compared to the previous dialogues with Ron and Barbara. Practice produces much better self-observation and reflection skills.

As coaches, we can suggest that additional coaching work would be helpful or that, from our perspective, the outcomes have been reached and it's a good time to complete. Depending on a number of factors, clients often choose to extend the coaching engagement. This is an ending of one phase and the beginning of the next. Continuation needs to be a win for both parties; both the client and the coach need to believe that continuing will be of service to the client. Continuation requires reconsideration of the purpose and outcomes. Coach and client are entering a new phase of the relationship; the context is different. So are the client and the coach.

In reengagement, sometimes we take a deeper pass at the same outcomes. Sometimes new outcomes are called for. Sometimes the structure (frequency, venue, or something else) of the coaching conversations changes. Being present in this moment requires looking at what's needed now. The client will presumably have become more self-generative, so a different meeting frequency or structure may better serve the development purpose.

A recommitment to purpose and outcomes, even if it's simply a reiteration that the same ones are still relevant and compelling, is important to ensuring that the conversation stays fresh and relevant. Let's see how the conversation with Jean addresses this.

COACH: You mentioned that things are still getting in the way of execution. Is that something that you'd like to focus on more?

JEAN: Yes. I know that some interruptions are inevitable. But some of the times I get off track, there's no one to blame but me. (hunches her shoulders slightly as she says this, and her brow furrows) I just get pulled off into some little unimportant task, and at the end of the day, I didn't get to the biggie! I'm not good at this.

COACH: Sounds pretty normal! So I hear a little self-judgment in that: "No one to blame but me." And I noticed that your brow furrowed. What did you notice?

JEAN: (pauses, reflecting) Yes, I noticed that tightening as well. I really think I should be better at this.

COACH: So what habit is that?

JEAN: It's my self-judgment. There's also resignation in it. *Jean is identifying the elements of the habit; there are somatic and emotional components.*

COACH: So touch your heart. *The core heart practice evokes compassion for herself and softens Jean.*

JEAN: (touching her heart, smiling; there's a longish silence) Okay. That's better.

COACH: And does that self-judgment and resignation relate to your ability to take action? *The coach is asking how the habit relates to the context. This is a question of relevance.*

JEAN: Well, that sense, that feeling happens during the course of every day. It's a subtle giving up on myself. I think that resignation is present when I see myself veering off track and not stopping myself. *Jean connects the present moment experience of the habit with something "out there" that is important to her.*

COACH: I know you are considering continuing our work together. Is this something that you would like to work on? *The coach raises the continuation question. Clearly there was some previous conversation about the possibility. The coach is extending neutrality. This is not a sell; it's simply a question.*

JEAN: Yes, I would. I've been considering extending our work together for two or three more months. I've got the new software implementation and a lot of extra testing as long as the Petersburg lab is down. Execution is at a premium! And I'm not good at this. I can use the help! *The coach is observing Jean's body slumping slightly. He notices Jean's self-assessments and feels a subtle sense of resignation within himself as a response. He notes his own response and sets it aside.*

COACH: So what's the outcome?

JEAN: Well, I want to get better at execution. Having the plans is great, and it has improved my execution a lot. But there's a long way to go, and the next three months are tough.

COACH: Listen to your language in this conversation, Jean. What do you notice? *The coach is requesting self-observation.*

JEAN: I'm feeling discouraged and a little overwhelmed. My resignation is creeping in! I can spot it! *Jean self-observes the habit, names it as separate from herself, and thereby disidentifies from it. This is the moment of realization. It is energizing; notice the sense of triumph in the last comment?*

COACH: Sneaky, isn't it? *The coach reinforces Jean's disidentification by referring to the habit as "it." Then the coach invites Jean to reorganize by articulating an outcome.* So, Jean, think like a coach. This is how you become self-generative. You have this little habit that creeps in, and it undermines you. In the planning area, you're really competent and self-generative. You make the move into planning easily. Now the trick is to translate this over to execution, and when you notice that habit of resignation, you shift it into simple, effortless execution. Make sense?

JEAN: Yes. I get it.

COACH: So craft this as an outcome: something compelling, worth working for, measurable. Put it in language that addresses your concerns and that you can mobilize yourself for. That's how you'll reorganize yourself. *Notice that the development of the outcome is already a reorganization move. Jean is practicing self-generation in the present moment through articulating an outcome.*

JEAN: So let's try this. I think the outcome is executing the most important things on my weekly and daily lists most of the time. I think we can create a measure and a tracking system. And I think working with this as a practice—working with the shift you identified, that's key. It's really like walking practice and planning practice. This is execution practice. How's that? *Positioning something as practice makes it a learning rather than a performance activity.*

COACH: How does that feel in your body?

JEAN: Feels energizing. I don't know how it's going to work. But I think it will work. It's like the other things we started on. They felt insurmountable at first. But seeing them as practice and learning to make these subtle moves paid off. This is worth working on.

The conversation continues; Jean and her coach get specific about this and other outcomes. The conversation concluded with two new outcomes and a recommitment to two existing outcomes that they agreed would benefit from additional attention. Jean and her coach agreed to another three months of work together, and there was a palpable sense of renewal and recommitment.

COMPLETION, AND BEGINNING

Sometimes after such an assessment, the client, the coach, or both declare completion. A declaration of completion and mutual satisfaction, made together with the client, is a wonderful moment. After all, our commitment to the client has been to build competence and self-generation. We can have very useful conversation during a completion about what the client will do to continue his development, coach himself, and be self-generative.

If the client declares that he is not satisfied, it is important for us to understand why and to consider what our part is in it. We may want to consider how we can make things right so that the completion is as honoring of both people as possible. There may be difficult things to look at.

We can also declare that we don't see the process working well, that we assess the client as having particular needs that we don't believe we can fill, or that we don't see an opening for further coaching. Of course, if we are completing, it's important to care for the client in the way we end it.

Completions provide another opportunity to be deeply present and to consciously choose how we complete. It is important to be aware that we are withdrawing our energy and attention from this particular kind of relationship. At the same time, we can simultaneously honor and appreciate the person with whom we have been in this relationship.

Here's a completion conversation after a successful engagement with Marc, the executive director of a nonprofit environmental organization. This conversation takes place after eight months of work together. Marc is a satisfied customer; he assessed himself as much more competent at three of the five outcomes, and has evidence. For the other two, he can cite progress. He feels complete and ready to move on. Marc and his coach have gone over their assessments of Marc's progress, and they are moving toward completion:

MARC: It's going to be interesting, being coachless for a while!

COACH: Coachless! Sounds like trying to find your way home in a blizzard without your vehicle!

MARC: Well, I don't think it's that bad. I *will* miss our conversations; it's been an extraordinary journey.

COACH: Yes, it has. I'm very honored to have shared it with you. (longish pause that is not at all awkward) Marc, I have a suggestion.

MARC: Let's hear it!

COACH: What if, instead of thinking of yourself as "coachless," you thought of yourself as "self-coaching." How would that change things?

MARC: I like that! In the sense of I'm my own coach? Is that what you mean?

COACH: Exactly. I mean that over the last eight months, we've intentionally been very explicit about everything that we've done. As a client, you've learned a lot about coaching. In fact, you've seen ways to work differently with your staff. So what would it look like to hire yourself as your new coach?

MARC: Well, it would be cheaper for starters. And scheduling would be easier. (laughs)

COACH: (laughs) Cheaper, yes, but I wouldn't count on the scheduling part! You might only have one calendar to deal with, but it will be lots easier to let yourself off the hook! *The coach is pointing to the central issue that it's always easier to organize around the urgent than around our own learning and development.*

MARC: (slightly startled) Yeah, you're right. This could be trickier than I thought.

COACH: How is that?

MARC: Well, I really have to be committed. It's easy to pay someone and then be committed to getting my money's worth. It's different to do something with no one watching. To do it just *because* I'm committed. (pauses) This actually raises the bar, doesn't it?

COACH: I think you're getting the idea! (chuckles) So, step into this, Marc. What would it take for you to carry this ball for yourself?

MARC: Well, I think it would be helpful to have a couple of others whom I talk with regularly. And to stay engaged with practices. I think I'll be doing practices for the rest of my life. And reading.

COACH: Good things to include. Now how will you organize these various things so that they're driven by an overall intention and an outcome? What's the purpose that ties it together? What makes it a development process, and not just a hodgepodge of activity? *The coach is inquiring about the organizing principles of this, and what Marc will orient to in the process.*

MARC: Wait, I thought we were saying good-bye! We're supposed to be winding up, and you're giving me the hardest assignment yet!

COACH: Well, you said you wanted to get your money's worth, right? So what if, in our last call, you design a process for developing yourself for the rest of your life? That makes our work look like a pretty good investment!

MARC: Hard to argue with that.

COACH: So, what's the purpose for doing this? What will it enable you to contribute?

MARC: I have a significant new initiative that I've been thinking about. It's a really big leadership move and involves coordinating with a number of other environmental groups nationally. I'm going to have to step up my game.

COACH: That's a worthwhile purpose!

MARC: Yes, it's huge.

COACH: So, sounds like you need yourself as a coach! How serious are you about being a self-generative, self-coaching learner as you step up your game? You absolutely know how to do it. It's just a question of commitment.

MARC: Well, I can feel a lot of energy and excitement. I'm very energized for this new project, and coaching myself could be really helpful. But tell me what you see as a structure. Then I can assess my commitment.

COACH: (pauses) What if you have a coaching session with yourself every two weeks? An hour. You put it on your calendar. You have specific outcomes. Fieldwork. Practices. The whole enchilada. Except you're the client *and* the coach.

MARC: (long pause as he considers this, draws himself up somewhat, and then speaks more slowly) This really is about my being self-generative, isn't it? I do know how to do this. I have the technology. I don't know how long I can commit to it. But this is clearly a worthwhile experiment. I'm willing to commit to this structure for three months, and then I'll see how it's going.

They move toward winding up. The coach voices his deep appreciation for what Marc has shared in coaching. They thank each other. They are complete.

At every point in a coaching engagement, we can hold our coaching in the larger context of the unfolding development story of each of us. For this period of time, we play a role in our client's story. He has played a role in ours. The hope is that we have each learned through sharing something precious along the way.

At some point, the coaching engagement is complete. At this moment, we and our clients move into whatever is next. Completions are an invitation to make this moment conscious and intentional.

I now speak directly to you. I am sitting at my window on a warm, sunny February day in the mountains of North Carolina, writing the very words that you are reading now. Here I am. There you are. Separated in time and space, and yet connected by these words.

When you finish *Presence-Based Coaching*, you and I will have completed something. Perhaps someday we will be in a different kind of relationship. Perhaps I will coach you, or you will attend a presence-based coaching retreat in North Carolina, or we will have lunch at a conference together. Right now, neither you nor I can know for sure.

So, for now, we move toward *this* completion. I invite you to look squarely at the questions that are uniquely yours to consider.

Being more present in your life will increasingly awaken you to your role in the extraordinary challenges that envelop us all. If you have experienced even some of what I aspire to reveal, then you have entered something from which you can no longer turn back. I hope you are engaging your own questions of relevance, meaning, and purpose. Although this can be uncomfortable, it also places you in touch with the developmental impulse and will eventually lead you to the deeper longing that is the direct experience of that impulse.

Your work is a playing field. It is your practice opportunity. You, in your unique world, have the opportunity to produce something different and new, an opportunity unprecedented in human history. It is exactly, squarely, in front of you, in whatever time and place you are reading these words.

⚜ PRESENCE PAUSE ⚜

Your world needs the best of you.

What new actions can you take? How are you called to contribute? And how can you begin to act from the largest possible picture of what is really important?

⚜ PRESENCE PAUSE ⚜

These are core questions. As you open to the developmental impulse within you, you may well discover that your role and contribution are different, richer, vaster than you ever could have anticipated. You will become more fully present. You will become more connected to the people and opportunities in your life, and will open to a bigger view of yourself and the contribution that is uniquely yours to make.

As a leader, and as a developer of others, you must be deeply committed to developing yourself. The developmental impulse continually invites you to transcend and include the person you have been. This continual waking up, this moving deeper into what the world is asking of you, is how you earn the right to coach.

It is an extraordinary person who chooses to develop himself or herself for the sake of . . . what? Your chosen playing field may be in the domain of business, of nonprofit work, of education, of parenting, of working to preserve the precious planet that gives us life. What is important to you? For the sake of what do you arise in the morning and go forth into your day?

Whatever your domain of practice, you have been given the opportunity to wake up. So, wake up. Now.

⚜ PRESENCE PAUSE ⚜

It is the final day of the ten-day seminar in Costa Rica that began with my discovering that I would be teaching entirely in Spanish.

We rise very, very early. Nine Latin American business school faculty members and I pack into two small vans and drive to the top of an active volcano. We sit together at the very edge of the crater, silent in a chilly dawn, each person contemplating his purpose as an agent of change. Great clouds roil the immensity around us, occasionally parting to reveal layered cliffs below, emanating acid smoke rising toward the sky. The moment is raw and staggeringly beautiful.

We marvel. We reflect and write. We sip tea.

We are together and alone in a great moment of presence. Each of us is experiencing awe-inspiring natural grandeur. Each of us is experiencing a timeless moment of choice in which we can evoke a new possibility.

After an hour or so, we head to breakfast. We spend a day on a mountainside, deep in conversation and planning, each of us solidifying the initial fragile sense of possibility and commitment, each of us preparing for bold new actions in the world.

It is the completion of something significant. And it is the beginning of everything that follows.

EXERCISE 12.1.

What's Next for You?

Take some time to consider and write about what's most important for you right now in your career and in your life.

For the sake of what are you developing yourself? To what purpose are you most deeply committed?

Then design, for yourself, the three core structures for development. (See Chapter Three for a review of these.)

- What person or person(s) can be your coach and development partner? Who will be deeply committed to you, competent to expand what you are able to observe, and skillful in designing the practices and fieldwork that enable sustainable change?
- What are the generative, ongoing practices that you are willing to commit to?
- In what domain, and in what competencies, is it important for you to develop? What specific practices and fieldwork will engage you in a robust and creative way?

Now, write down your immediate next steps to move this forward. Affix times and dates to these actions. Start now.

CHAPTER SUMMARY

- The principles and moves of presence-based coaching can be applied to many different kinds of clients; it's critical to meet people where they are.
- Entry points provide a great opportunity to invite the client into an experience of presence. For a prospective client, feeling and sensing something new is energizing and shows something about what coaching can be. Establish relevance and immediacy in the opening conversation.
- Continuations should be conducted consciously and intentionally. Done well, they open opportunities for self-assessment and for practicing self-generation. Extensions of coaching are invitations to make conscious choices about what is needed now, which may be quite different from what was needed earlier in the engagement.
- Completions are beginnings in disguise. They mark the beginning of what's next. With presence, we are in contact with the developmental impulse, and we work with the client to make the completion and transition as conscious as possible.
- The completion of this book opens the question of what you will do next. Get clear about the purpose for which you are developing yourself. And commit to a development partner or coach for yourself, to a regime of generative practices, and to specific fieldwork in your domain. Start now.

Coda

To be awake is to be alive. Time is but the stream I go a-fishing in.

Henry David Thoreau

When you were born, you cried and the world rejoiced.
Live your life so that when you die, the world cries and you rejoice.

Cherokee saying

WE DRIVE OUR RENTAL CAR, LOADED WITH CAMPING gear, kids, empty Cheetos bags and soda cans, and the assorted flotsam and jetsam from an extended family road trip, up the long road into Yosemite National Park. I have looked forward to seeing Yosemite Valley, having seen photos of it all my life, but frankly, my expectation is of great postcard scenery and lots of tourists. My plan is to quickly see the valley, and then leave to get out to our campground to set up for a few days of camping and hiking with the kids.

We pass through a long tunnel, right before the scenic overlook that provides the first view of the valley. We park the car, I grab the camera in case there is a good shot, and we walk over to check out the view. Although I've seen countless Ansel Adams calendars, I am totally unprepared for what happens next.

What lies opened before me is far beyond anything I imagined. There is El Capitan. Half Dome. The Merced River. Vast expanses of raw granite and golden light. I have seen pictures and know the names, but have never felt the grandeur, purity, and vastness of this landscape. I am transfixed. It feels as if my chest is opened wide; I am exhilarated, gasping for breath, tears rolling down my face. My whole body is alive, electrified. Any possibility of words is erased by an indescribable sense of exaltation. I can do nothing other than stand and weep, nearly overcome by this felt experience of awe and sublime beauty.

After a minute or two, the feeling fades, and some sense of orientation returns. The kids are antsy to go, and we head down into the valley for more Cheetos. Writing this fifteen years later, a trace of the same feeling returns, readily accessible even now.

My experience in Yosemite was aliveness, the full sensation of life. Greater aliveness is the inevitable result of practice and of presence-based coaching. It is our birthright. When we move deeper into ourselves, into the moment-by-moment experience of life, we find ourselves more and more fully alive. This, ultimately, is of far greater value than any other product of coaching. It is through our aliveness that we rediscover what it is to be human.

Business and leadership and coaching (and marriage and friendship and parenting and community) are only the domains in which we most frequently practice and learn. At the same time, what is available to us is greater than anything we can imagine when we restrict our attention to success in these domains.

Professional efficacy and personal development are inseparable. As we become self-generative, we have more to offer others who are in different places on a similar journey. We become increasingly able to support others skillfully in their own unfolding. We develop ourselves in order to support others. And as we support others, our own developmental edges are inevitably revealed, furthering our own growth. Our development is intertwined with the development of those around us.

The more fiercely we hang on to our familiar identity and ways of being, the more challenging and bumpy the ride is likely to be as we are inevitably called to be more. Yet the constant process of becoming present, of letting go of attachments in order to respond creatively to what is emerging, opens us to life itself. We discover that we can see everything as practice. We can ease up and not take ourselves so seriously.

What is revealed when we enter into presence is greater and greater. We become more deeply connected with ourselves. And we come to experience ourselves as an integrated, belonging part of an ever-expanding system around us: our whole organization, our community, our culture, the planet, all of existence.

When we are present with ourselves and connected to the systems around us, we experience ourselves as more and more interdependent with the whole. By following the developmental impulse, we inevitably become committed to making a contribution. We care for more, and we care more deeply. We love everything. We clearly see that how each of us lives helps to shape our collective unfolding story, the final chapters of which are as yet unwritten.

We end by discovering, through presence, our true nature as a full participant in the miracle of life.

This is the real promise of this book. It is this for which we have been longing all our lives.

This is the way home.

Table of Moves and Practices

THIS OUTLINE GATHERS THE INNER MOVES, GENERATIVE
practices, and relational moves from Chapters Four to Twelve.

INNER MOVES

Orienting

- Orienting to a coaching model
- Generative orienting to your client
- Orienting to your purpose
- Orienting to your client's purpose
- Orienting to coaching outcomes
- Expanding the context

Holding

The relational field

- Sensing the field
- Sensing qualities in the field
- Extending qualities into the field

Silence and possibility

- Holding the certainty of possibility

- Holding the client's potential
- Holding silence

GENERATIVE PRACTICES

Mind

- Core mind practice: Sitting
- Naming
- Self-observation of a habit
- Letting go of an attachment

Body

- Core body practice: Centering
- Observing versus sensing
- Body scan: Directing attention within the body
- Experiencing somatic responses to others
- Self-observation with somatic awareness
- Centering through a reaction
- Take on a body practice

Heart

- Finding compassion for others
- Core heart practice: Touching your heart
- Kissing practice: Observing versus sensing 2.0
- Integrating three core practices in a quick self-regulation move
- Gratitude practices
- Connecting through the heart

RELATIONAL MOVES

Moves for Self-Observation and Realization

Reflect

- Name our own experience

- Reflect observations
- Reflect what is produced in us by our client

Invite internal awareness

- Invite self-observation
- Invite presence
- Track sensation
- Access the intelligence of the body and heart

Focus the field

- Bring relevant factors into the conversation
- Create immediacy
- Spotlight habits in real time
- Spotlight aliveness

Challenge identity

Moves for Reorganization

Shift perspective

- Shift frame of reference
- Access future possibilities now

Reorganize around center

- Center
- Center in a commitment

Build competency in self-regulation

- Extend what's needed
- Identify internal somatic resources
- Make internal processes explicit
- Connect with the heart

Mobilize commitment

Moves for Stabilization

Design fieldwork

- Design self-observations around conditioned tendencies
- Design self-observations around a new behavior or action

- Design relevant practices
- Invite clients to take on generative practices
- Identify relevant body practices
- Design complementary learning actions

Work jointly

Create new "facts on the ground"

Moves for Entry, Continuation, and Completion

Entry

- Invite the client into presence
- Establish relevance of present moment to larger concerns
- Reveal client's habits gently
- Jointly develop purpose and outcomes

Continuation

- Invite clients to self-assess progress
- Validate and benchmark progress
- Share assessments and possible next steps
- Renegotiate purpose, outcomes, and structure

Completion

- Jointly share assessments
- Address outstanding issues
- Jointly design ongoing self-generative actions for client
- Declare completion

Purpose Exercise

LTHOUGH THIS EXERCISE IS NOT STRICTLY PRESENCE-BASED coaching, being clear about your own purpose is fundamental to orienting yourself as a coach. Orienting to purpose is described in Chapter Four.

There are many processes available for creating a purpose statement; this is one. A quick Internet search will find others, and Appendix C has other purpose-related resources. I highly recommend, if you have not done so, that you engage in such a process. (Note that, with minor changes in the questions, this same process could be used for yourself or clients around life purpose.)

EXERCISE B.1.
Develop a Purpose Statement as a Coach

If you've not done so, spend some time developing a statement of your purpose as a coach.

Begin by taking some time alone, preferably in an inspiring and relaxing environment, to write responses to the following questions. Allow yourself to be present and creative as you do so; if you have practices that bring you into presence, use them before you begin writing.

Use these questions to guide your exploration:

1. In your work with people, what gives you the greatest joy?
2. In your work with people, when do you feel most alive, optimistic, and grateful?
3. What historical figures and relationships have inspired you and taught you? What do you admire in them?

4. What are the five or six values about learning that you hold most dear?
5. What are your innate strengths and skills?
6. Who are the people in your life to whom you have contributed the most? How did you do so?
7. What is it that you teach, mentor, or inspire most skillfully? Most passionately?
8. What regrets do you have about how you've coached people in the past?
9. Imagine that you're eighty-five years old and looking back over your life. What are you most grateful for? What do you want to be remembered for? What have been the most important things that you've learned? Contributed to others?
10. What would others, who know you well, say are your real contributions in life?
11. What possibilities in the world do you most strongly believe in? What gifts do you have that are relevant to bringing forth those possibilities?
12. Consider the skills, beliefs, and values listed above. How might you offer these in service to the growth and development of others?

Take time to write in response to these questions. It is best to do this over several sessions and let them percolate in the background in between. Then write a concise sentence or two that answers these questions:

- What is it that you offer to those you coach?
- To whom will you offer this?
- What value is created by your coaching? What difference will your coaching make to your clients?

That's your purpose statement. Write it up and post it where you can see it and be reminded. Live in it, recognizing that it might change and shift as you develop.

Annotated Bibliography

T HE FOLLOWING BOOKS PROVIDE ADDITIONAL READING. SOME of these have been significant influences in my own work; others were chosen because they add diverse and complementary perspective to that offered in *Presence-Based Coaching.*

You will notice that the fields of business, coaching, somatic psychology, leadership, emotional intelligence, spirituality, therapy, philosophy, Buddhism, and neuroscience are all represented. As an integrative work, *Presence-Based Coaching* draws on a wide range of influences. This short list is intended to provide some starting points and necessarily omits much worthy work that has also contributed much to my own. Suffice it to say that there is much in here to enrich your exploration.

References are correlated with a specific chapter, although this seemed at times almost arbitrary. Books are alphabetized by author; my top recommendation for relevant reading in each chapter is highlighted in bold text. (Order links for all these books can be found at http://dougsilsbee.com/books/pbc/biblio.)

I have grouped the books for all of Part Four into one section. Because of the nature of Part Four as a synthesis of everything that came before, it's difficult to find sources that are unique to those chapters. I simply included several other books that I have found useful.

Silsbee, D. *The Mindful Coach: Seven Roles for Helping People Grow.*
Marshall, N.C.: Ivy River Press, 2004.
> My first book explores the nexus of mindfulness and coaching. Based in Buddhist practice, the importance of self-observation is in recognizing and

setting aside the habits that get in the way of real service to our clients. The Septet Model provides a road map for the coaching conversation and is built around seven voices that the coach plays, as determined by the emerging needs of the client. Lots of exercises for coach self-development are included, as well as links to free online coach self-assessments. This book is a natural partner for *Presence-Based Coaching*.

CHAPTER ONE

Halpern, B., and Lubar, K. *Leadership Presence: Dramatic Techniques to Reach Out, Motivate, and Inspire.* New York: Gotham, 2004.

Rooted in theater, these authors have created a practical guide for developing leadership presence: "the ability to connect authentically with the thoughts and feelings of others." Lots of exercises make this a practical and fun experience in building authenticity as a leader.

Moss, R. *The Mandala of Being: Discovering the Power of Awareness.* Novato, Calif.: New World Library, 2007.

Offers a description of the territory of presence and describes the mechanisms by which we get pulled away and how we can return. Moss is a brilliant writer and offers a new map of the territory of being.

Scharmer, O. *Theory U: Leading from the Future as It Emerges.* Cambridge, Mass.: Society for Organizational Learning, 2007.

Scharmer explores a model for presencing, in which groups and individuals move into a different awareness and inner state. Scharmer claims that accessing the inner state from which future possibilities are ready to emerge is essential to leadership. Offers many business examples.

Tolle, E. *The Power of Now: A Guide to Spiritual Enlightenment.* Novato, Calif.: New World Library, 1999.

This simple book became an international best-seller and offers readers a cognitive understanding of presence along with a direct experience of it. Tolle's contribution to making the experience of presence explicit for a wider audience is significant, and he embodies this in a powerful way. A wonderful book. Businesspeople with little interest in the spiritual aspect will be better served by Scharmer (above).

CHAPTER TWO

Leonard, G. *Mastery.* New York: Plume, 1992.

A beautiful, elegant, simple, and profound book. A must-read for anyone concerned with human development and anyone taking on a consistent practice of any sort. Leonard, based on his long-standing work in aikido, offers the keys to mastery in any discipline. These keys include proper instruction, practice, and surrender.

Schwartz, J. M., and Begley, S. The Mind and the Brain: Neuroplasticity and the Power of Mental Force. New York: HarperCollins, 2002.

This lucid and fascinating intellectual journey through quantum physics, neuroscience, and Buddhism describes the research that has led to the startling and profound discovery that we can literally rewire our brains through directed attention and repeated practice. The research is presented against the background of some of the deepest questions we face: Is there free will? What is consciousness? For those interested in the scientific grounding for how mindfulness and practices build sustainable behavior change, this is the starting point.

Strozzi-Heckler, R. *The Anatomy of Change: East/West Approaches to Body/Mind Therapy.* Boston: Shambhala, 1984.

An exploration of how the body stores and is shaped by life's events. An important discussion of how we embody our conditioned tendencies (habits) and how somatic awareness leads to a stronger sense of ourselves, and more meaningful contact with others.

Wilber, K. *A Brief History of Everything.* Boston: Shambhala, 2000.

Wilber is one of the most notable philosophers of modern times. With a prodigious intellect, he has given us a comprehensive map of the evolution from matter to life to mind to spirit and how human development mirrors the larger patterns of this unfolding. This book provides a sometimes humorous overview of Wilber's thought, and a big picture story of how humans "transcend and include" as we progress along our developmental journey.

CHAPTER THREE

Flaherty, J. Coaching: Evoking Excellence in Others (2nd ed.). Boston: Elsevier/Butterworth-Heinemann, 2005.

One of the most profound and inclusive books on coaching. Grounded in a big picture of how humans change, this book is a gift to the field. Flaherty integrates the work of some of our greatest thinkers into a flexible and elegant approach to coaching; his work has been a significant influence on my own.

O'Neill, M. B. *Executive Coaching with Backbone and Heart: A Systems Approach to Engaging Leaders with Their Challenges.* San Francisco: Jossey-Bass, 2000.

One of the best coaching books available for people working with top leaders. O'Neill breaks down the coaching process into a clear methodology, backed by sound principles. Her focus on presence and the use of self in coaching is refreshing.

Whitworth, L., Kimsey-House, H., and Sandhal, P. *Co-Active Coaching: New Skills for Coaching People Toward Success at Work and in Life.* Palo Alto, Calif.: Davies-Black Publishing, 1998.

An early classic in the coaching field, this book provides a good, question-driven framework for coaching. It is included here because of the emphasis on self-management for the coach. The authors developed an extraordinarily successful leadership program building on the principles described here.

CHAPTER FOUR

Leider, R. *The Power of Purpose: Creating Meaning in Your Life and Work.* San Francisco: Berrett-Koehler, 2005.
> A philosophical and practical exploration of the need for purpose in our lives. Leider provides lots of practical exercises. For people engaging the questions of purpose, meaning, and contribution, or facing retirement or a reexamination of what their life is for, this is the place to start.

Swimme, B. *The Hidden Heart of the Cosmos: Humanity and the New Story.* Maryknoll, N.Y.: Orbis, 1996.
> Swimme, a mathematical cosmologist, describes how we have come to understand the exact location of the true origin of the universe. Looking back to the Big Bang, Swimme's elegant and poetic prose will startle you, orient you, and provide you with a powerful realization of exactly where you stand in the order of things.

Wegela, K. K. *How to Be a Help Instead of a Nuisance: Practical Approaches to Giving Support, Service, and Encouragement to Others.* Boston: Shambhala, 1996.
> Wegela explores the territory of helping, cultivating compassion, and being a resource. Through mindfulness, she offers practical wisdom and guidance for being present with others. This thoughtful book will help you be more available with your clients and less wrapped up in your own distractions.

CHAPTER FIVE

Boyatzis, R., and McKee, A. *Resonant Leadership: Renewing Yourself and Connecting with Others Through Mindfulness, Hope, and Compassion.* Boston: Harvard Business School Press, 2005.
> This important business book on emotional intelligence argues that the cumulative effects of challenges and stress make it very difficult for leaders to avoid becoming dissonant. Their prescription for harried executives? "Soft" practices that develop mindfulness, hope, and compassion while renewing the body, mind, and emotions. Lots of exercises and references for further reading.

Goleman, D., Boyatzis, R., and McKee, A. *Primal Leadership: Realizing the Power of Emotional Intelligence.* Boston: Harvard Business School Press, 2002.
> The third in Goleman's series of books on emotional intelligence, this far-reaching book describes six distinct leadership styles and how each is appropriate for and resonant in specific situations. The book includes an interesting and substantial exploration of neuroanatomy as it relates to emotional intelligence and leadership. The authors conclude with suggestions about how to develop emotionally intelligent leaders and organizations.

Johanson, G., and Kurtz, R. *Grace Unfolding: Psychotherapy in the Spirit of the Tao-te-ching.* New York: Belltower, 1991.
> This simple and beautiful book takes a series of themes ("welcoming," "empowering," "seeking truth," and others) and, in a very few pages briefly

explores the significance of each for the helping relationship. As coaches, we can orient to these, and they will shape how we are present for our clients.

Lewis, T., Fari Amini, F., and Lannon, R. *A General Theory of Love*. New York: Vintage, 2000.
> Written by three physicians, this book explores love, emotions, psycho-biology, and relationships in a poetic exploration of how humans bond. Understanding the nature of limbic resonance is important in working with the relational field that we establish with our coaching clients. This reassuring book will remind you of what it means to be human and of the possibility of fulfillment and happiness that comes latent in our bodies.

CHAPTER SIX

Bennett-Goleman, T. *Emotional Alchemy: How the Mind Can Heal the Heart*. New York: Harmony, 2001.
> Offers wisdom on working with difficult emotions. Mindfulness, short-circuiting habits, shifting perceptions, and making conscious choices about our relationships with our thoughts and emotions will sound familiar to readers of *Presence-Based Coaching*. A very useful book on working with difficult emotions.

Gunaratana, B. H. *Mindfulness in Plain English*. Somerville, Mass.: Wisdom, 2002.
> A thorough, practical introduction to meditation and mindfulness. How to meditate, what to do with your mind and body, how to work with problems and distractions, ways to carry mindfulness into everyday life. Common sense and down to earth.

Hayes, S. C. *Get Out of Your Mind and Into Your Life: The New Acceptance and Commitment Therapy*. Oakland, Calif.: New Harbinger, 2005.
> An exciting book for people who want to be their own coach. A rich exploration of the contribution of our minds to suffering, this is essentially a workbook for becoming familiar with how our minds create our own suffering and how we can move to acceptance and presence. Based in solid research, this practical book goes far past the shallow prescriptions of the self-help genre to offer rigorous practices that more closely resemble Buddhism than popular psychology.

Mingyur Rinpoche, Y. The Joy of Living: Unlocking the Secret and Science of Happiness. New York: Harmony, 2007.
> A delightful book that explores Buddhist teachings in a thoroughly modern narrative. Reading it, one can't help but feel happier! The interwoven threads of mindful awareness, neuroscience, and quantum physics provide a fascinating and at times humorous story about what it means to live a mindful, happy life. Highly recommended for skeptics.

Siegel, D. J. *The Mindful Brain: Reflection and Attunement in the Cultivation of Well-Being*. New York: Norton, 2007.
> A robust exploration of well-being and awareness, grounded in a rigorous integration of brain science, personal experience, and professional clinical

application. For those looking for a deeper exploration of what's going on beneath the surface of awareness, and interested in bringing this knowledge to bear on helping others, this will be an important book.

Chapter Seven

Gendlin, E. T. *Focusing.* New York: Bantam, 1978.

A tiny classic centered around why some people seem to be able to change readily while others get stuck in old patterns that prove difficult to change. Gendlin argues that being able to access the "felt sense," a somatic sensibility within our bodies, is critical to being able to change. This book shows us how to access the felt sense in a clear, simple, step-by-step approach that is nonetheless profound.

Kabat-Zinn, J. *Full Catastrophe Living: Using the Wisdom of Your Body and Mind to Face Stress, Pain, and Illness.* New York: Delta, 1990.

Kabat-Zinn is best known for developing mindfulness-based stress reduction (MBSR), a program that has well-documented physical and psychological health benefits and has been replicated in many other places. This book is practical and accessible and designed to enable the reader to learn the basic MBSR program at home. Full of practices, this is a comprehensive and useful book. Supplementary meditations and body scan CDs can be ordered from http://mindfulnesstapes.com.

Levine, P. *Waking the Tiger.* Berkeley, Calif.: North Atlantic Books, 1997.

An overview of Levine's fascinating work with trauma. Levine presents a revolutionary theory about how our fight/flight/freeze reactions are stored in the body, determining our unconscious and habitual reactions.

Strozzi-Heckler, R. *The Leadership Dojo: Build Your Foundation as an Exemplary Leader.* Berkeley, Calif.: Frog, 2007.

The most recent of Strozzi-Heckler's books, the one most focused on leadership and the one most accessible to a business audience. This work lays out the centrality of the somatic self in developing leaders. Integrating martial arts, body work, psychotherapy, meditation, and educational psychology into an elegant synthesis, this book is must reading for anyone concerned with developing authentic leaders. This author's work is a significant influence on my own; I often provide this book to coaching clients.

Chapter Eight

Childre, D., and Martin, H. *The Heartmath Solution.* San Francisco: HarperCollins, 1999.

Provides specific techniques for accessing the heart's intelligence and maintaining clarity in the midst of stressful and emotional events. This work is heavily researched and provides the basis for training programs, tapes, and other resources used widely in business and other high-stress professions. This classic book is very practical, with tools and exercises throughout.

Chödrön, P. *The Places That Scare You: A Guide to Fearlessness in Difficult Times.* Boston: Shambhala, 2001.

Chödrön, a teacher in the Tibetan Buddhist tradition, offers practical guidance for cultivating compassion and loving kindness and extending it to others. This is a great book for those interested in a mindfulness-based approach to compassion and the heart.

Kouzes, J., and Posner, B. *Encouraging the Heart: A Leader's Guide to Rewarding and Recognizing Others.* San Francisco: Jossey-Bass, 1999.

Two of the best-selling authors in the leadership field present this practical and easy-to-read approach to communicating caring and appreciating employees in a business environment. Loaded with business examples and practical suggestions.

Pearsall, P. *The Heart's Code: Tapping the Wisdom and Power of Our Heart Energy.* New York: Broadway, 1998.

Gathers in one place a lot of current information about the heart as an energy system with its own intelligence. Heavily footnoted, this book is a good starting point to learn more about the power of the heart, connecting with your own heart, and connecting with others.

PART FOUR

Budd, M., and Rothstein, L. *You Are What You Say: A Harvard Doctor's Six-Step Proven Program for Transforming Stress Through the Power of Language.* New York: Crown, 2000.

This easy-to-read book provides a practical approach to working with the body, mood, and language to be more fulfilled and effective in life. Budd, a physician, goes far beyond a simple self-help book; his teachers include some of the heavyweights in psychobiology, linguistics, and somatics. This is a good starting point for busy readers.

Howe-Murphy, R. *Deep Coaching: Using the Enneagram as a Catalyst for Profound Change.* El Granada, Calif.: Enneagram Press, 2007.

Integrates presence, somatic and heart intelligence, mindfulness, generative practices, and fieldwork with the Enneagram (a framework of nine personality structures) into a practical coaching structure. The strong developmental orientation in this book makes it a valuable contribution to the field. Highly recommended.

Leonard, G., and Murphy, M. *The Life We Are Given: A Long Term Program for Realizing the Potential of Body, Mind, Heart, and Soul.* New York: Tarcher/Putnam, 1995.

Two pioneers of the human potential movement make a case for long-term practice that integrates the body, mind, emotions, and spirit. The authors include a specific *kata* or routine; other elements could easily be included. A good field guide to integrative cross-training.

Shafir, R. *The Zen of Listening: Mindful Communication in the Age of Distraction.* Wheaton, Ill.: Theosophical Publishing House, 2000.

Shafir puts mindfulness into practice with a guide to listening fully to others and understanding how different interpretations might create confusion, and mindful self-listening, so that your communication is likely to be clearer.

Web-Based Resources

THE FOLLOWING RESOURCES ARE AVAILABLE THROUGH THE Presence-Based Coaching website at http://dougsilsbee.com/books/pbc:

- An online annotated bibliography, including updated resources not mentioned in the book, and order links
- Downloadable templates and practices
- Free online coach self-assessments
- Links to other websites with rich collections of practices
- Links to coaching resources that feature similar and complementary approaches
- Descriptions and dates of upcoming coach training and presence-based leadership development retreats
- A calendar of the author's public speaking engagements and workshops

Notes

INTRODUCTION

1. D. Silsbee, *The Mindful Coach: Seven Roles for Helping People Grow* (Marshall, N.C.: Ivy River Press, 2004).

CHAPTER ONE

1. M. B. O'Neill, *Executive Coaching with Backbone and Heart: A Systems Approach to Engaging Leaders with Their Challenges* (San Francisco: Jossey-Bass, 2000), p. 17.
2. P. Senge and others, *Presence: An Exploration of Profound Change in People, Organizations, and Society* (Boston: Society for Organizational Learning, 2004), p. 13.
3. L. B. Halpern and K. Lubar, *Leadership Presence: Dramatic Techniques to Reach Out, Motivate, and Inspire* (New York: Gotham, 2004), p. 3.
4. R. Quinn, *Deep Change: Discovering the Leader Within* (San Francisco: Jossey-Bass, 1996), describes the ubiquitous tendency to feel overwhelmed and withdraw. "As performance levels fall, stress goes up, and vitality and drive wane. Our focus narrows, and we increase our commitment to our existing strategies, leading us toward greater difficulty" (p. 55). Quinn describes the alternative as deep change.
5. A slightly different definition is explored in depth in D. Silsbee, *The Mindful Coach: Seven Roles for Helping People Grow* (Marshall, N.C.: Ivy River Press, 2004), p. 14. Both definitions distinguish between coaching and related activities. My definition also borrows from James Flaherty, whose work has been very influential in my own.
6. J. Flaherty, *Coaching: Evoking Excellence in Others,* 2nd ed. (Boston: Elsevier/Butterworth-Heinemann, 2005). Flaherty also describes three

products of coaching, two of which are similar to what I'm describing here: "long-term excellent performance," "self-correction," and "self-generation" (pp. 3–5).

CHAPTER TWO

1. D. Whyte, "Working Together," in *The House of Belonging* (Langley, Wash.: Many Rivers Press, 2004).

2. Attachments and aversions are important components of the Buddhist taxonomy of consciousness, and are described as the source of suffering. D. Silsbee, *The Mindful Coach: Seven Roles for Helping People Grow* (Marshall, N.C.: Ivy River Press, 2004), pp. 32–36, offers more detail on attachments and aversions, and places them in the context of coaching. Lama Surya Das, *Awakening the Buddha Within: Tibetan Wisdom for the Western World* (New York: Broadway Books, 1997), provides more on the Buddhist context for these terms. An Internet search will quickly find many other references.

3. Daniel Goleman, and others in the emotional intelligence field, refer to this neurological phenomenon as an "amygdala hijack," in which the fast-reacting limbic system, focused on survival, overrides our best cognitive reasoning about how to respond to the situation. The automatic nature of such reactions is a great illustration of habits in action. D. Goleman, *Emotional Intelligence: Why It Can Matter More Than IQ* (New York: Bantam, 1997), describes this phenomenon.

4. E. Langer, *Mindfulness* (Reading, Mass.: Addison-Wesley, 1989), describes this thought experiment.

5. James Flaherty places self-generation centrally in his discussion of coaching in one of the best coaching books available. He describes it somewhat differently than I do here. See J. Flaherty, *Coaching: Evoking Excellence in Others*, 2nd ed. (Boston: Elsevier/Butterworth-Heinemann, 2005).

6. An extensive body of emerging research documents precisely how practice with directed attention literally rewires the brain, creating new neural pathways that support the new habit. J. M. Schwartz and S. Begley, *The Mind and the Brain: Neuroplasticity and the Power of Mental Force* (New York: HarperCollins, 2002), is a great starting point for exploring this. See also D. Rock and J. Schwartz, "The Neuroscience of Leadership," *Strategy and Business*, Summer 2006, and available at http://www.strategy-business.com/press/freearticle/06207.

7. Flaherty's third product of coaching, self-correction, addresses this ongoing need for self-regulation and requires the diligent practice of much of what I am discussing here. See *Coaching*.

8. R. Strozzi-Heckler provides compelling examples in *The Leadership Dojo: Build Your Foundation as an Exemplary Leader* (Berkeley, Calif.: Frog, 2007), pp. 55–59, 78–79.

9. By this I mean that she was organizing herself to serve in a new role; at the same time, she could include her historically useful behaviors in this new role as appropriate. As Miles learns to walk, he'll still be able to crawl; as Janet learned to develop others, she could still step into the weeds and solve problems when that was required.

CHAPTER THREE

1. D. Goleman, R. Boyatzis, and A. McKee, *Primal Leadership: Realizing the Power of Emotional Intelligence* (Boston: Harvard Business School Press, 2002), p. 141, states that "improvement plans crafted around learning—rather than performance outcomes—have been found most effective." This is a significant opportunity to improve much of the coaching delivered in business.
2. J. Flaherty has a useful discussion about openings for coaching in *Coaching: Evoking Excellence in Others*, 2nd ed. (Boston: Elsevier/Butterworth-Heinemann, 2005), pp. 61–70.
3. Richard Strozzi-Heckler speaks of a set of similar distinctions as the "triad of power." He describes three sources of power: the self, a community of fellow learners that demand more of us, and a combination of ontological (generative) and ontical (designed to develop a specific skill) practices. Personal communication with the author, February 2008.
4. Strozzi-Heckler places generative practices in a continuum of embodied behaviors including reflexes, habits, routines, practices, and generative practices. See *The Leadership Dojo: Build Your Foundation as an Exemplary Leader* (Berkeley, Calif.: Frog, 2007), pp. 81–83.
5. S. Gilligan (ed.), *Walking in Two Worlds: The Relational Self in Theory, Practice, and Community* (Phoenix, Ariz.: Zeig, Tucker & Theisen, 2004), p. 111.

CHAPTER FOUR

1. More information on the Septet model and on coach training retreats teaching the model is available at http://dougsilsbee.com/books/tmc.
2. J. Flaherty, *Coaching: Evoking Excellence in Others*, 2nd ed. (Boston: Elsevier/Butterworth-Heinemann, 2005), p. 70.
3. S. Covey, in *The Seven Habits of Highly Effective People* (New York: Simon & Schuster, 1989), pp. 106, 128, has useful discussion about personal mission statements. R. Leider, in *The Power of Purpose: Creating Meaning in Your Life and Work* (San Francisco: Berrett-Koehler, 2004), discusses purpose extensively and provides suggestions for clarifying purpose.
4. S. Salzberg, *A Heart as Wide as the World* (Boston: Shambhala, 1997), pp. 89–91.

CHAPTER FIVE

1. This phrase is attributed to Carl Rogers, a pioneer therapist, who believed that effective client relationships relied on an atmosphere of total acceptance. C. R. Rogers, "A Theory of Therapy, Personality and Interpersonal Relationships, as Developed in the Client-Centered Framework." In S. Koch (Ed.), *Psychology: A Study of Science*, vol. 3, pp. 184–256 (New York: McGraw-Hill, 1959).

2. The resulting sense of intimacy and connection can be explained as limbic resonance: "a symphony of mutual exchange and internal adaptation whereby two mammals become attuned to each other's internal states." T. Lewis, F. Amini, and R. Lannon, *A General Theory of Love* (New York: Vintage, 2000), p. 63.

PART THREE

1. Based on Wilber's work, the Integral Life Practice Starter Kit (Integral Institute, 2005, http://myilp.com), provides a set of practices in the domains of body, mind, spirit, and psychoemotional domains. DVDs and a practical, commonsense guide encourage anyone to begin "body/mind/spirit cross-training."

CHAPTER SIX

1. K. Weick and K. Sutcliffe, *Managing the Unexpected: Resilient Performance in an Age of Uncertainty*, 2nd ed. (San Francisco: Jossey-Bass, 2007), pp. 32–41.
2. S. S. Hall, "Is Buddhism Good for Your Health?" *New York Times*, Sept. 14, 2003.
3. D. Silsbee, *The Mindful Coach: Seven Roles for Helping People Grow* (Marshall River, N.C.: Ivy River Press, 2004), pp. 38–48.
4. J. Flaherty, *Coaching: Evoking Excellence in Others*, 2nd ed. (Boston: Elsevier/Butterworth-Heinemann, 2005), pp. 193–202, describes the principles of self-observation and provides a number of examples in personal, business, and relationship domains. Also, a significant portion of *The Mindful Coach* addresses the topic of self-observation as coaches. More in-depth discussion and coach-specific self-observations can be found throughout *The Mindful Coach;* the treatment here is necessarily briefer.
5. Attributed to Shunryu Suzuki-roshi, source unknown.

CHAPTER SEVEN

1. R. Strozzi-Heckler, *The Leadership Dojo: Build Your Foundation as an Exemplary Leader* (Berkeley, Calif.: Frog, 2007), p. 79.
2. Eduardo Galeano, *Walking Words*, trans. Mark Fried (New York: Norton, 1995), p. 151.
3. Thomas Hanna is generally credited with modernizing the Greek term *soma* to refer to "the body as experienced from within, where we experience mind/body integration." See T. Hanna, "What Is Somatics?" *Somatics,* 1986, 5(4), 4–9.

4. The term *somatic literacy* was, as far as I know, first used by P. Linden, "Somatic Literacy: Bringing Somatic Education into Physical Education," *Journal of Physical Education, Recreation, and Dance,* Sept. 1994, 65(7), 15–21.

5. This centering practice uses the dimensions of length, width, and depth, as described by Strozzi-Heckler, *The Leadership Dojo,* pp. 123–125. Another description of this centering practice can be found there.

6. Many people find verbal guidance helpful in doing the body scan. Jon Kabat-Zinn has created a series of guided meditation CDs, available at http://mindfulnesstapes.com. The Series 1 CD contains an extensive forty-five-minute long body scan exercise. He provides body scan descriptions in *Coming to Our Senses* (New York: Hyperion, 2005), pp. 250–253.

7. This research is referenced in S. C. Hayes, *Get Out of Your Mind and Into Your Life: The New Acceptance and Commitment Therapy* (Oakland, Calif.: New Harbinger Publications, 2005), p. 49.

8. J. M. Schwartz, *The Mind and the Brain: Neuroplasticity and the Power of Mental Force* (New York: HarperCollins, 2002), states: "Introspection, willed attention, subjective state . . . can redraw the contours of the mind, and in so doing can rewire the circuits of the brain, for it is attention that makes neuroplasticity possible" (p. 339).

9. Described in J. Stevens's "Introduction" in M. Ueshiba, *The Art of Peace* (Boston: Shambhala, 2007).

10. R. Strozzi-Heckler, verbal communication, October 2006.

CHAPTER EIGHT

1. J. M. Kouzes and B. Z. Posner, *Encouraging the Heart: A Leader's Guide to Rewarding and Recognizing Others* (San Francisco: Jossey-Bass, 2002), p. 119.

2. P. Pearsall, *The Heart's Code* (New York: Broadway Books, 1998), pp. 72–74, describes many elements of this intelligence and provides extensive references.

3. R. Howe-Murphy, *Deep Coaching: Using the Enneagram as a Catalyst for Profound Change* (El Granada, Calif.: Enneagram Press, 2007), p. 173.

4. D. Goleman, R. Boyatzis, and A. McKee discuss the emotional center of the brain and explore the neurology of emotional intelligence in *Primal Leadership* (Boston: Harvard Business School Press, 2002).

5. Y. M. Rinpoche describes the *tonglen* practice in *The Joy of Living* (New York: Harmony, 2007), pp. 187–188. Another description can be found in Pema Chödrön, *The Places That Scare You* (Boston: Shambhala, 2001), pp. 55–60.

6. This exercise is modified from Irmansyeh Effendi and the Padmacahaya Institute for Inner Study. More information on the heart and links to workshops can be found at http://heartsanctuary.org.

7. From testimony provided to the National Civil Aviation Review Commission in a public hearing on May 28, 1997. http://www.library.unt.edu/gpo/NCARC/testimony/swa-te.htm.

8. Brother David Steindl-Rast, a Benedictine monk, has a wonderful website dedicated to gratefulness at http://www.gratefulness.org. Here, you can find many practices and other resources with gratitude as a theme.
9. Kouzes and Posner, *Encouraging the Heart,* p. 150.
10. R. M. Rilke, *The Book of Hours: Love Poems to God* (New York: Riverhead, 2005), p. 98.

CHAPTER NINE

1. R. Strozzi-Heckler, *The Anatomy of Change: East/West Approaches to Body/ Mind Therapy* (Boston: Shambhala, 1984), provides a good overview. His work integrates approaches from Wilhelm Reich, Randolph Stone, Ida Rolf, and many others.
2. M. B. O'Neill, *Executive Coaching with Backbone and Heart: A Systems Approach to Engaging Leaders with Their Challenges* (San Francisco: Jossey-Bass, 2000), pp. 33–37.

CHAPTER TEN

1. Richard Strozzi-Heckler has a discussion of centering in commitments in *The Leadership Dojo: Build Your Foundation as an Exemplary Leader* (Berkeley, Calif.: Frog, 2007), pp. 126–128.
2. Self-regulation is one of five main areas of competency in Daniel Goleman's taxonomy of emotional intelligence in *Working with Emotional Intelligence* (New York: Broadway Books, 1998), pp. 26–27. (The others are self-awareness, motivation, empathy, and social skills.) I describe self-regulation as a subset of reorganization, implying the more subtle moves of maintaining a state as distinct from mobilizing ourselves for something new, as is implied by "reorganization."
3. "Limbic resonance supplies the wordless harmony we see everywhere but take for granted... The limbic activity of those around us draws our emotions into almost immediate congruence." T. Lewis, F. Amini, and R. Lannon, *A General Theory of Love* (New York: Vintage, 2000), p. 64.

CHAPTER ELEVEN

1. J. M. Schwartz and S. Begley, *The Mind and the Brain: Neuroplasticity and the Power of Mental Force* (New York: HarperCollins, 2002), explores this in depth in the context of an intriguing philosophical discussion of the concept of free will.
2. The term *activator* comes from the work of Darya Funches and is an element of her REAP model for personal and organizational transformation. Personal communication, June 1995.
3. M. Budd and L. Rothstein, *You Are What You Say* (New York: Crown, 2000).

Index